PSYCHOLOGICAL INVESTIGATIONS

Psychological Investigations

A Clinician's Guide to Social Therapy

LOIS HOLZMAN AND RAFAEL MENDEZ, editors

Brunner-Routledge
New York and Hove

Published in 2003 by
Brunner-Routledge
29 West 35th Street
New York, NY 10001
www.brunner-routledge.com

Published in Great Britain by
Brunner-Routledge
27 Church Road
Hove, East Sussex
BN3 2FA
www.brunner-routledge.co.uk

Brunner-Routledge is an imprint of the Taylor & Francis Group.
Printed in the United States of America on acid-free paper.

10 9 8 7 6 5 4 3 2

Library of Congress Cataloging-in-Publication Data
    Psychological investigations : a clinician's guide to social therapy / Lois Holzman
and Rafael Mendez, editors.
        p. cm.
    Includes bibliographical references and index.
        ISBN 0–415–94404–X (hbk.) — ISBN 0–415–94405–8 (pbk.)
    1. Social adjustment. 2. Social psychiatry. 3. Social networkx—Therapeutic use.
I. Holzman, Lois, 1946– II. Mendez, Rafael, 1949–

RC455.4.S67P78 2003
362.2—dc21   2002155072

Acknowledgments

Our thanks to the hundreds of clients, therapists, students, colleagues, and coworkers, who have created social therapy. We are especially grateful to the following people:

- Our production team—Murray Dabby, Joan Fleischman, John Fraire, Esther Farmer, Maggie Gouldin, Warren Liebesman, Manny Straehle, and Kim Svoboda—for their painstaking work transcribing and editing the original audiotapes.

- Therapists, therapists-in-training, and students in Fred Newman's teaching and supervisory sessions for their ability to create stimulating conversation with him.

- Colleagues in Holzman's online courses whose dialogue helped shape the final manuscript.

- Sheila McNamee and Will Wadlington for their enthusiasm for the project and their own efforts in creating a new psychology.

- George Zimmar at Brunner-Routledge for his support for the project.

- Fred Newman for his unlimited capacity to give.

Contents

Foreword

Psychological Investigations is a refreshing and confronting antidote to the usual academic press. If expecting from the title to have a "guide" or "recipe steps" to social therapy, readers will instead surprisingly find themselves engaged in a creative endeavor: Dialogues about social therapy.

Participants in learning forums such as colloquia, seminars, and supervision groups pose *questioning* questions to Fred Newman—philosopher, therapist, community activist, playwright, and director—about the practices and theoretical underpinnings of social therapy. Newman, who is undeniably a gifted teacher, does not answer the questions, instead he discusses them. Mendez and Holzman do not tell the reader what Newman does, Newman performs it and the reader experiences it. This collection is truly a gift as recorded and transcribed dialogues between students and teacher are rarely available.

Social therapy stands at the edge among those therapies influenced by postmodernism and its challenges to psychological science. Within the social sciences in general, postmodernism as a social theory offers a challenge to inherited positivist assumptions and practices of knowledge development and acquisition, knowledge as truth, the objectivity of knowledge and knowing, and knowledge as an individual product. In particular it confronts the nature of psychology, calling for a critical examination of the dominant psychological discourse that embraces the notions of universal truths about the nature of human beings and their behavior, a core or bounded self, the conceptualization of problems, and deficit-oriented language and the conventions that flow from them.

Newman and his colleagues take a radical position toward truth-referential psychology and human behavior as its unit of analysis and target of change. Referring to social therapy as a nonepistemological practice of method, social therapists make a strong plea for an activity-theoretic paradigm in place of a descriptive truth telling paradigm. They passionately plea for revolutionizing the culture of psychology and its practices into that which people can transform themselves into who they are not and their world into what it is not. They adamantly believe that psychology and social practice go hand-in-hand, and that psychology therefore must address the often oppressing social, political, and economic conditions in which people live. Toward this, Newman and his social therapy colleagues rely on a blend and creative application of the works of Russian learning and developmental psychologist Lev Vygotsky and the ordinary language philosophy of Austrian philosopher Ludwig Wittgenstein, placed on a background of a Marxian methodology that calls for social change.

Social therapy is a group therapy that provides a context and process for personal growth and development, helping people to develop what they want to develop and to perform their lives differently and creatively. It is based on the premise that people grow as a social unit. They do not develop and grow individually, on their own so to speak, but that these are relational activities. Likewise, transformation is a collective activity not an individual one.

The social unit in social therapy is the group. Participants build the group, creating a community with each other that provides the environment for growth where they immerse themselves in relationships and learning experiences. Helping to build the group is a precursor to emotional growth. Building the group is creating the conditions and the performatory environment in which people can relate and converse in ways that are generative and invite emotional growth.

In *Psychological Investigations* Newman performs what makes social therapy a distinct group therapy and what makes it radical. His performance provokes, stimulates, and compels us to rethink our theories and practices and to keep them abreast of the global changes and associated consequences that we encounter in our daily worlds.

Harlene Anderson
Houston-Galveston Institute
November 2002

Preface

As psychology begins its second century, we find ourselves at a crossroads. For some, the question is, "Whither psychology?" For others, the question is, "To be or not to be?" Both questions encapsulate the motion in the discipline—the re-alignments, reconceptualizations, and re-evaluations occurring on both method-ological–philosophical and pragmatic terrains. Within this context, many clinicians (psychologists, psychotherapists, counselors, social workers, et cetera) are rethink-ing the foundational issues of their practices. What is a therapeutic relationship? What does it mean to help another person? Indeed, what is "the other"? What is therapy talk good for? Do therapists—and should therapists—*know* what they're doing? *Psychological Investigations* raises these questions, and takes readers through a process of exploration—with some answers, but many more questions discovered along the way. This book and social therapy (its subject matter) are a part of what is going on in psychology, which, it seems to us, is a much-needed *cultural* transformation. What does this transformation look like?

First, there is psychology's responsiveness to changes in the broader culture. Many in psychology recognize that they must go where the interest and money are in order to be relevant and survive, and they are attempting to create a psycho-logical niche in other disciplines, for example, medicine and health care, sports, business, conflict resolution/negotiation, terrorism, and trauma. One promising effect is that boundaries are becoming blurred—between psychology and other disciplines and between so-called pure and applied research.

Another related change is the effort to reform psychology by changing the subject from "what's wrong" to "what's right." In just a few years, mainstream psychology has all but dropped its "*d*-words" in favor of "*p*-words"—we've gone from nearly a century of talk of deficits, disorders, and disabilities to speaking the language of positive traits, prevention tactics, and potential. Many of those who have switched from negativity to positivity (from *d*'s to *p*'s) have done so without recognizing the need to rethink their methods of study and help, given that they changed the subject matter. Nevertheless, this change is still a progressive step, for while these psychologists still insist that psychology is an objective science, they are changing the topic of conversation, and that in itself can open some doors and build some new partnerships. Already it has put academic psychologists in touch with people and organizations that, for years, have been practicing positive youth development, positive education, and positive therapy in their communities.

A more radical change is under way among those psychologists who question the whole enterprise called psychology and go outside traditional boundaries to develop theories and practices for how to see, study, and support people to create new ways to be together. Many loosely gravitate to the term postmodern, to characterize their view that the tenets of modern science—such as truth, reality, and objectivity—no longer should be considered foundational, that we and the world we live in are emergent, complex, and not predictable, and—that this is not a problem! Perhaps, these innovators say, rather than trying to rule subjectivity out of order, we need to accept our self-reflexivity and devise methods to study human life subjectively. Perhaps we should take seriously that human beings are social and that the self-contained isolated individuals that psychology taught us we were don't exist. Perhaps understanding human life needs to be *a cultural and philosophical activity*, rather than a scientific one. Perhaps people the world over would be better served if theorists and practitioners looked at the human landscape with a painter's, poet's, storyteller's, and playwright's sensibilities instead of with the biologist's and physicist's scientific tools. The entertainment of such possibilities suggests that psychology itself is becoming more of a cultural activity.

Psychologists are beginning to see things they never saw before—process, possibility, and performance (more *p*-words). Psychology has traditionally been fixated on what is, and set itself up as the authority on what it is to be human and on who particular humans—individuals and groups of all kinds—are. Part of the transformation occurring in the field is the recognition that human beings are not just who we are but also *who we are becoming*. Psychologists are beginning to see (and see the importance of seeing) process and not just product or outcome.

A related phenomenon is the beginning of a shift from prediction to possibility. Prediction has been a mainstay of psychology since its beginnings, in spite of significant failure to predict what people will do. The more radical of psychology's innovators are abandoning prediction in favor of focusing on understanding and supporting people's capacity to create new possibilities out of what currently exists.

Finally, performance—both on formal stages and off—has become something of a hot topic in psychology. Once process and possibility become important, then behavior (the official subject matter of psychology) becomes less interesting. For increasing numbers of theorists and practitioners, the human capacity to perform—to create endless situations, scenarios, stories, characters, and characterizations—is where the excitement, the growth, the challenge, and the help lie.

A renewed interest in the philosopher Ludwig Wittgenstein and psychologist Lev Vygotsky has played a key role in psychology's emerging concern with process, possibility, and performance. Their ideas—Vygotsky's search for a dialectical method to study human activity as social, historical, and cultural, his understanding of child development as "performing beyond" ourselves, his notion of language completing thinking, and Wittgenstein's argument against private language, his insistence that language is to be understood and experienced as a form of life, his notion of language games— have been both a catalyst for these new concerns and a product of them.

Social therapy, the subject of this volume, has both benefited from and contributed to the flowering of innovative, postmodern practice and debate. Founded over 30 years ago by Fred Newman, social therapy—and its related community-based projects in education, youth development, and theater—was cultural, postmodern, and performatory long before these terms became popular. However, it is psychology's movement toward the cultural, the applied, and the postmodern that has created the environment in which social therapy is now seen as an important theoretical and practical contribution. In addition to the books and articles exclusively devoted to social therapeutic method published in the last decade (see Appendix), discussions of the approach appear in psychotherapy and psychology publications of various schools of psychology and therapy, including humanistic, critical, social constructionist, constructivist, and systemic. As more scholars and practitioners, disaffected from traditional psychological understandings and clinical models, search for new ways to approach many of the challenges and injustices of today's world, social therapy becomes increasingly relevant.

Psychological Investigations: A Clinician's Guide to Social Therapy presents social therapy as it is taught to clinicians by its founder—psychotherapist, philosopher, playwright, and political activist Fred Newman. Part One sets the stage. The two editors—in different ways—introduce readers to social therapy and to Newman. Rafael Mendez, a social therapist trained by Newman in the 1980s and currently assistant professor of psychology at Bronx Community College in New York City, sets the stage with the story of how he came to be "teaching Newman" to undergraduates. Lois Holzman, director of the research and training center where social therapy is developed and taught, narrates the intellectual history of her almost 30-year collaboration with Newman and the ongoing development and key characteristics of social therapy, creating the context for the teaching dialogues that are the remainder of the book

Part Two consists of a series of dialogues drawn from transcripts of teaching and supervisory sessions between Newman and therapists. Organized topically, the dialogues show social therapy as an improvisational, investigatory, development-focused method, and address practice issues of concern to clinicians and students of various schools of psychotherapy and counseling. Chapter 1 introduces the core issues of social therapeutic practice, including its understanding of development, creativity, improvisation, and performance, and how it deals with questions of identity, truth, and the language of problems. Chapter 2 focuses on the group process of social therapy, from how to begin a social therapy group to how to "speak to the group." The next two chapters advance this conversation— Chapter 3 with dialogues on how to develop the social therapeutic relationship and Chapter 4 with dialogues addressing particular challenging therapeutic situations. The integration of social therapy with other fields, such as medicine, body work, self-help, and spirituality is addressed in Chapter 5. Chapter 6 returns to core issues, this time from a more philosophical and political perspective. The book concludes with comments from therapists and therapists-in-training who participate in Newman's training and supervisory sessions addressing how they make use of the teachings in their practices.

Designed for psychotherapists, clinical psychologists, counseling psychologists, social workers, and others involved in the mental health and human development fields as practitioners, supervisors/trainers, scholars/researchers, or students/trainees, *Psychological Investigations* is an invitation to anyone interested in ways to create activistic, socially oriented, culturally based practices of living.

Lois Holzman and Rafael Mendez

PART ONE

Setting the Stage

RAFAEL MENDEZ

The Town Hall theater in New York City's Broadway theater district is full to capacity. In a few minutes the evening's program will begin; already preparations are being made to close the entrance doors. I'm concerned that some of the hundreds of people I've invited will arrive just 5 minutes late and miss the opportunity to hear Dr. Fred Newman's annual psychology lecture. There is a buzz in the theater. Most everyone is noticing the uniqueness of the crowd; the diversity of the audience is captivating. Of the 1,500 people in attendance, there are those one would expect to be attending a psychology lecture—helping professionals, psychologists, physicians, counselors, social workers, and psychiatrists. But this is not the American Psychological Association. What makes this event unusual is the mix of people—many hundreds of New Yorkers, young and old, from many different neighborhoods, and all ethnicities and walks of life. This is a community event.

For nearly 30 years, Newman has spoken to community audiences on advanced topics of psychology and philosophy. He has long believed that it is the ordinary people of the world who need to have and practice the most advanced concepts, so that they can change everything. Each year, the audience grows, as more and more people become involved with and/or are impacted by the psychological, educational, and cultural projects that practice his method of reinitiating human growth. Activists, participants, financial contributors, supporters, and students in these projects have invited their friends and coworkers to the lecture so that they can be introduced to an approach to human development and experience Fred's unique way of teaching.

I am one of the organizers of this evening's event. I'm a college professor, a community organizer, and a therapist. I invited everyone I know to attend. As I walk around the theater, in most every section a group of my students wave and say hello. More than 250 of my students are in the audience. Finally, I spot who I'm especially looking for, Watts. A former student of mine, Watts now works as

1

a drug counselor in a residential facility in Harlem where he was once a resident himself. Watts is interested in learning how to use psychology to help his neighbors and community. He reminds me of me when I was younger. Fascinated by the approach I presented in class, he asked to learn more. I invited him to participate in the committee that organized tonight's event. Watts has a talent for organizing. I want to meet the people he brought to the lecture.

As he introduces me to the busload of residents and counselors he brought, I feel proud of his success and development. He has organized an often-abandoned grouping of people to hear the lecture with the intriguing title *Changing Everything: An Introduction to Social Therapy*. Like so many others, Watts loved the title and thought his coworkers and clients would be intrigued to learn how to do just that. Watts introduces me to his contingent. They're feeling welcomed.

As I take a few steps further there's a large group of students from my Bronx Community College Group Dynamics class. They are standing and waving as if they were at Yankee Stadium. They're excited tonight. As a class, they have been performing on stage learning a new methodology and psychology called social therapy from me and from Fred Newman's books. Tonight, they get the opportunity to hear from the author of their textbook directly.

Fred Newman founded social therapy in the mid-1970s as a nonepistemological therapeutic approach. More than a decade earlier, he had left the machine shops of the Bronx to study philosophy at City College of New York and then earn his doctorate in the philosophy of science from Stanford University. He didn't remain in academia long. Over the past 30 years, as a teacher, therapist, political activist, theater artist, and author, Fred has brought many diverse and unlikely people together to build something new, a *development community*. He has written numerous books and articles, for both popular and academic audiences, describing how the community works and what it has learned about growth and development. His plays attract growing audiences to the Castillo Theatre in New York City that he built as a performance laboratory. He inspired the creation of a youth leadership training program, the Development School for Youth, which introduces public high school youth to corporations and Corporate America to them. He is the founder and co-executive director of the All Stars Talent Show Network, the largest antiviolence, prodevelopment youth program in the country. He is an extraordinary therapist and leads weekly group therapy sessions, workshops, and classes.

In developing social therapy, Fred has been influenced by the writings of the Austrian philosopher Ludwig Wittgenstein and the Russian psychologist Lev Vygotsky. In 3 decades of therapeutic work, Fred has blended Wittgenstein's understanding of language and his concept of language games with Vygotsky's concept of zones of proximal development and his tool-and-result methodology to create an approach to helping people learn to perform their lives differently and creatively. Social therapy helps people to create who they want to be. Critical to this therapeutic approach is what Newman calls "philosophizing with a small p." He believes that philosophizing is not about learning what the great philosophers said; rather, it's doing philosophizing in our everyday life. Philosophizing is an activity that allows us to experience our lives not only in the immediacy of society's here and now, but at the same time as part of the continuum of human history. This, Fred maintains, is a critical human activity. In the absence of philosophizing, it's exceedingly difficult for us to see ourselves in the juncture where history and society meet. Philosophizing about ordinary matters of life is how Fred believes people can learn to think critically and to discover how to continuously create our lives. I have had the good fortune to be one of Fred's collaborators, and as a member of the development community I've participated in creating many community organizations and projects based on the practice of social therapy. I've seen firsthand the enormous personal growth that comes with participating in the activity of philosophizing. And I've found a way to bring this activity into the urban community college classroom.

I first met Fred Newman in 1978. I was earning my doctorate in clinical-community psychology at Boston University. A friend introduced me to Newman's efforts to build a new kind of therapy center called the Institute for Social Therapy and Research. I was captivated by how it was organized. The Institute worked intimately with, and simultaneously supported, the New York City Unemployed and Welfare Council, a union of welfare recipients. This was precisely the type of community-oriented activistic psychology I wanted to practice.

Some years earlier, in 1972, I was like Watts. I wanted to do something to help my community, but did not know how. Politicized yet still politically naïve, I had just returned home to the South Bronx from the Vietnam War, where I was an air traffic controller. I served in the Mekong Delta, 100 miles south of Saigon, in a lawless area where the contradictions of the war were stark. I returned home to yet another war zone. The South Bronx was on fire. During the 1970s, there were more fires in the South Bronx than in any city in the world. The plight of my community has since been well documented; the epidemic of arson for profit by landlords devastated the South Bronx, giving it all the appearances of a war zone. People lived in fear that their apartment building would be the next to burn. The devastation left few people untouched; in retrospect, what was most destroyed was the existence of community.

Returning from Vietnam, I didn't have any idea what I wanted to do. I had brief jobs as a roofer and a security guard before landing a job through the Teamsters Union loading and driving a truck delivering cigarettes and candy to local stores. The Watergate scandal, President Nixon, the Vietnam War, and the future of the country were on many people's minds, including mine. I was moved by these social and historical events to want to be a more active participant in shaping what was happening in my community and country, with virtually no idea how to do that. I was an alienated, working-class Puerto Rican, restless and angry. Ignoring the advice of my friends and family, who reminded me that I barely graduated high school with a general diploma, I quit my job and enrolled at Bronx Community College.

It was at Bronx Community College and later at City College of New York that I first learned of psychology. I became fascinated with the idea not only that people could be damaged by life experiences but that they could also be helped to repair the damage. Naïvely, I had always thought people were how they were, and that was how they would always be. I was especially attracted to the community mental health movement and its goal of a mental health center in every community to respond to social concerns and help people in need. I took every psychology class I could, including fieldwork at Jacobi Hospital and Bronx State Hospital, where I worked with the so-called mentally ill. A professor who admired my passion gave me a lead on a job as a community advocate and counselor with elderly people who were destitute and alone. I loved the job and the older people I cared for. It seemed to me that through psychology, I had a job that mattered and a way to make a difference. It also seemed like a cool professional job, a lot better than delivering cigarettes.

But I also was not entirely happy with psychology as I found it. I thought it could be advanced in ways that made it more sensitive to the significance of social conditions and less oriented to the individual in isolation. With the experience of the war still fresh, I was arrogant enough to think I could use psychology and the community mental health movement to do something about the devastation of the South Bronx. I remember finding older people near death in their apartments and bringing them to the hospital where they received the finest of care, only to be returned to the same wretched conditions that made them ill. I thought there must be a way of combining the science of clinical psychology with the advocacy of community organizing.

Imagine my shock when I was accepted to Boston University's clinical-community doctoral program in psychology in 1977. Even though I had graduated with honors from City College and was awarded a scholarship, I was totally intimidated by the idea that I belonged in graduate school. I thought that I would be immediately discovered as a fraud. Instead, it wasn't long before I was the one who discovered fraud. The community mental health movement had died long before I learned about it in school. Community was now a mere footnote to psychology's obsession with the self. I was completing my doctoral work when I first met Fred Newman. He gave me an opportunity of a lifetime—and I took it.

Fred and I are alike and different. Fred is Jewish and I am Puerto Rican. He came of age in the1940s and 1950s, I in the 1960s and 1970s. Yet we both grew up poor and working class in the South Bronx. We both left home for the first time during an American war, he going to Korea and me to Vietnam. We both went to City College as war veterans. Fred also worked odd jobs; when he was young, he sold programs at Yankee Stadium and delivered groceries. He worked with his older brother as a machinist, a tool and die maker. (He often speaks about this experience of making the special kinds of tools that tool and die makers do. He has brought to psychology and community organizing what every machinist knows—that new kinds of tools must be designed to create results; the tool and its result are part of the same process.)

When he returned from the Korean War, Fred had no desire to be a machinist. He says (only half-jokingly) that he wanted to do something as distant from the work of a machinist as possible, something that had no practicality—and studying philosophy seemed to fit the bill. Following graduate school and after a few years teaching philosophy, Fred—politicized by the Civil Rights Movement and the Anti-Vietnam War movement and frustrated by the hypocrisy he found at the university—left academia to do community organizing. It was as a community and political activist and radical therapist that he discovered that the abstract conceptions of philosophy were indeed very practical. And I, initially attracted to psychology because it was practical (I thought it would help me help my community), have been fortunate to be a beneficiary of Fred's discoveries about the practicality of abstract philosophical concepts.

It was in 1979, shortly before I was to begin my clinical fellowship in psychology at Harvard Medical School, Children's Hospital in Boston, that I was invited to attend a staff meeting of the New York Institute for Social Therapy and Research, the therapy and research and training center Fred and a handful of colleagues had just founded. Fred and Lois Holzman were leading a discussion of their manuscript, *The Practice of Method*. I had this extraordinary experience of not having any idea what they were talking about while simultaneously recognizing that it was groundbreaking and revolutionary. I told Fred that an Institute for Social Therapy was needed in Boston, and he invited me to build one. While completing my clinical training, I organized a study group of young professionals to read and discuss *The Practice of Method*. We opened the Boston Institute for Social Therapy a year later. I was its first director, saw patients, and trained new social therapists.

The Boston Institute continues today, but in 1984 Fred invited me to return to New York City. He reminded me that there were more Puerto Ricans in the Bronx than there were people in Boston, and that is where I was needed. At that time, the Bronx was known for its political corruption. Both its borough president and Democratic Party leader were convicted of racketeering in 1979. Fred thought I could make a difference if I entered the political arena. So, doctorate in hand, I began doing community organizing and independent electoral politics. As a community organizer, I participated in developing a broad network of independent educational, cultural, and mental health organizations that practiced Fred's methodological approach.

My electoral political work in the Bronx was part of a larger effort to create an independent electoral political movement in New York and the rest of the country. Long before Ross Perot, Fred understood that creating political alternatives meant creating a social environment where people could break out of the constraints of the two-party political system. Odd as it sounds, at the time many registered voters believed that if they were registered as a Democrat, they had to vote Democratic. People thought it was illegal to vote otherwise. We set out to create an independent political movement to create the conditions for people to see electoral politics differently.

In 1988, my colleague Dr. Lenora Fulani (also a CUNY graduate, with a doctorate in developmental psychology) ran for President of the United States as an independent. Although she was on the ballot in all 50 states and earned federal matching funds, few people heard of her campaign. When she introduced herself as running for President, people would ask, "President of what?" It was incomprehensible that an African American woman could run for President, much less as an independent. Nevertheless, her independent campaign paved the way for Ross Perot's independent campaign 4 years later and created an environment in which independents could make inroads at the local level.

With Fred as my campaign manager, I ran for many elected positions against some of the most corrupt and entrenched New York City politicians. Most baffling to many observers and supporters alike was that I didn't run for positions that I could possibly win. I ran against politicians who would otherwise have gone unchallenged. For example, in 1989, I ran for City Council President, New York City's second highest office, against a millionaire with a multi-million-dollar budget. I spent a mere $6,000 and garnered 25% of the vote (over 210,000 votes), winning the South and Central Bronx and almost every Latino district.

I began teaching as a graduate student and continued teaching as an adjunct professor at the College of New Rochelle in the South Bronx and at Bronx Community College during the time I was involved in electoral politics and running for office. At first, I taught because it was fun to be with students. I loved their ambition and enthusiasm. I was a teacher who understood a lot about psychology, its value and limitations. I was a public figure and knew something about how the world worked, so my students seemed eager to learn from me. But I wasn't skilled as a teacher. Most students will tell you that there is a difference between a good teacher and someone who has expertise and knowledge. I taught through the strength of my personality. When I became a full-time instructor, I began to examine my pedagogy. I began to focus my teaching toward supporting students to learn *how* to learn and to recognize that learning to learn could and should be fun.

For the past 8 years I have been an assistant professor (I earned tenure in 1998) in the department of social sciences at Bronx Community College, my alma mater. It is quite a privilege to teach on the same campus where I was once a student. I experience an affinity with my students, since I was once where they are now. Quite a lot has changed within the City University of New York (CUNY), of which it is a part. In 1972 when I enrolled, there was a policy of open admissions and free tuition. It is doubtful I could have entered or afforded college without such policies. Today, increasing tuition (the university hasn't been free since 1977) and admission standards threaten to deny many poor and working-class students of color an educational opportunity. CUNY, like so many other colleges and universities, has responded to conservative political pressure and is instituting placement exams. Thousands of high school graduates accepted to CUNY are failing the placement tests and thus begin their college work with a cycle of remedial classes that too often fail to prepare them to pass their placement exams. Last year, only 27% of the 6,770 students who took remedial instruction were able to pass the placement exams.

I am struck by the lack of creativity that characterizes the "back to basics" approach at our college campuses today. It seems sadly ironic that as we have entered the 21st century our educational system is implementing policies that revert back to the teaching methods of the 1950s. Creativity is virtually absent from the fossilized environment of our schools, and I believe its absence is related to the difficulty our students are having with learning. Given this crisis in education, many students are underdeveloped.

Rather than promoting creativity and critical thinking, our schools focus on acquisitional learning. In the information age, education has come to mean the acquisition of propositional knowledge, for example, "I know this, I know that." Learning in the college environment often looks like this: The contemporary college student exits the classroom, reaches for her or his laptop computer, goes online to one of the many websites such as ASK.com or Screwschool.com, and finds prewritten essays on any and every topic. Students are then ready and able to find immediate answers for their professors on what they are supposed to *know*. They are becoming skilled at the knowing game.

Students learn where to find the "right answer" and accumulate information, but rarely learn how to think and create. The primary activity they are required to do is to recall information (terms, definitions, facts) that has been identified by the professor as "what will be on the test." Whether in the form of a multiple-choice test or an essay, the students are rarely asked to think, but to repeat what they have been told is important. This is what passes for learning at most colleges.

I believe the pedagogical response is not to go back to basics, but to reinitiate development—having students go beyond themselves. It's a methodology I learned from Fred and it's very different from remediation. One of the most valuable things I've learned from Fred is the practice of challenging traditional assumptions about learning (and involving my students in this activity). In my classes, I work to support my students in creating new learning environments (what Lev Vygotsky, as I learned from Fred and from Lois Holzman, called zones of proximal development) in which learning is the activity of doing what you do not know how to do. When people are asked to create something, they are placed in a position of having to reorganize what they know to produce something new. What they produce is a product of their activity, not what was predetermined by their professor as what they should remember. The activity of being creative is process oriented, involving helping people step out of how they typically view things, to break out of categories and see things anew. Creative activity, as opposed to acquisitional learning, promotes human development. It is the creative activity of *you not being you.* It is taking you and stretching you, as you go beyond your self and your identity. This dialectical process of you being you and not you simultaneously is the developmental process of becoming. Creative activity includes internalizing and making use of the examples of others, but it is not being exactly like them. Rather, it is using models in the social process of actually creating something new, what Newman and Holzman (again, after Vygotsky) call creative imitation.

The course I teach, called Group Dynamics, is unlike traditional college courses; there is no defined curriculum, no list of key terms to know, and no right answers. When I was first assigned this class I surveyed the traditional psychology textbooks. I noticed that their definition of group was fundamentally different from Fred's. The traditional psychological understanding is that a group is a collection of individuals with a common purpose or a common context. Through my early experience with Fred training as a social therapist and providing supervision to those training in social therapy, I learned a different concept of a group—an entity distinct from the individual members who constitute the group.

 When Fred trains therapists to practice social therapy, a critical focus is on developing the therapist's skill in seeing and relating to the group rather than to the individuals who comprise the group. A social therapist would ask, "How is the group doing?" or "What does the group want to do?" The philosophical belief in the existence of the group as an entity is fundamental to social therapy, where the therapist treats the group, not any individual member. This understanding of group challenges traditional psychology, and it also challenged me to think more radically about the way I wanted to teach my Group Dynamics course.

I decided to use Fred's popular books, *Let's Develop! A Guide to Continuous Personal Growth* and *Performance of a Lifetime: A Practical-Philosophical Guide to the Joyous Life* as textbooks for the course. To advance my own skills at being creative, I enrolled in a personal development course at Performance of a Lifetime, an improvisational program inspired by Fred's social therapeutic approach aimed at the development of adult creativity. There I learned improvisational activities that engage people in the activity of *performance*, the self-conscious activity of producing how we are in the world. Using this cultural-performatory approach supports people in breaking out of their predetermined social roles that often impede our development through the internalization and identification with prescribed roles ("Oh no, I couldn't do that; that's not me!"). Adapting this approach to my Group Dynamics course allowed me and my students to break out of our roles as professor and student and create a new learning environment, one where I could aim to teach the class (the group) rather than the individuals and together we could focus on the group's development.

At first I used an ordinary classroom and had my students reorganize the chairs to create a stage area so they could perform improvisational activities and skits based on their reading of *Let's Develop* and *Performance of a Lifetime*. The roars of laughter so disturbed other classes that I had to seek a different location. I chose an auditorium, which turned out to be ideal. The odd setting makes it clear from the beginning that this is no ordinary class. The students perform their activities on stage, in front of a live audience.

Through Fred's books, I have introduced my students to the significance of philosophizing and performing. For example, after my students read "Giving in a Culture of Getting" (a chapter from *Let's Develop*), I ask them to improvisationally create a skit with two different endings. Creating different possibilities out of similar circumstances gives them the opportunity to engage in the philosophical activity of considering questions like, when do we decide to be giving? Who do we give to? Why do we give? Is there a developmental value to giving?

By philosophizing I mean being self-conscious of the ordinary day-to-day activity of making mundane decisions in our lives. Through the activity of philosophizing students learn to think critically. I ask them questions to explore the assumptions of how we think. I'm seeking to create a conversation without assuming that either they or I *know* anything.

At times, they are assigned to create cultural productions for the college campus. Last semester, for example, they produced a forum on therapeutic conversations. They invited a guest speaker and organized students to attend the event. At the forum, the students performed skits about the experiences that they had visiting physicians and counselors, and having the experts not listen to them as they gave their professional advice. The humor of the skits not only made clear the significance of the forum's theme, but simultaneously created an environment where the guest speaker could lead an open and lively dialogue.

By creating, producing, and performing cultural events daily in class and occasionally for the college campus, the students are engaged in a primarily collective activity, rather than a primarily individualistic one, and thereby are building a community among themselves. Performers work to make their on-stage partners look good, a fundamentally *giving* activity that challenges the competitive character of most learning environments. Students say that what we do is in stark contrast to their other classes where they rarely meet their fellow classmates and are tacitly discouraged from sharing knowledge so that each person can look good compared to others. In these ways, my teaching raises philosophical questions for them that challenge their notions of schoolwork and learning.

My students are confused—often from the first day to the final class—but they are creative, creating, alive, and performing. Indeed, their confusion and experience of not knowing is a condition for development. This is what Fred means by nonepistemological. They have to engage the traditional notions of the "self" and the associated therapeutic conceptions, "know yourself" and "identity." Students get introduced to Ludwig Wittgenstein's understanding of private language, and engage the question of creating meaning rather than just using language. They play with the intellectual history of concepts such as identity, self, and other, and how these concepts impact on their daily lives.

These discoveries regarding performance, development, and community underlie the unique structure of my classes. Students build learning environments that promote their learning and development collectively, as a class. I have found this methodological approach to be a significant response to the crisis in education and the failure of psychology to respond to the myriad social issues that people are facing. It supports students in creating new social environments where they can perform and create culture—new ways of seeing and being. My fellow professors have asked me how I could possibly teach without a curriculum. I respond by saying, "How could students create if the class is already predetermined?" It's been my experience that the creativity my students produce always exceeds my expectations.

I am particularly enthusiastic about this current effort, *Psychological Investigations*, because it presents Fred as the extraordinary teacher that he is. I have seen how Fred's books have influenced my students far beyond the classroom. So many of them, after taking my class, ask, "What else has Fred written that I could read?" This book is for them as much as it is for those interested in training as therapists or those considering advanced training.

All of which brings us back to Town Hall. What will Fred say about how to change everything? Like most everyone in the theater, I am at the edge of my seat, barely containing my anticipation. Fred is a great orator and master storyteller. He never fails to be provocative, intriguing, profound, and yet quite ordinary. From his opening remarks, his distinct methodological understanding is evident. He thanks everyone for coming to the event and then, with his characteristic charm, pokes fun at the title of his lecture while simultaneously revealing his understanding of what it means to change everything. He says, "There is a paradox of giving a talk entitled 'changing everything.' That is, that giving talks changes nothing. It is not me who is going to change anything. It's you, and the thousands of people like you, who have the capacity to change everything. So if you came to hear an inspirational talk, you came to the wrong place. You are the inspiration, not me."

In the following days the students in my Group Dynamics class are alive with questions. "I loved the event, but I thought it was supposed to be a psychology lecture. Why did he talk so much about paradoxes?" "Wow, it was very interesting, but what was he talking about? What is a . . . I'm not sure how to pronounce it . . . paradigm?" "I loved the crowd. I've never been to anything like that. I liked how everybody was together. I liked the part about community, and that we need to have community." "I felt like I understood what he was saying, and that he was saying something important, even though I can't say what it is that he said." The lecture was a wonderful opportunity for my students to experience the larger development community that they are participating in building.

I told my students that what I thought was so special about the audience at the Town Hall theater was that it was filled with ordinary people from all walks of life, like them, sharing this experience and having their many different responses to it. I tell them that Fred does not believe that paradigm shifts occur as a result of a new paradigm being introduced to society from high on up, such as a scientific institution or government. Rather, he believes that paradigm shifts are the product of social-cultural transformations produced by the masses of society and that this takes years if not decades to produce. He does not make a distinction between the activity of transforming paradigms and the cultural activity of creating new environments and activities and building community. I remind my students that Fred is continuously attempting to organize new cultural activities of people seeing in new ways by creating community together.

As a community organizer, I helped Fred build an independent political party to help people see that they can create new conceptions of democracy and democratic participation, allowing for new coalitions among people who otherwise might not come together—building community. As a professor, I support students to create a new learning environment that is not predetermined, where they can philosophize, play with abstractions, perform and create culture, and build a community where they are free not to know, where they are free to creatively learn and develop.

I see how lucky I am, at this time in history, to find my job as an educator fulfilling. I am fortunate to introduce to you, as I do my students, some of the teachings of Dr. Fred Newman. The abstractions contained within them are of very practical value to my students in the Bronx and, I believe, to ordinary people the world over.

Creating the Context

An Introduction

LOIS HOLZMAN

A DISCOVERY OF MOTIVE

Why *Psychological Investigations*? Why this title for a collection of thoughts from and conversations with a man who believes that psychology is a myth, a pseudoscience, a scam?

The answer is simple. That man, Fred Newman, really likes the title. He gets a kick out of it. As an academically trained philosopher of language and science, Fred was influenced very early on by the iconoclastic philosopher Ludwig Wittgenstein, and still considers Wittgenstein's posthumously published *Philosophical Investigations* to be one of the most brilliant and important books ever written. In the early stages of compiling this volume, Fred told me that he always wanted to write a book called *Psychological Investigations*. And although he did not, strictly speaking, write this book, it does contain his words and I was more than happy to grant his wish. Beyond that, however, the title is perfect for this collection of conversations on social therapeutic method. Fred's social therapy, in both form and content, is a collectively organized and practically oriented investigation into psychology by ordinary people.

Psychological Investigations pays tribute to Wittgenstein and ties the book's contents to his philosophical method. For this reason, the title is somewhat provocative, no doubt striking some readers as presumptuous, which is consistent with who Fred is—someone who always provokes. The essence of his provocations (always delivered, as long as I've known him, lovingly and ruthlessly) is twofold: He thinks big, and he thinks/speaks/lives dialectics. Over the decades, I've come to believe that those who see the bigness but miss the dialectics often think Fred is arrogantly overstating things. One of my goals in putting this book together was to highlight Fred's practice of dialectics in the therapeutic arena.

Fred understands dialectics—more specifically, dialectical materialism—as a methodology for transforming the world, as opposed to a point of view or position from which to view the world. Put simply—and in deference to Marx—

13

dialectics is not an interpretation of reality but a changing of it. Dialectics is a rejection, in people's practice, of all forms of objectification and dualism (e.g., particularized entities, inner thoughts and outer reality, mind and body, people and environment, feelings and actions), and of any amount of distance between activity and contemplation/reflection on that activity in favor of monistic relationality, continuous historical process, human activity. In other words, to practice dialectics is to live (as fully as possible, given our thingified culture) as a relational and historical being. As Fred put it in one of his training sessions:

> I think there's a certain methodology that's required to give meaning to the interrrelatedness of all things in history. The traditional, causal, objectivistic ways of talking tend to suggest that we can particularize certain events. What's necessary is to be able to talk about how things are historically, to convey that what we're communicating with each other is not just some reified particular, is not only a new method, but a whole new meaning of methodology. The new methodology is dialectics.

Social therapy, the approach to helping people grow emotionally that Fred has created, is the practice of that new methodology. In academic circles, we often characterize social therapeutic methodology as a therapeutic synthesis of Wittgenstein and Vygotsky. No one comes closer to Wittgenstein than the Russian psychologist Lev Vygotsky in articulating a new meaning of methodology and a new, noncausal, nonobjectivist understanding of language. The similarities between Wittgenstein and Vygotsky have not gone unnoticed by scholars—for example, Shotter (1996, 2000)—and Fred and I have participated in some of the ongoing debates that take place in the pages of journals and the meeting rooms of academic conferences. The basis for the contribution we have to make to these intellectual discussions is Fred's practice, a working synthesis of Wittgenstein's philosophical method and Vygotsky's psychological method. Social therapy did not begin this way; rather, it evolved in this direction as Fred began to see the therapeutic dimensions of Wittgenstein's and Vygotsky's work and, simultaneously, as he and I began to see the Wittgensteinian and Vygotskian dimensions of social therapy. Over the years, social therapy has been greatly enriched by this therapeutic synthesis; perhaps it is also adding another dimension to the intellectual community's understanding of these two great thinkers.

Fred and I have written together since 1979 when we self-published *The Practice of Method* (through our then year-old Institute for Social Therapy and Research in New York). The monograph was an ambitious and eclectic attempt, especially since our organization barely existed and Fred's and my intellectual partnership was about 2 minutes old. We brought together many issues and varied conceptual frameworks that we found relevant to understanding human subjectivity, particularly the subjective constraints on—and potentials for—ordinary people to effect radical social change. Marx, Vygotsky, Chomsky, Freud, Quine, Gödel, and Wittgenstein were among those whose work we discussed. Subtitled *An In-*

troduction to the Foundations of Social Therapy, in another sense the monograph was the first of many attempts to share something of what Fred does when he does therapy and the ways in which we believe the social therapeutic method was/is important to pay attention to.

Social therapy was relatively new then. Fred and some lay therapists he had trained had been practicing for only about 5 years, and I had been studying and teaching it for just 3 years. A young developmental psychologist/psycholinguist then, I was rapidly learning analytic and Marxist philosophy (and politics and community organizing) from Fred. At that time, social therapy had no voice (not even a fringe one) in institutionalized psychotherapeutic/psychological discourse of either the traditionalists or radicals. We wrote *The Practice of Method* to learn something about social therapy and about our voice. We hoped that it would provoke.

In the 20-plus years since, we have continued to write in order to learn and to provoke; we have trained our voice to be (sometimes) in tune with the institutionalized discourse, even as we always try to reorganize the totality of that discourse. We've made up new terms, like *social therapy*, *clinical history*, and *the practice of method*; we've appropriated terms from other disciplines or relatively obscure psychological theory, like *tool-and-result methodology* and *activity-theoretic*; we've made attribution to its methodological influences, like *Vygotskian–Wittgensteinian synthesis* and *Marxist*; and we've put together terms that have recognition in psychology, like *developmental, clinical approach*. We've even gone the "anti-" route—*anti-psychology, anti-paradigm, anti-therapy*. Currently, we emphasize social therapy's basis in performance, creating phrases like *a cultural-performatory approach, performative therapy,* and *performance social therapy*. Naming is the name of the game in Western culture (and the global economy)— and it's a game we no doubt will continue to play.

Fred and I have even become prolific by academic standards, having had six books published by academic presses in the past 8 years. We have come to find ourselves occupying a position of modest influence within a newly emerging progressive psychology movement marked by an appreciation for a cultural approach to understanding human life. Despite whatever success we have had in this arena, however, our attempts to share social therapy with our colleagues and other practitioners have all failed. Despite the far greater success of the *social therapy practice* (the thousands of people who have been helped by participating in the therapeutic activity and the hundreds who have been trained), no one but these participants themselves have a clue as to what social therapy is. How are we to understand this failure?

On the one hand, some of our academic critics have said that our work is understandable only if you participate in it (e.g., Nissen, Axel, and Jensen 1999). We tend to agree. The (perhaps irreconcilable) difference between the mode of understanding of the academy and that of the social therapeutic group and community certainly suggests it. After all, the scholarly distance presumed to be required for so-called objectivity is what we are critiquing, in practical-critical fashion, in social therapy, and so, in our view, objective criteria are not valid tools to evaluate it. As we see it, the kind of understanding that can be derived from a distance is, despite its claim to objectivity, necessarily subjective. It imposes an interpretive subjectivity rather than being historically subjective. When academic colleagues attempt to understand our work without participating in it, they wind up relating to our radical rejection of objectivity as a methodological flaw or moral shortcoming, rather than allowing our embracing of self-reflexivity to impact on their own scholarly practices, including the practices of participation and understanding.

On the other hand, the failure to present social therapy to those who do not participate in it has also to do with how we have been presenting it. Perhaps Fred and I have been too theoretical and overly concerned with articulating social therapeutic methodology and its differences, as we see them, from epistemological methodologies. Perhaps, in being practical-critical, we have been insufficiently practical! We have not shown actual social therapeutic practice very often. Several times over the years, I have tried to write a deconstruction of social therapy group conversation/activity. With the exception of one excerpt from a social therapy group that appears in *The End of Knowing* (Newman and Holzman 1997), drafts remain unsatisfying and unfinished. At my urging, Fred agreed a few years ago to ask one of his ongoing therapy groups if they would allow a few sessions to be videotaped. I thought that if we showed a few groups in their entirety and as they happened, unencumbered by my researcher's deconstructionist analysis, people might be able to gain an understanding of social therapy. We produced videotapes of two sessions and distributed them, raw and unedited, to several colleagues. While the videos might have shown Fred's practice of social therapy from a video camera's point of view, neither our colleagues nor I found the videos very illuminating or satisfactory. The reason may have something to do with the fact that in viewing any therapy, one is inclined to look for "therapeutic moves," which makes it difficult to see the *relational activity*. This way of viewing is particularly distortive in the case of social therapy since there really aren't any such moves to discern.

With *Psychological Investigations* we take a different tack. Perhaps if we share some of how Fred teaches social therapy, the reader will begin to glimpse his practice. Perhaps illustrations of Fred in dialogue with practicing therapists and therapists-in-training will reveal more about his method than a gloss on 5-minute snatches of therapeutic discourse or 2 full hours of group process "captured" on camera. For years I have attended the training and supervisory sessions that Fred leads for staff and trainees. I have always loved these sessions and in putting this book together I have discovered a reason why. I think that Fred's uniqueness and significance as a therapist can be seen in his teaching and training. (In fact, what he does as a therapist is more like teaching and training than it is like therapy.) Surely this can be *experienced* by participating in his therapy groups, but after several failed attempts I have come to accept that it cannot be *seen* in that context. Social therapy is too slow, too uneventful, too ordinary, too unstructured, too pointless. In contrast, teaching and supervisory sessions (appear to) have a point—participants want help with specific issues in their practice as therapists. And such sessions have a recognizable structure—questions are asked and responses are given. For example, a social therapist describes a particularly difficult session and asks what to do next, a trainee asks what it means to build the group, a therapist trained in narrative approaches who is taking an introductory social therapy class wants to learn more about how the social therapeutic belief that human beings are always performing is manifest in doing therapy, and so on.

What is special about Fred Newman's way of doing therapy—and why I believe his work should be studied by psychotherapists—is that it dialectically synthesizes a philosophical sensibility with a practitioner's experience and concerns and an artist's penchant for creativity. It is this quality that I think might be glimpsable in the teaching and training dialogues that are the contents of *Psychological Investigations*. And that, I have discovered, is the meaning of the title to me.

Fred has had no formal training in psychology, psychotherapy, or social work. He was not taught the various skills and tools with which a professional is supposed to relate to mental illness or to help people in emotional distress. He did, however, have several things going for him when he began to practice in the early 1970s: philosophical know-how, particularly in the philosophy of science and of language; a revolutionary's passion for and belief in social transformation; a machinist's appreciation for how (and that!) things are made; a working class humanism—and a comfortableness with madness. Added to the mix, since the late 1980s when he began to write and direct plays, has been a theater practitioner's approach to the creative process.

Over the 30 years that he has been developing, practicing, and teaching his style of therapy, these elements have intertwined and matured into a sophisticated approach to reinitiating emotional growth. Social therapy is an art form. At the same time, it is primarily methodological rather than substantive or explicative. This combination makes it unique among therapeutic approaches—arguably, perhaps it's not even therapy. And as art and methodology, it is at once theoretically irrelevant to the psychotherapeutic tradition and exceedingly useful to practicing psychotherapists. It is this very quality that has made social therapy, although sometimes initially daunting, embraceable by therapists of many different schools of therapy. Throughout the remainder of this introduction, I intersperse snatches of dialogue between therapists, trainees, and Fred to help illustrate the characteristics of social therapy I want to focus on and to preview what lies ahead.

A PHILOSOPHER'S PRACTICE

Abstraction is something that is dangerous unless it is engaged in by the masses. I think abstraction is not simply something that CAN be done by the masses, I

> think it is a critical developmental activity for the masses to engage in. People
> must know how to philosophize.*

In the opening paragraphs of his 1996 book *Performance of a Lifetime*, subtitled
A Practical-Philosophical Guide to the Joyous Life, Fred asks us to imagine those
moments when we are immersed in the pressing practicality of everyday life, as
when we're standing in front of the meat counter at the supermarket debating
whether to have chicken or hamburgers for dinner. It is during these "mundane
societal moments" that, he urges, we most need to philosophize (Newman 1996,
29). We need to let ourselves experience the paradox that is the human condition—the intertwining of our banality and grandness, our simultaneous bigness
and smallness, our dialectical "location" in history and society. If we can, for
example, experience the "chicken or hamburgers" question simultaneously in its
societal significance and its historical triviality, then we can enjoy a moment of
historicalness—our gaze is diverted from the societal mirror and we glimpse ourselves as the collective producers (along with every other person, past, present,
and future) of the cultural-historical totality of our species' life.

Without this experience, Fred contends, we remain alienated, estranged, and
too often miserable, seeing ourselves and others as merely the products of the
societal here and now who are entirely determined by the particular circumstances
of our individuated lives. However, having this experience over and over again,
we come to appreciate our historicalness, which allows us to live joyously. What
is required is philosophizing—to Fred, the social, dialogic activity of asking *big*
questions about *little* things like "chicken or hamburgers" (Newman 1996, 29–
30). This kind of philosophical activity helps us out of psychological subjectivity—a me-centered, particularistic universe—and into historical subjectivity—the
beginning-less and end-less totality of the world, including the human species
and each and every other human being.

Helping people to experience this paradox of human life is one manifesta-
tion of how Fred has tried to make use of formal concepts in his therapeutic work.
He has become convinced, from decades of doing therapy, that abstraction plays a
vital role in human development, a view that is informed by philosophical rather
than psychological concepts. The relationship between particulars and totalities,
decidability, theories of proof, paradox, contradiction, if and how our thinking
and speaking are related—these and other thorny subjects that have occupied great
minds in the philosophy of science and language and the foundations of mathematics are what ordinary people need to become able to think about. These meth-
odological/philosophical puzzles have, for Fred, as much if not more relevance to
emotional and cognitive growth as the abstractions of mainstream psychology
(for example, concepts such as permanence of the object, temporality, causality,

---

*This and subsequent quotations that open sections of this introduction are from
Fred Newman.

generalization, and prediction). In fact, without engaging methodological/ philosophical concepts, we are left imprisoned by the dominance of psychological objects, devoid of any understanding of the philosophical assumptions on which they are based, the role these objects play in shaping our perceptions, understandings and experiences, and the social relations they perpetuate.

Dogma

Therapist-in-training: What is it about psychology that makes it difficult to embrace new approaches? I work in a very traditional clinical environment, and the "knowers" want to plug patients into the old way of doing things. So I wonder how long it will take for psychology to wake up as other disciplines, like the arts, have.

Fred: Well, my answer is going to be unduly philosophical but bear with me. I think it's very hard for psychology—as opposed to the arts or physics or architecture—to do this because psychology has no subject matter. And having no subject matter, it becomes all the more authoritarian about the statements that it makes about what it takes to be its subject matter, because it hasn't one! Nothing is more dogmatic than the activity of defending what isn't. If you check out the history of the world, you'll see that the most dogmatic statements made have been about things whose existence is highly questionable. Psychology, in my opinion, falls into that category.

No small part of what we're trying to do in our ongoing conversation with psychology is to engage this fundamental issue. In our opinion, the stuff that has ontologized psychology isn't a proper subject matter for understanding human growth and development. I think that has made it shockingly dogmatic and less useful than a cultural study of human growth and development, with activity as the subject matter, might be.

Transforming Totalities

> The overriding question in social therapy is, "How well is the group performing its activity?"

One formal (abstract) concept that Fred believes can make a difference in people's lives is that of the group, a much-debated issue in the history of both Eastern and Western thought. To him the question "What is a group?" is fundamental to engage, not only in doing group therapy but in all areas of life. This is because our understanding of groups impacts profoundly, in ways that we don't typically realize or recognize, on what we do. Do groups exist at all? Or are they nothing more than individuals arrayed in varying formations, with "group" being simply a shorthand term for describing particular collections of people? How we answer that question plays a major role in what we do.

With regard to social therapy, this question about abstractions is nothing if not practical. Therapeutic help in social therapy derives from the group's development as a social creative unit. The social therapeutic activity consists of transforming the group again and again and again, so—if groups don't exist, how can we transform them?

What Is a Group and Why Does It Matter When You're Doing Therapy?

Fred: In years of doing group therapy, my experience is that there are some people, whether they articulate it or not, who hold to the position that the group is nothing more than a collection of individuals. All kinds of moral, ethical and pragmatic things follow from that position. If a group is just a collection of individuals then it almost follows immediately that what you should do in the group is figure out how each of the individuals can get their fair share.

This is a fundamental issue, not just in therapy but in life. It raises the question of the existential character of relationships. Are relationships real things, or are they reducible to the elements that make them up? I don't deny that there are individuals but I take individuals to be secondary to relationships. As I see the world, it's filled with groups, relationships, combinations, and what people do as individuals is to be understood in terms of a certain stage of our growth and development in a fundamentally relational world.

I would identify the Western tradition as a positivist tradition, sometimes called in fancy philosophical language a nominalist tradition, in which we tend to see the world as ultimately reducing to the basic elements, to the particulars. In the last years of the 20th century, there has been a profound change to a recognition that what is fundamental is not the individual, nor the element, but the relationship. That change is what I identify as postmodernism, and it's in that sense that I consider myself to be a postmodernist. I take relationships, groups, sets—these kinds of abstract things—to have genuine, real, critical existence.

That is a pretty big issue for me, one I see as impacting on some of the most mundane things that we do. How we relate to each other depends on the extent we think there *is* such a thing as a relationship. When people say, "I'm in a relationship with so-and-so," the first place that I'm inclined to go to in therapeutic work is, "What precisely do you mean by saying you're in a relationship? Is there something called 'the relationship' that has a different quality of existence than you-and-the-other-person?"

One of the first questions I raised in family therapy was, "Who's on the side of the family?" Often people would look at me as if I was out of my mind; they took the question to be absurd. And in some ways I can see why someone would take it to be absurd, because a presupposition of that question is that there is something identifiable as the family which is different from the people who make it up. I'm not saying they're wrong and I'm right, but there's a profound difference in point of view if you accept that there is something called "the family," "the relationship," "the group." So a great deal turns on what our abstract assumptions are.

Therapist-in-training: In social therapy groups, people's actions and thoughts shape the kind of group that exists. Doesn't that suggest that the group is the sum of individuals and the product of individual acts?

Fred: I would agree that what people contribute shapes the kind of group that it is. On the other hand, people don't make those contributions in isolation; they make them in the context of a group. The existence of the group, after all, is a critical presupposition for people to be doing things that shape the group. It's not as if there's a moment when everything's a blank. Human beings don't exist on desert islands, a la Robinson Crusoe. We are a social species. There's a difference between saying "people shape the group" and saying that the group has no existence independent of that activity. The notion that what we create can be reduced to us as individuals is simply not the case, in my opinion. That is the fascinating dialectic of our species— we can change things, we do change things, we transform things, but we never come onto the scene unshaped by the social arrangement in which we do those things. I think creation is continuous, never *ex nihilo*.

Therapist-in-training: Maybe it doesn't matter whether there's such a thing as a group but only what you believe, in terms of how you act.

Fred: Well, you're raising a very complicated philosophical question. Some people believe things and they take what they believe to be characteristic of how things are. Others believe things but don't hold to there being a correlation between their beliefs and how things actually are. So in some respects the answer to your question depends on what you mean by belief.

Some beliefs seem to have little to do with what we do, while others profoundly inform it, for example, the belief that we should not cross the street if the light is red because "a car might hit us." I put belief (or disbelief) in "the existence of the group" in this latter category. While you can do all kinds of things not believing in the existence of the group, if you do not believe in the existence of the group you cannot come to terms with the possibility that the growth and transformation of the group might transform you. If you only believe in the individual, then you will be disposed to think that you are in the group for your own individual growth or advancement, and that there's no particular connection necessarily between your growing and the growth of the group.

This is the fundamental concept that I am trying to engage in social therapy. The task, if you will, of people in social therapy is to collectively transform this thing called the group, because it is the activity of transforming the environment that is transformative of all of those who participate in that. The group is not just a context for individuals to grow individually. And yes, this is a continuous struggle in social therapy, and that makes sense to me because we all have been socialized to see ourselves fundamentally as individuals. I am not arguing against individuality but against the *fundamentality* of individuality.

We have had taken away from us a sense of sociality. If you want to speak in grandiose terms, that's what I think is wrong with the world. We've lost a sense of our sociality in favor of a notion of the individual. And while this was a huge, progressive advance during the Enlightenment, the fetishization of the individual over the last couple of hundred years has deprived us of a sense of sociality, of community, of history, of spiritual location. I think that is at the root of what is sometimes identified as the great moral crisis in the world. I don't think it's the case that people are bad people now and they used to be good people. I think what *has* been the case is that the loss of our sense of sociality in this age of the individuated entity has been a profound sociocultural change. No small part of social therapy is to help people modestly regain that sense because the process of regaining that sense is emotionally curative.

Therapist: If groups are just collections of people, then there is a beginning when people enter the room. But if groups have an existence in and of themselves, then maybe the question of beginnings doesn't even enter into the picture. Is that consistent with what you're saying?

Fred: Yes. Certainly you can identify 7:15 as the time the group begins. So there is an innocuous sense of beginning that is functional. But if we mean *the point before which there was nothing*—that's a troublesome conception in my opinion. Moreover, the same is true of endings. A lot of people say that their therapy group is wonderful but that they don't think it's applicable to other environments. But what has to be understood, in my opinion, is that you *can't* leave it behind. Our life experiences go with us.

A painful characteristic of our culture is that we have been led to believe in the notion of starting all over again. Now, cognitively or intellectually people might not believe that, but emotionally many people do subscribe to it. It's often the case that when we explore what it is that people really want, what it is that's really bothering them, we discover they want to have another chance. That is a very seductive belief, but I believe it stands in the way of human growth.

That belief is related to the reductionistic bias that somehow or another we can redo the building blocks. But there are no erasures. Our life is a continuous relational process. That doesn't mean we can't evolve, but we

help people grow as who they are

can't go back and start again. So a critical part of what happens in social therapy is finding ways to help people grow *as who they are*. If you stop being who you are, then you can't have any growth at all. There has to be some kind of continuity in order for there to be any growth at all. I don't think this is philosophically trivial, because I think people walk around at some level thinking of their capacity for change in this kind of way: "I don't want to be like that." This is not a presupposition that is conducive to transformation and growth. The starting point of growth is radical acceptance—you can't grow unless you accept where you're growing from.

Therapist: Who is the "you" that's changing?

Fred: The relational you is changing, which is different from the relational me. All that I'm urging is that we break out of the notion of the thoroughly isolated, totally separate *you*. That conception of you has had a very dominant place in Western culture. The very brilliant philosopher Leibniz pointed out that no single thing ever changes; it's never happened in the history of the world. Even for the smallest units, if something changes, it relationally transforms the entirety of the world.

Therapist-in-training: Some days I feel that the group is a group; other days it feels like a collection of individuals.

Fred: Are there days it feels like both?

Therapist-in-training: Sometimes it feels like it goes from one to the other. I think I dichotomize—one or the other—and this contributes to how I see whether the group is doing well or not, to some judgment I'm making.

Fred: Maybe this is a measure of your need to dichotomize. I'm urging that you have a look at whether it has to be one or the other. The dichotomistic way of thought is pervasive in our culture. I have no appetite for that any longer; I have no particular need to answer the either/or question. Answering the either/or question is distortive.

Therapist-in-training: I guess I'm still trying to answer the question "What is a group?"

Fred: OK, that's fair, but maybe you want to think in terms of not having to answer the question in terms of the dichotomy between groups and individuals. That very way of thinking about it is going to limit the kinds of answers you come up with. No small part of the brilliance of some of the great proofs in foundations of mathematics is that they literally had to create a new concept of proof. And the response of a lot of people was, "Then it's not really a proof." Maybe what we're working on here is not simply what a group is, but finding some ways of talking about what a group is that don't posit the dichotomy between groups and individuals. I've seen people grow dramatically off of that. If we were limited by the traditional means of understanding or describing, that wouldn't happen. So I'm suggesting you try that on.

Engaging Alienation

Our very human interactions—our talking to each other, our touching each other, our being with each other in all the ways in which we do that—are fundamentally a creative process. I'm interested in helping people to grow developmentally through a process of better understanding—in a practical and activistic sense—their capacity to create. In my experience, this is the best chance we have of helping people deal with the terrible pain that they frequently bring into therapy.

It's Wednesday night a little before 6:30. In a few minutes, a social therapy group will begin at the East Side Center for Social Therapy in Manhattan, one of about forty social therapy groups that take place around the country every week. This particular group—fondly, if not very creatively, referred to as the Wednesday Night Group—has about 25 participants. These women and men hang out together for two hours a week and make small talk. They create conversation, perform philosophy, and tell stories. They laugh, cry, sometimes bore each other, and touch each other emotionally. Each week, they create their own cure, their own development—and change the world.

Each week, the group works to transform itself because it is in that activity that all who participate transform. This is the basis of the social therapeutic method: (1) Change occurs socially; and (2) totalities, not particulars, change. I suspect that many therapists pay lip service to (1) and do not believe (2)—they try to get their clients, qua individuals (i.e., particulars), to change. Fred has no interest in changing people, even if that's what most people come into therapy wanting, because he doesn't believe that's possible unless you use coercion. He relates to people as creators of change/changers of totalities, in this case the group—not as objects to be changed. He supports the group to continuously create emotional growth. His task as therapist is to direct the group in transforming itself as a way for people to regain a sense of their sociality as human beings, something which has been lost in our individuated, commodified, and alienated culture. He helps the group to move around and disturb the alienation that is as much a part of our environment as the air we breathe.

By alienation I mean the way we see people and things as separate and distinct particular entities. We have learned to give primacy to these particulars, and only secondarily (and only sometimes), out of the necessity of trying to make sense of the world, do we connect some of them. We don't see process or connections. We don't see the social processes that create the things that fill our lives, and we don't see the interconnectedness of everything and everyone. We don't see that we the people created and continue to create the stuff of the world, whether that be a box of corn flakes, a CD, a language, a "drug problem," a family, a global economy, a political party, the Brooklyn Bridge, a love affair, war, wealth, poverty, or our emotions. Instead, we relate to all these things as having an independent existence, as if they came from nowhere and just "are." Seeing and relating to things in this way—torn away from the process of their creation and their creators—is the normal way of seeing in our alienated culture.

Alienation deprives us of our power. It deprives us of the joy of experiencing our sociality. It deprives us of the capacity and energy for creative activity that we had as little children and with which we and our families created our emotional, social, and cultural development. It makes us mad and at the same time adapts us to our madness. No surprise, then, that alienation constantly looms its head, as both friend and enemy to the group.

I continuously wonder at the way psychologists and psychotherapists have ignored alienation. Is it perhaps accepted as a given, a constant, and thus, unchangeable and uninteresting? Or is it that alienation—at least the preceding characterization of it which is in the Marxist tradition—is simply not known among U.S.-trained psychologists, who typically are not well versed in Marxism or, more generally, philosophy?

A STORYTELLER'S PRACTICE

A big assumption in therapy is that what people talk about matters. Well, I don't think it makes a bit of difference what the group is talking about on any given night. I think we can create and do emotional developmental work with whatever it is that people bring into the therapy room.

I have never been a very good teller of stories. I'm not sure why. I seem to have at least some of the requisite abilities, like attention to detail, sense of plot, and curiosity about people. I'm a pretty good listener and observer, appreciate the absurd, have a sense of the ironic. Maybe it's how all these abilities are put together. Maybe—invoking a typically vague psychological term—it's my temperament. I am, temperamentally, more scientific than artistic. I'm inclined to want to make sense of things, to discover patterns. I'm told that I "show my thinking" (how I am getting from here to there), especially when I teach.

Unlike me, Fred Newman is a terrific teller of stories. This is one of his most attractive characteristics, at least to me. He has a knack for creating interest in what others might pass over, for wowing you with the exquisiteness of the utterly ordinary. Although well versed in the latest scientific findings and theories and formally trained in the philosophy of science, Fred has an artist's—not a scientist's—sensibility. Throughout our 25-year friendship and collaboration, we have been fascinated by this difference between us as we have worked and played with it.

Fred's primary interest is not in the stories themselves, but in the activity of story making. He has come to believe, through 30 years of doing therapy, that the value of telling stories is the transformative power of the activity. Storytelling is a centuries-old human practice, but it is also the methodology of a new mode of understanding that has the potential to help us create a new way to live. For this reason, Fred is pleased to see the growth of narrative approaches to psychotherapy that are part of the postmodern movement. He has commented that, "The emancipation that postmodern therapies provide comes from people transforming their life activity based on a new postscientific understanding of the 'storiness,' the cultural mythicality, the human authorship of human consciousness." His own therapeutic approach is designed to expose the fictional nature of "the truth" of our everyday language and our everyday psychology, not to create a new truth disguised as a better story. This kind of liberation from truth-based referentiality, he believes, is essential to emotional growth (and many other developments, as well).

Fred helps people see stories for what they are and for what they are not. The stories we tell ourselves and others about our lives, while they are typically taken as an accounting of events that have occurred, are as much a part of what happened (as much a part of our history) as "what happened." The telling of stories continues the ongoing process of "what happened." But to the extent that we mistake our stories for the events they are purportedly about, we can get locked into interpreting our lives in terms of these "truths" about ourselves. We distance ourselves from ourselves—from our "past," which we take to be fixed and determining of who we are now, and from our current relational activity (the telling of the story), which we take to be a description of what happened. We thereby fail to experience storytelling itself as something that we are doing now and that is continuous with—and part of creating—our history. Thus it is that, from Fred's point of view, the bondage of literality and truth-referentiality is the bondage of psychological subjectivity. Developmental freedom, particularly the freedom to create emotionality, is to be found in historical subjectivity.

The Language of Children

Fred: Speaking and listening do not require knowing what you're doing. If they did, children would never learn to speak. But as adults we insist that a condition for doing these things is that you know what you're doing, and it is this insistence that is at the root of people's experience of alienation. I've been doing therapy for 30 years now and have come to see that what you have to do is help people to participate in group, to listen and speak, without having the foggiest idea of what's going on.

Therapist-in-training: You've said that in social therapy you help people talk like children. Does that mean that children are not so self-centered?

Fred: Children are very ego-centered but they are not _about_-centered. Adults are deeply about-centered. They insist that everything they say _has_ to be about something. Children don't make that requirement of speech, at least before a certain stage in their development. At some point, they are socialized very forcibly to make aboutness a criterion of speech.

Therapist-in-training: So then when people come into therapy, one of their assumptions is that a lot of what goes on in their lives is about them. Is it the aboutness that's problematic?

Fred: Sometimes it's about them, sometimes not, but it's _always_ about something. Our question is, "Is everything _about_ something?" What if a lot of things going on in your life aren't about anything at all?

Creating Meaning (Thoughts on Speaking and Thinking)

Fred and I share a love/hate relationship with language. When our paths first crossed in 1976, we recognized in each other a keen interest in language and a respect for its infinite creative power (and also for its tyranny). However, it would be years before we would share our views on language in any detail. We were too far apart, with my views having been formed by the analysis of literature and the study of linguistics and his by the formal study of philosophy, in particular philosophy of language and of science, and by some early efforts in creative writing. I was learning to look at language scientifically, while Fred was learning the philosophical underpinnings of scientific inquiry and gaining an appreciation of its limitations. (What we did talk of, almost immediately, was psychology, perhaps because neither of us had much use for it.) However, in fits and starts over the many years of collaboration since first meeting, we have created thousands of hours of fascinating conversations out of our common and different ideas about language, about language about language, about meaning making, and about "aboutness" itself. And we treasure—to borrow a poetic phrase from our friend and colleague Ken Gergen—the "dances of difference" we have thus created. As I share our histories—distorted of course by who we have become and what we now think—the scientist-artist difference between us (no doubt part of that distortion) will occasionally be seen.

LINGUISTICS AND LANGUAGE

I was trained as a developmental psychologist quite by accident. My passionate interest was in language—what it is, what it does for us, what we do with it, how it is learned/acquired, how it varies from culture to culture, from person to person, and from situation to situation. Even as a child, I was an observer of linguistic behavior—noticing that some people talked a lot and others hardly at all, some were fun to listen to and others boring, with a few you felt you were

really talking together and with most others you didn't—and wondering where all
the variety came from (perhaps these questions were the origins of my scientific
bent). Once I learned to read and write, written language fascinated me just as
much. I made newsletters and magazines and kept a diary until I was a teenager.

And I read a lot. I have no memory of anyone advising me on what to read, or
making any decisions about what kind of books to read. (Neither my mother, who
left school after finishing eighth grade, nor my father, a high school graduate,
were what you'd call readers. The only books in our house were a few *Reader's
Digest* condensed novels.) However, looking back, I realize that I would choose a
genre and stick with it through several books or authors. The first were fairly
typical for a girl growing up in the 1950s—the Bobbsey Twins series and all of
Walter Farley's horse novels. After that, when I was about 10, came biographies
and autobiographies (the one I still remember is by Althea Gibson); beginning at
12 and through early high school, I read American plays, especially Arthur Miller
and Eugene O'Neill; then it was on to what I later learned were masterpieces—
The Psychopathology of Everyday Life, *A Tale of Two Cities*, *Jean-Christophe*, *An
American Tragedy*, *The Grapes of Wrath*, *All the King's Men*, the essays of Sir
Francis Bacon. English was my favorite subject in school and I loved the creative
writing assignments of Mr. Herzog, who had us imitate various genres and styles,
and both good writing and bad (I remember having to write an essay in the style
of Jonathan Swift and a story using as many clichés as possible).

Meanwhile, in high school classes I was more aware than ever of the gap
between the articulate and the inarticulate, observing that while many of the smart
kids were articulate and many of the dumb kids were not, there was not a one-to-
one correlation. In fact, I was a smart kid who was not terrifically articulate!
Speaking, thinking, writing, conversing, asking questions, answering questions,
creating with language, parts of speech, patterns, accents, dialects, genres . . . what
were these about, how were they related, what makes someone inarticulate—these
were things I wondered and wondered about—silently.

Until my last semester in college, when I took a course entitled Modern
English Grammar that turned out to be an introduction to structural linguistics.
What a joyful experience it was to discover that other people wondered about
these things, too—and made their living at it to boot! I could hardly believe that
studying language was a legitimate intellectual pursuit. As I immersed myself in
the course, I fell in love with linguistics—the discovery that utterances, words,
and sounds had form, function, and history thrilled me. I believed I had found my
professional home. This was very important to me at the time. I had been search-
ing for a discipline to be passionate about—having first tried psychology but rejecting it for being entirely experimental and laboratory-based at the time and
place I studied it, and then "falling back on" English literature because I had
learned to play the analytic and interpretive games required of a lit scholar reasonably well.

I entered the Ph.D. program in linguistics at Brown University and spent a year learning the basics of structural linguistics, through both seminar and field-work experience. I was fortunate to work on two projects in which I was learning by talking to "real people." As one of an army of researchers for the new edition of the *Dictionary of American Regional English (DARE)*, I traveled to villages and towns of Rhode Island, visiting elderly people who had lived in the state all their lives. Armed with a tape recorder and interview protocol, I asked them questions designed to elicit words, phrases, and pronunciations that were known to be particular to regional dialects (e.g., "What do you call the thing the rain goes into on the side of the house?"). The other project was an assistantship teaching English to foreign graduate students. Both projects put me smack in the middle of very rich and constant linguistic variation—reminiscent of my childhood concerns with articulateness and inarticulateness, variation in style and conversational ease.

Deciding to move back to New York, I left Brown University and transferred to the Columbia University linguistics department, which had a very different approach to linguistic analysis from Brown's. The orientation of the faculty, and therefore of the doctoral training, was exclusively theoretical, and I experienced levels of abstraction entirely new to me. On the one hand, I was drawn to transformational and generative approaches to language and was especially excited by the sophistication of Chomsky's work. On the other hand, my passions simply weren't stoked by the exercise of painstakingly delineating the underlying (i.e., mental) linguistic knowledge presumed to be possessed by any speaker. Nevertheless, I learned many things in this program, with the most valuable being about my own interests and views. I realized that I was interested in the process of producing language and linguistic phenomena and not in the mental structures that were supposed to make language possible. I accepted abstraction as a part of any linguistic analysis, but believed that analysis rooted in and tied closely to people's actual language activity was less abstract and therefore had more validity. This issue of the abstraction of linguistic analysis was to continue to intrigue—and elude—me throughout my years of becoming a developmental psychologist. It was only when I met Fred and encountered, through him, the abstraction of philosophy that I began to get a handle on it.

EXPLANATIONS AND EXPLAININGS

Fred was good with language from a young age. A marvelous improviser, he's told me that he had that skill as far back as he can remember. Language variation, however, is not something he ever gave much thought to and linguistic analysis didn't, and still doesn't, interest him. Artistic rather than scientific, Fred liked to play with language, not analyze it. But his decision to study philosophy when he did led him to look at language under a microscope.

When Fred entered the graduate program in philosophy at Stanford University in 1959, a revolution of sorts was occurring in the field. The study of ideas, which has been the traditional subject matter of philosophy, was being supplemented—indeed, at Stanford and many other universities, supplanted—by the study of language. No longer were ideas (e.g., truth, reality, beauty, the good, etc.) so compelling; rather, it was the language that we (both philosophers and ordinary people) use to talk about ideas that held fascination. In particular, the branch of philosophy known as analytic philosophy was devoted to exposing the meaninglessness of traditional philosophical analysis and argumentation, while at the same claiming that there was value in analyzing the language of philosophy. Fred was drawn to this subject and approach, as well as to the closely related new areas known as philosophy of mind and philosophy of science. Two topics came to interest him—historical explanation, a subject he met in an early graduate course and then explored in his dissertation, and mental language, a topic he was drawn to in his brief postdissertation teaching career. Both are interesting to take a look at because of how they shaped Fred's conception of language, his development as a methodologist, and his practice of social therapy.

In the 1950s, philosophers of language, of science, and of mind began to seriously (i.e., philosophically) discuss the intellectual exercise known as history. What did historians do? What form of thinking did they employ? Were they like scientists, who used a model of deduction and sought to explain the phenomena under study in terms of general laws? What was *explanation by history*, anyway? Debate centered around two competing positions on the nature of historical explanation. One, put forth by Carl Hempel in the 1940s, claimed that explanation in the field of history followed the same model as explanation in the fields of science, that is, it adhered to general laws like causality. In everyday language, Hempel was arguing that all explanation, whether in biology, physics, or history, was an attempt to provide answers to "why" questions. The other position, put forth by William Dray in the 1950s, contended that not all explanations follow a causal-deductive model and, in particular, that the accounting that historians do is often a description of what happened or how something happened, and not an explanation for why it happened. In other words, Dray claimed, Hempel's model did not apply because historians don't explain, they describe. Fred initially sided with Hempel because when you scratched the surface of Dray's seemingly clear-cut explanation–description distinction, things looked pretty fuzzy. Granted historians describe, but wasn't it the case that any given description makes sense only to the extent that it is explanatory? Aren't descriptions a specific type of explanatory accounting and not, as Dray contended, a completely separate and distinct analytic tool? And besides, it seemed that historical explanations were comprehensible only if they were subsumed under a general law (an implicit causal-deductive model).

However, Fred changed his position midstream in the writing of his dissertation (published as *Explanation by Description* in 1968). Influenced by the new philosophical writings on language, he began to consider the nature of events, description, and explanation in ways that neither Hempel nor Dray had; he examined them outside the framework of analytic philosophy. Reflection on certain claims of the new analytic tradition—for example, the claim that any event has potentially an infinite number of descriptions, and the claim that explanations are not explanations of events, but of events under description, which means that the language of the description is what determines whether the description is deducible from the explanatory law—suggested to Fred that the philosophical enterprise was limited. He began to question whether the very nature of philosophical analytic abstraction—as exemplified in this approach to historical explanation—was an overdetermining and distorting factor. Ultimately it would be Wittgenstein who inspired Fred to make a complete break with analytic philosophical determinism. Along the way, though, Fred met the important works of philosophers W. V. O. Quine and Thomas Kuhn.

Quine, a Harvard logician and revered American pragmatist, was among the philosophers critical of a philosophical school emerging in the 1930s and 1940s known as logical positivism. This was an attempt to construct logical foundations for all of modern science and to resurrect and justify empiricism. Quine took on logical positivism with great rigor and bite, and many believe that he did more than anyone else to "demolish" it. His concise and influential essay, "Two Dogmas of Empiricism," completely undermined the basic tenets of logical positivism (Quine 1963, first presented in 1950). Quine demonstrated that these tenets (he called them dogmas) of *reductionism* and *the analytic-synthetic distinction* were untenable. Quine's critique played a major role in Fred's development as a methodologist and, to this day, he never tires of teaching the significance of the "two dogmas."

The popularity of analytic philosophy had all but turned the philosophical enterprise into a method for creating methodological/philosophical generalizations and through them an understanding of particulars, a method that proved to have great value in science but little or none in the social sciences and practical areas of human life. Among the mounting critiques of philosophy's attempt to explain/justify/become science was one with broad and lasting cultural impact—Thomas Kuhn's *The Structure of Scientific Revolutions* (1962). In this work, Kuhn provided a sociological deconstruction of the scientific activity. He argued that scientific explanation could not be reduced either to a priori philosophical concepts or to empirics (raw data). In describing how modern science was created over the 16th to the 20th centuries, Kuhn introduced the notion of paradigm—a model, way of seeing, or worldview. Scientific explanation involves the generating of paradigms. Science evolves through a series of paradigm shifts, the revolutionary process whereby one worldview breaks down and is replaced by another.

The logical positivists thought of explanation in terms of abstract philosophical analysis that logically determined what an explanation was. Quine thought of it in terms of linguistic analysis, Kuhn in terms of paradigms. What was common to all three, however, was the underlying and unexamined assumption that explanation (whatever it was) had to exist in order to account for *explaining*. But didn't this beg the question; wasn't accounting for explaining as if it had to conform to an abstract conception of explanation circular? Maybe explainings didn't need explanation but were worthy of analysis qua *activity*. This notion of activity, barely formed at this time, was to become central to Fred's thinking and to the practice of social therapy.

Once Fred completed his dissertation and was intellectually "free," he broke out of the confines of analytic philosophy and explored other schools of thought. He returned to writings in philosophy of mind (for example, those by Hampshire, Ryle, Strawson, and Winch), which he initially read at Stanford in courses taught by the esteemed contemporary American philosopher Donald Davidson. He read and was greatly impacted by Sartre's existentialism (even writing an article on "The Origins of Sartre's Existentialism" that appeared in the philosophy journal *Ethics*) and began to delve into other existential writings and phenomenology. Compared to the sterility of analytic philosophy, existentialism and phenomenology seemed very much in the world and alive! Recently, Fred commented that these schools of thought served as a bridge that led eventually to his passion for history and Karl Marx. It was only years later, after a decade or more of political and community organizing, that Fred—now a Marxist—returned to philosophy. Most significantly, away from the academy, he got reacquainted with Wittgenstein.

Wittgenstein, whom Fred had read in graduate school but had not seriously studied until some years later, was a rare intellectual giant who carried out a brilliant piece of work, came to believe it was all wrong, and admitted that publicly—and proceeded to carry out another, just as brilliant. The first work, the *Tractatus Philosophicus* (published in 1921), was an attempt to reduce language to its logical form and, while Wittgenstein repudiated it, the *Tractatus* (as it is called by those in the know) became the springboard for the logical positivists and other schools of philosophy that claimed Wittgenstein as their father. The later writings (e.g., *The Blue and Brown Books [BB]*, *Philosophical Investigations*, *Culture and Value*) were a complete turnaround. In them, Wittgenstein put forth a method of doing philosophy without foundations, theses, or premises, philosophy that eschewed generalizations and abstractions. He had no use for philosophy modeled on science: "You can fight, hope and even believe without believing scientifically" (*Culture and Value* 1980). Explanation was, for him, part of the "mental mist which seems to enshroud our ordinary use of language" (*BB* 1965, 17) and produced philosophical muddles and confusions. Wittgenstein devised ways to expose the "pathology" embedded in our language and in the ways we think about language, about thinking, and about the relationship between our language and our thoughts (e.g., that we seek causes, correspondences, patterns, generalizations, etc.). He wanted people to see the activity of language, for it was language as activity, as forms of life, that could prevent such muddles.

In Wittgenstein, Fred found a completion of his own thinking about the activity of explaining and, even more, of his discomfort and worries about philosophical abstraction.

A DIALOGIC INTERLUDE

In 1993, Fred and I taught a 4-week class at the East Side Institute entitled "Vygotsky, Wittgenstein, and Social Therapy." Among the 60 people who attended, most had some familiarity with social therapy as either clients or practitioners, although for the 10 to 15 professors and students from nearby universities who attended, it was all new. During this time, Fred and I were having frequent conversations as part of the process of writing drafts of what ultimately became part of our 1996 book, *Unscientific Psychology: A Cultural-Performatory Approach to Understanding Human Life*. We decided to continue our conversation in class and see what emerged in that context. The following is an excerpt from the first session.

Lois: My history with philosophy is closer to that of everybody here than yours is, so I thought it might be helpful if I began—as someone who has not had formal training in philosophy but has been learning from you.

As an undergraduate, I had an introduction to philosophy course that I didn't get much out of, in part because of how badly it was taught. Then, as I was being trained as a developmental psychologist, the only way I thought about philosophy and psychology was realizing—and wondering about the fact—that little kids ask all kinds of questions that are philosophical, or thought to be philosophical, like "what's that, why is that, how'd that happen, where'd that come from," et cetera. And then they stop asking them—I think in part because adults get tired of answering them. It wasn't really until we started to work together that philosophy became real for me. One way it did is that it was then okay to ask, or give voice to, these questions. At the same time, it was very exposing because I realized how few questions I had. All these questions I had as a kid . . . that capacity is so repressed that when you made it okay to ask questions, I had very few questions. And I'm not alone in that, I'm sure.

So I want to invite you, as someone with formal training in philosophy, to help us, without formal training in philosophy, come to know what philosophy is and what its value is, by addressing your relationship to philosophy, which I think of as conflicted. By that I mean that I think to you it's both not of any value (at least how philosophers have come to do it) and at the same time it is obviously of great value.

Fred: I don't want to pass this off to Wittgenstein and not answer for myself, but in the spirit of talking about Wittgenstein, he was very conflicted about this very issue—what philosophy was and, inextricably tied to that, whether it had any value. I think Wittgenstein says in his writings that there's something about our human capacity to abstract, to generalize, to create language that gives us an extraordinary ability to do things with each other and with nature. At the same time, however, it leads to the generation of, if you will, philosophical and/or psychopathological abstraction, the creation of thoughts and ideas and ways of thinking, and so on, which keep us distant from anything resembling what is really history. I think Wittgenstein is saying that, in some respects, philosophy is to be understood as a species-pathology. It varies from grouping to grouping, age to age, and so on, but it's so pervasive that it comes to be identified as more normal than normal. Philosophy is the ability to do these things, like abstracting, generalizing, et cetera, gone wild. If philosophy has a use at all, it's to get rid of the pathology of philosophy itself. It's a kind of vaguely Pasteurian conception of immunization—that in some ways you have to use philosophy to destroy the dread virus of philosophy. I think that that's his view on what philosophy is. And I basically agree, which is, in a sense, why I gave up doing philosophy ultimately and started doing psychology—which I think is profoundly impregnated with philosophy. In fact, I don't think there's very much there except philosophy. Philosophy and pretty much four noteworthy experiments—that's what psychology seems to me to be.

Philosophy *is* questioning. In some sense, it's nothing but questioning. It's not even, particularly, answering. It has more to do with replacing the activity of having answers with the activity of asking questions. But that's not so easy to do and not so easy to learn, because we've been so conditioned by a paradigm, effectively a philosophical paradigm, of questions being primarily the occasion for giving answers, that it's kind of hard to deal with the activity of simply asking questions without so overidentifying them with the activity of giving answers. It's a very answer-dominated culture we have created, it seemed to Wittgenstein and it seems to me.

So I think what you were raising is very insightful and very interesting. In some sense, if I were to try to help everybody as a trained philosopher (and probably a trained philosopher is the person who can be of least help in all of this, but since that's what we got, what the hell—we've learned to use what we got around here), what I would try to help you to do is to ask lots of questions without wanting any answers. That's the activity I would urge you to try out, if you want to learn something about what philosophy is—to search out more and more questions, but have no interest at all in finding the answer to them.

Lois: Let me ask a further question without wanting any answer to this question.

Fred: Was that first question sufficiently unanswered?

Lois: Yes, it was sufficiently unanswered! Thank you! I think of psychology as very harmful and, as you say, a myth. You just said that psychology is 99% philosophy with about four good experiments, or experimental findings. I still think of psychology and philosophy as different on this, because psychology *is* looking for answers. If I understand what you're saying and want you to speak more about, what you and Wittgenstein mean by "the value of doing philosophy is destroying it" is that the positive aspect of philosophy is asking questions without looking for answers, but, in our answer-dominated society, what happened is that it developed into another institution, one that is seeking answers.

Fred: Yes. What Wittgenstein is attempting to destroy in destroying the old philosophy is answers without questions. Just answers. Traditional philosophy is nothing but answers.

Lois: Can you give one example of an answer in philosophy?

Fred: "I think, therefore I am." Who asked? Who in the world ever asked that question? If you study traditional philosophy you'll find these endless answers and if you think about it for a moment you'd wonder, "Who ever wanted to know the answer to this question?"

Does that indicate that these answers are less pernicious? No, what it actually indicates is they're more pernicious. Answers without questions are truly problematic for people and the world. Philosophy, I would argue and I think Wittgenstein would argue, has much to do with how life is conducted in our culture. It has an enormous degree of impact and over-determines our culture—our ways of looking at the world, our ways of seeing, feeling, hearing, touching, understanding language, understanding meaning, human nature, on and on and on. Our life is permeated with these philosophical abstractions, which are, as I said, answers to unasked questions that shockingly overdetermine our moment-to-moment life.

As I see it now, what had troubled me about the abstraction of linguistic analysis was what Fred's analytic philosophical studies had led him to reject—objectification. By objectification I mean the investigative practices that stem from the presumption that phenomena are study-able only from a distance. The typical scientific way of getting this distance is to posit a set of abstract general principles and/or model to which the world—the phenomenon, what people do, your data and so on—must conform. In analytic philosophy these took the form of principles of logic and deduction; in linguistics they took the form of deep structures, transformational rules, and taxonomies of phonological, grammatical, and semantic linguistic forms. In both cases, the phenomena in question are understood to be determinate; that is, they are either logically or linguistically determined.

Wittgenstein's method of philosophical investigation was, among other things, a practical critique of determinacy. Language as *activity* and *form of life* is indeterminate ("Only in the stream of thought and life do words have meaning," *Zettel* 1967, para. 173). In effect, Wittgenstein created a method of deconstruction that introduced indeterminacy into the investigation of language, a topic Fred repeatedly turns to in his teaching of social therapy.

A DEVELOPMENTALIST'S PRACTICE

What has become very important to me in doing therapy is helping people to come to know who they are—not by seeing what they're made of, but by seeing what they make.

For at least the first 5 years that Fred and I worked together, every few months he would say to me, "What are people talking about when they talk about development? I can't grok it." This was both fascinating and frustrating to me; on the one hand, I thought development was at the core of what we were attempting to create in social therapy and other projects and, on the other hand, I talked to him all the time about developmental psychology and couldn't figure out what he didn't understand. As I became more comfortable with thinking philosophically, especially about science and language, I began to understand Fred. It was what developmental psychologists did that he couldn't understand, because it seemed to have nothing to do with people developing. To Fred, the activity of developing, like the activity of explaining, was endlessly interesting, but development—like explanation, abstract and reified—was not. However, it wasn't until I shared with Fred the work of Lev Vygotsky and my excitement for it that the activity of developing became conceptually important in his work.

Development and Developing

Trained as a developmental psychologist, over the years I have come to all but reject that label as encapsulating a discipline that is antithetical to my beliefs and to my practice. I prefer to think of myself as a developmentalist—a word that captures an attitude and activity of supporting people to utilize, as fully as is possible, their creative capacities to grow and develop throughout their lifetimes. Here's some of how I now understand the transformation.

While in graduate school (I switched to psychology after my year of theoretical linguistics at Columbia), I loved the framework that the developmental paradigm provided. Piaget's stages of cognitive development were especially compelling to me. My first graduate seminar in developmental psychology at Teachers College, Columbia University, was entitled "The Child's Conception of Space," and Piaget's book by that name was our only text. I was hooked—by the elegance of Piaget's argument, the painstaking care and clarity of his observational reporting, and the self-confidence of his interpretation. Looking back, I now think that what so attracted me had little to do with Piaget's theoretical position, research method, or findings. What excited me was the intellectual exercise he was engaged in—and in which he engaged me. I designed and carried out some Piagetian quasi-experiments of my own, a contemporary variation of his classic "three mountain task." (In this task, a child is seated in front of a three-dimensional model of three mountains set on a table. A doll is placed in different seats around the table. The child is asked first what he or she sees and then what the doll sees.) Contrary to Piaget's findings that children described what they themselves—and not the doll—saw, I found that children younger than his subjects were able to take the perspective of someone else and describe what "the other" saw.

In the graduate seminar, this discrepancy led to some important discussions about research paradigms and theory generation—and about the perspective of the researcher. I had not set out to replicate Piaget's study; perhaps our findings were due to differences in experimental conditions. To what extent were Piaget's findings—and mine—a product of the time and place in which we worked? How much did Piaget's claim of childhood egocentricity influence how he carried out his research and how he interpreted what he heard and saw? Was he looking for evidence of the inability to take the perspective of another, while I was looking for nothing in particular? And what of Piaget's overall task—to understand how children acquire knowledge of the world—and the theoretical/philosophical perspectives (mentalism and constructivism) that are embodied in that task? This last question leads, of course, to an even larger philosophical issue, namely, what is meant by knowledge, but we didn't get that far in the graduate seminar.

The issue that intrigued me most at the time was how dependent on children's verbalizations Piaget's research and theoretical writings were. Much of the support for his claim of childhood asocial egocentricity came from inferring a particular kind, level, and process of thinking from what children said and, further, presuming that this inferred kind, level, and process of thinking was expressive of particular knowledge about the world at that stage of development. Even as a philosophically naïve graduate student, this struck me as much too a heavy burden to place on "Yes," "No," "I don't know," "The doll sees a little hill next to a big one," "This group has more," and many other instances of child talk in experimental settings. (Referring back to the discussion on linguistic and philosophical abstraction, I was questioning whether these utterances had to have an explanatory accounting.)

The assumption of a correspondence relationship between speaking and thinking came to trouble me more and more as I became increasingly committed to understanding how children learn and develop. However, it wasn't until I completed graduate school that I began to seriously engage the biases of this assumption. Instead, I embraced what I took to be positive about Piaget—in particular, his conception of the child as active and constructive—and threw myself into the task of developing a research paradigm to understand the emergence of early child language. As graduate research assistant to Lois Bloom, I worked closely with her, collecting, transcribing, and analyzing data from child–adult interactions, from roughly the time the children were 18 months to 3 years of age (today we would call these data "conversations"). We believed that children's utterances during these early years could not be understood in terms of idealized grammatical categories of the adult language, nor in isolation from the context in which they are uttered. Rather, they could be comprehended in terms of patterns of semantic, syntactic, and pragmatic categories that were fundamentally expressive of (and, perhaps, inseparable from) children's actions and interactions and people and objects.

Unlike Piaget, who posited schemas and operations inside the child's mind in his effort to explain how human beings come to operate on the world in terms of logical and/or scientific thinking, Bloom and I (and eventually a whole group of graduate student researchers) were wary of such blatant mentalism and teleology. We thought of our work as descriptive, not explanatory (as if it was simple to separate the two)—more akin to linguistic and anthropological concerns than to philosophical problems about the nature of mind. We saw our goal as describing child talk in concert with nonverbal context, rather than in comparison with adult talk. (Borrowing a distinction used in anthropological linguistics, we characterized what we were doing as "letting the categories emerge from the data"—an "emic" description—rather than imposing adult categories on the data—an "etic" description). To the extent that we made knowledge claims, we tried to confine ourselves to what children knew about language and not venture to posit what they knew about "the world." Bloom's work since then has shifted back to an explanatory mode. In *Language Development from Two to Three*, Bloom's 1991 compilation of previously published papers from the longitudinal child language research program, she frames our original studies in far more mentalistic terms than we did in the originals; for example, "what the child has 'in mind' determines what the child says (and interprets) what others say" (p. 4). Moreover, although still critical of research that begins with adult grammar for its portrayal of children as passive, she nevertheless attributes an important role to teleology in developmental theory.

I loved the challenge of this work, especially the interplay of participant observation, data analysis, and theory construction. I was thrilled when we made discoveries that contributed to developmental psychology's knowledge base (especially when our findings contradicted conventional wisdom). As an intellectual exercise, I found it immensely satisfying. Yet I wondered if our elegant analyses had anything to do with the children we were studying. I couldn't reconcile the gap between our categorizations of their talk and their language-learning lives; the complexity of our descriptions of what was going on linguistically and nonlinguistically came nowhere near capturing the richness of their—essentially social—activities. I began to question whether it was possible to really learn anything about how children develop through this kind of intellectual exercise. I didn't have an alternative, but still I couldn't accept that we *had to* isolate variables—to separate out from the total interactive activity what the child said, and then relate to what the mother or I said, what we were doing together, or what went on 5 minutes or 5 days earlier as *context*? I was uncomfortable with what seemed to me the artificial split that this made between inside and outside, between psychological and social, and between child and environment.

Years later, I was able to articulate more clearly my disagreements with Piaget and came to realize that, as groundbreaking as his work was, it contributed as significantly as did Freud's to psychology's conception of the autonomous, individuated subject. Both presuppose an inner (private mental) world and an outside (social) world; both take the biological as structurally and ontogenetically primary. That Piaget viewed the child as active did not change this in any significant way; Piaget's active child is only instrumentally active—a child's interactions with physical objects are important only to the extent that they stimulate internal mental schema. It was also years later that I learned that there were terms in philosophy of science for what was troubling me—reductionism and dualism.

Upon completion of my PhD in developmental psychology, I joined the research lab of Michael Cole at Rockefeller University. An experimental psychologist turned maverick cross-disciplinary explorer of human cognition, Cole was enthusiastic about the promise offered by noncontemporary and non-Western approaches to understanding learning and development. He was putting together a team of researchers from different disciplines to study the differing conditions of everyday and school thinking and learning and their impact on development. I was excellently trained by Bloom in observational, ethnographic methods of studying children in their everyday settings. I knew developmental psychology well and was skeptical of its value. I had an emerging view of development and learning as social, cultural activities. I was, indeed, ready for the radical departure from tradition that I found there.

The key methodological issue for us in Cole's lab (the Laboratory of Comparative Human Cognition) was validity. Specifically, the question we posed was, "If psychological theory and findings are generated in the laboratory (or under experimental conditions designed to replicate the laboratory), how can they be generalized to everyday life?" In other words, did they have any "ecological validity" and, if not, could we develop a methodology for a psychology that *was* ecologically valid? We considered the laboratory as a methodology and not merely a physical location. For it seemed to us that naturalistic and observational research conducted in everyday life settings was guided as much by the laboratory's methodological assumptions as any research conducted inside a psych lab. Conversely, much of what happens inside the laboratory during an experiment is what happens everywhere—but in the lab, it is ignored because the experimental paradigm disallows it. We hoped our research would not only expose the pervasive laboratory biases of how children's learning and development were studied and understood, but also help us create a new, ecologically valid set of investigative practices. Ultimately, our goal was to impact positively on the inequality and inadequacy of American schooling.

The main project I worked on—with Cole, anthropologist Ray McDermott, and radical behavioral psychologist Ken Trauppman—was a 2-year study of 8- to 10-year-old children in which we observed and interacted with them in a variety of school and nonschool settings in order to see and experience how various cognitive acts, such as remembering, problem solving, reading, reasoning, and others, were alike and different in the different settings. When we talked to "regular people" about the project, we said we wanted to find out some things about "how come kids who are street smart are school dumb."

We went looking for individual cognitive acts in non-school settings, but we couldn't find any—in informal settings, children solved problems and remembered things together, not in isolation from each other. About this time, Cole, along with three of his colleagues, had just finished putting together a translation of some of Lev Vygotsky's writings (what became *Mind in Society*; Vygotsky, 1978). We found in Vygotsky corroboration for the positions we were formulating. Cognition is a social and cultural achievement that occurs through a social process of people constructing environments to act on the world. It is located not in an individual's head, but in the "person–environment interface." This is what an ecologically valid psychology of learning and development needed to study (Cole, Hood, & McDermott, 1978). From this perspective, when we looked at children who were having problems in school, we didn't see their cognitive or emotional difficulties. Instead, we saw a complex, socially constructed cultural scene involving many people and institutions. We concluded that learning disability, for example, does not exist outside of or separate from the interactive work (joint activity) that people do that, intentionally or not, creates "displays" of disability (Hood, McDermott, & Cole, 1980; McDermott & Hood, 1982).

All this was very exciting for me. It offered an accounting of what had troubled me about the naturalistic, observational research paradigm I employed with Bloom in studying early language development. It was a clear alternative to Piagetian constructivist mentalism. It seemed an escape from the trap of the individualist paradigm that dominated developmental psychology. "Context" moved from the background to share equal footing with "person." And yet . . .

Through many conversations about this work with Fred, my old question—what did the intellectual exercise of researching development have to do with the life process of children developing?—resurfaced. We weren't making generalizations, looking for patterns, or applying a model. But was it the case that by studying the concrete and real-life situations children are in, we were studying their actual life process? Eventually I saw the objectification that remained in the ecological validity approach (and ethnography in general). We claimed to be free of the biases of laboratory methodology because we were studying people in their everyday life situations in such a way that we did not exclude a priori those elements that laboratory methodology excluded. And certainly we were able to see new things when we looked at social scenes and displays instead of formal cognitive tasks, and at the person–environment interface instead of at individuals. But while what we saw might have been new, our way of seeing was the same. We were still seeing at a distance, as observers with a scientific gaze. For us, the environment was an experimental context after all, one in which we hoped to get a "true"—rather than a generalized—picture of what was "really" happening. But for the children, this was not an experiment—it was a scene in their ongoing life performance. As I see it, the work of a developmentalist is to see, show, study, and create this performance—a very different task from that of a developmental psychologist.

A New Psychology of Becoming

> *If there's any single formulation that recurs in therapy again and again, it's people saying to someone they're often paying a substantial fee to, "I can't really do any of what you're suggesting because that's not who I am." Well, I frequently respond, hopefully not cynically or negatively, "What in the world are you doing here in that case? If you can't be or do or create who you're not, then why would you go anywhere for help?"*

The "discovery of development"—that is, the study/practice of the process of creating life performances, or the activity of developing—didn't happen at the Rockefeller University lab (it was, after all, a lab!). I say this in no way to deny the significance of the ecological validity project nor to minimize the influence Cole and his followers have had in bringing a social-cultural perspective to developmental, educational, and cognitive psychology. It is just that these advances in the academic fields have little to do with helping masses of people to exercise their capacity for creating developmental activity.

The work Fred, I, and others were doing in our noninstitutionally affiliated environment—Fred is fond of calling it "walls without a university"—allowed us to "discover development." It was an environment in which we saw the developmentalist in Vygotsky, something that was overlooked (probably not seeable) in the Cole lab. However, seeing the revolutionary nature of Vygotsky's conception of development and its relevance to social therapy did not come quickly. Fred and I worked and wrote together for about a decade before we added Vygotsky to "our team." I was involved in helping to create an experimental Vygotskian elementary school (the Barbara Taylor School) and exploring cognitive and language learning from a Vygotskian perspective strongly influenced by a social-therapeutic, dialectic understanding of method (Holzman, 1997). When I began to look at social therapy in Vygotskian terms, Fred and I had a qualitatively new way of talking about our work. Social therapy groups were akin to Vygotsky's zones of proximal development, in which the joint activity of creating the "zone" is what creates emotional growth. Relating to people in therapy as revolutionaries (something Fred had been speaking and writing about) was, in Vygotsky's words, relating to them as "performing a head taller than they are." And so on.

Here is how Fred recollected the transformation (our developmental activity) a few years after we had begun our revolutionary reading of Vygotsky and when we had just completed the manuscript that would become *Lev Vygotsky: Revolutionary Scientist*:

Vygotsky is how we learned together to write about our work. It's an interesting irony: Vygotsky is very anti-about, and we're even more anti-about than Vygotsky, and we used Vygotsky to help write about our work. But he does, after all, have a distance from our work—namely, he never even knew of it—which makes it possible for us to give expression to our work through him in ways which are very difficult to give expression to without him. So he's this marvelous spokesperson for social therapy, which doesn't diminish who he is at all. (from a 1993 interview)

Having Vygotsky as a new voice did much more than help us understand social therapy in a new way; it greatly advanced the practice. The activity of developing became the centerpiece of social therapy. As we came to understand it (and as "our Vygotsky" understood it), development is not a stage or state, but an activity—a joint, relational activity of continuously shaping and reshaping totalities (e.g., the person–environment interface). Development doesn't happen to us; we create it. For we are simultaneously who we are and who we are becoming. Environments for growth (Vygotsky's zones of proximal development) are ones in which we are related to by ourselves and others as who we are becoming. Fred's therapy groups literally became Vygotskian zones of emotional development. Social therapy clients talk development talk all the time. They may not know Vygotskian theory, but they know that their therapist is a developmentalist.

Therapist-in-training: Are there certain things that social therapy tries to develop?

Fred: For decades, people have asked us, "Doesn't your concept of development, either explicitly or implicitly, include some kinds of particular things that you want to develop? Doesn't the notion of development have to have an end?" I think that characterization would be a distortion of what it is that we're doing. We're trying to help people *practice the art of development.* I don't think we have some kind of hidden agenda. Yes, many of us in this room would agree on some things that would be good things to develop. But people will have to creatively determine for themselves what is to be developed. This is a big improvisation; this is not a scripted play, neither mine nor yours or anybody else's.

THE DIALECTICS OF COMPLETION

Vygotsky: (Hesitant) Well, Miss Braun, Dr. Wittgenstein (gesturing to Wittgenstein) . . . Dr. Wittgenstein and I have a somewhat unusual . . . "presenting problem."

Braun: And what is that, Dr. Vygotsky?

Wittgenstein: (Clipped and critical) He is too slow, Dr. Braun . . . too polite. Here's the problem. Vygotsky and I never knew each other when we

were alive. He died in the 30s. I died in the 50s. Now . . . 40 years later—
against our will—we have been brought together—"synthesized"—by
a number of people, including, I am told, two Americans named Newman
and Holzman, whom I understand trained you in this performatory therapeutic method you call social therapy.

Vygotsky: (Calming Wittgenstein down) Don't be so harsh, Ludwig. Don't be
so harsh. You see, Miss Braun, it's not that we don't like each other. Dr.
Wittgenstein is a brilliant philosopher and he has written extensively
about the philosophical foundations of psychology. We agree on a great
deal.

Braun: Then what's the problem?

Wittgenstein: (Harshly) The problem, Braun, is that we didn't agree to be put
together. (*The Myth of Psychology*, Session One, "Beyond the Pale," a
play by Fred Newman, in Newman and Holzman 1997, 158–162)

Until I met Fred, I wasn't at all interested in therapy. I knew almost nothing about
it; no one I knew ever told me they were in therapy and I myself had never felt the
need or considered it. To the extent that I thought about it at all, I didn't believe in
what I took to be its premise—that getting an explanation or interpretation for
how you were feeling automatically changed how you were feeling. What initially struck me about social therapy was that it was a way of helping people with
whatever emotional pain they were experiencing without diagnosing their problem, analyzing their childhood, or interpreting their current life. This was a completely new idea to me, one that fit with my budding understanding that all of
what we do is social activity. In social therapy, the clients, mostly in group settings, are charged with the task of working together to create an environment in
which they can get help, because in the activity of developing the group, all develop emotionally. They create their own "cure" by creating new emotional activity.

Fred also had disdain for therapy, or, more accurately, for its premises and
paradigm. He rejected the notion of an inner self that therapist and client needed
to go deeply into; such concepts and the philosophical dualisms upon which they
are based were things he was quite familiar with from studies of analytic philosophy, especially Wittgenstein's arguments against an inner life and private language. However, in the late 1960s he went into therapy and, like many people,
found it profound and transformative. As Fred tells the story, that therapy was so
incredibly helpful raised a "nasty" contradiction he had to deal with: "It never
occurred to me that some of the attitudes and beliefs I had about what I took to be
some of the mythic and irrational qualities of therapy were inaccurate. It didn't
make sense that it should work; it didn't make sense that it should be so successful. So I had to deal with the fact that therapy is of incredible value to lots of
people, and the question that kept occurring to me was, 'How in the hell could this
thing possibly work? What made it work?'" (Newman, 1999).

The answer Fred found emerged as he developed his own therapy practice—
a therapy devoid of most of the premises of therapy. "It occurred to me that the

entire model of what therapy has come to be identified as—getting into the mind and somehow reshaping it—has little or nothing to do with what makes people better. I began to reconsider the process that was taking place, not in terms of some notion of a kind of mental surgery to find out what were the deeper internal mental phenomena and restructuring them, but in terms of *what was going on between human beings* that was leading people to give some expression to emotional life" (Newman, 1999).

During the 1970s and 1980s, Fred continued to do therapy and train others in his method, social therapy. As the practice developed, he came to understand better how it worked from an analytic philosophy and dialectical perspective. One of the things that was going on in the process of social therapy was the challenging of the psychological picture of human life, especially cognitive and emotive life, as individuated, isolated, and internal—a fundamentally distortive picture of life-as-lived. Social-therapeutic conversations were, in part, a process of demystifying language, because it is our language—especially our language of emotions—that has become rigid and reified and leads us to experience the events in our lives and our feelings as individuated products, not as part of the continuous social process of creating our lives.

In this respect, Fred came to realize how strongly his therapeutic work was influenced by Wittgenstein. He shared with me his realization that Wittgenstein's philosophical method was essentially a form of therapy. I began to read Wittgenstein's work for the first time, and together we explored this notion of Wittgenstein as therapist. We found that others had commented on this, including Gordon Baker, the prominent Wittgensteinian scholar, who recommended that "scrupulous attention" be paid to Wittgenstein's "overall therapeutic conception of his philosophical investigations" (Baker, 1992, p. 129). In 1993, while in Great Britain on a speaking tour, Fred and I paid a visit to Baker at Oxford to learn more of his thinking on this matter. His corroboration of Fred's therapeutic practice as Wittgensteinian spurred us on to articulate the method of social therapy in these terms. We tried out our ideas at informal and formal presentations within our community and at scholarly conferences of philosophically oriented psychologists. We gave a fairly extensive formulation of our ideas in print in our 1996 book *Unscientific Psychology: A Cultural-Performatory Approach to Understanding Human Life*. In part, we wrote:

> Wittgenstein's antiphilosophical philosophy (his antifoundationalism) provides critically important methodological tools for a new, humanistic, developmental-clinical practice/cultural-performatory approach to emotional life. His self-appointed task was to cure philosophy of its illness. (Ours, as we will try to show, is closer to curing "illness" of its philosophy.) We are all sick people, says Wittgenstein. No small part of what makes us sick is *how* we think . . . especially how . . . we think about thinking and other so-called mental processes and/or objects. . . . It gets us into intellectual–emotional muddles, confusions, traps, narrow spaces; it torments and bewilders us; it gives us "men-

tal cramps." We seek causes, correspondences, rules, parallels, generalities, theories, interpretations, explanations for our thoughts, words and verbal deeds (often, even when we are not trying to or trying not to). But what if, Wittgenstein asks, there are none? (Newman and Holzman, 1996, p. 167)

To our understanding, Wittgenstein had developed a method to help free philosophers from the muddles they get into because of the way the institution of language (how we use language and understand what it is) locks them into seeing things in a particular way. His method was to "suggest, or even invent, other ways of looking . . . possibilities you had not previously thought. . . . Thus your mental cramp is relieved" (Wittgenstein, quoted in Monk, 1990, p. 502). Likewise, we saw social therapy as a method to help ordinary people get free from the constraints of language and from "versions of philosophical pathologies that permeate everyday life" (Newman & Holzman, 1996, p. 171), so as to have the opportunity to be makers of meaning and not just users of language.

However, something was still missing. If the expressionist conception of language was inaccurate, what was it that was going on when people are speaking? If our thoughts, ideas, feelings, beliefs, and so on are not somehow "transported" from our minds to other people through language and other means of communication, what is happening? If language is not a mediator between an inner life and outer reality, then what is it? How is it possible for people to make meaning together? Excitement, clarity, and discovery were to come through a reexamination of the work of Lev Vygotsky.

When I first shared my enthusiasm for Vygotsky with Fred, it was Vygotsky's overall method, his grasp of dialectics, his discovery of what we came to call tool-and-result methodology that excited us (Holzman & Newman, 1979; Newman & Holzman, 1993). We had seized upon a statement Vygotsky made which we found remarkable—here was an entirely new way of understanding method as something to be practiced, not thought up and then applied to "real life":

> The search for method becomes one of the most important problems of the entire enterprise of understanding the uniquely human forms of psychological activity. In this case, the method is simultaneously prerequisite and product, the tool and the result of the study. (Vygotsky, 1978, p. 65)

Vygotsky helped us to see social therapy as the practice of tool-and-result methodology. More important, he helped us see all of human development as tool-and-result activity—the activity of creating developmental environments (Vygotsky's zones of proximal development, zpds) is inseparable from growth. To Fred, Vygotsky's understanding of children's language development was profoundly relevant to adults' emotional development. Vygotsky had shown that in the zpd of early childhood, children are supported to do what is beyond them, to perform who they are becoming (even as they are who they are), and that this process of creating the zpd is the joint (ensemble) creation of their becoming language speakers.

They learn to speak by playing with language. Vygotsky's accounting was completely coherent with the activity of social therapy, in which people are supported by the therapists to do what is beyond them (create the group), to perform who they are becoming.

Fred had discovered the therapeutic dimension of Vygotsky's remarkable research. Therapeutic work is actually development work: helping people to continuously create new performances of themselves is a way out of the rigidified roles, patterns, and identities that cause so much emotional pain (and are called pathologies). In social therapy, people create new ways of speaking and listening to each other; they create meaning by playing with language.

Having found the therapeutic in Vygotsky, Fred now was to find the answer to his long-standing search to understand language as the activity of making meaning, a question only partially answered by Wittgenstein. I remember the day it happened. I had been rereading Vygotsky's *Thinking and Speech* (earlier English versions were entitled *Thought and Language*). I came upon some passages I hadn't really noticed before. Vygotsky is discussing the relationship between thought and word. He deconstructs the accepted understanding that we express our thoughts through language and shows how this could not be the case or children would never learn to speak. His own view of thinking and speaking was put so oddly I couldn't make sense of it, even though it immediately felt "right" to me. I was very excited—I had discovered something important and I had no idea what! I went to Fred and said, "Listen to this!"

> The relationship of thought to word is not a thing but a process, a movement from thought to word and from word to thought. . . . Thought is not expressed but completed in the word. We can, therefore, speak of the establishment (i.e., the unity of being and nonbeing) of thought in the word. Any thought strives to unify, to establish a relationship between one thing and another. Any thought has movement. It unfolds. (Vygotsky, 1987, p. 250)

> The structure of speech is not simply the mirror image of the structure of thought. It cannot, therefore, be placed on thought like clothes off a rack. Speech does not merely serve as the expression of developed thought. Thought is restructured as it is transformed into speech. It is not expressed but completed in the word. Therefore, precisely because of the contrasting directions of movement, the development of the internal and external aspects of speech form a true identity. (Vygotsky, 1987, p. 251)

Vygotsky's new way of looking at language and thought as one dialectical process, one activity, puts an end to efforts to try to link the "inner" (thoughts) and the "outer" (language). For as we understand his radical thinking/speaking, there are not two separate worlds, the private one of thinking and the social one of speaking. There is, instead, the complex dialectical unity, speaking/thinking. The child would not be able to perform as a speaker (and thereby learn to speak) if thinking/speaking were not a completive social activity.

Here was the answer to Fred's question—a nonexpressionist understanding of language that focuses on language as activity. As he described this discovery some years later:

> One of the immediate implications that I drew from this extraordinary new picture was that if speaking is the completing of thinking, if what we have here is a *building* process, which has different looks and different dimensions and different forms at different moments, but is all part of a continuous process of building, then this undermines the notion that the only allowable "completer" is the same person who's doing the thinking. For, if the process is completive, then it seemed to me that what we're looking at is language—and this goes back to Wittgenstein—as an activity of building. That is, what is happening when speaking or writing, when we are participating in a dialogue, discussion or conversation, is that we are not simply saying what's going on but are *creating* what's going on. . . . And we understand each other by virtue of engaging in that shared creative activity. (Newman, 1999, p. 128)

Fred and I continued to develop our method and to articulate it theoretically, with me primarily in child development and education and Fred in therapy. In our work, it became clearer and clearer that the human ability to create with language (to complete, and be completed by, others) is, for adults as well as for little children, a continuous process of creating who we are, a tool-and-result of the activity of developing.

In *The Myth of Psychology*, the play from which I chose a few lines to open this section, "Dr. Braun" (social therapist Bette Braun playing herself) helps Vygotsky and Wittgenstein with the difficulty they have with being "synthesized." She helps them examine the intellectual and emotional muddle they are in—fearing that they are being "violated" by the process, "watered down," or suffering a loss of their individual identities. Braun encourages them to see that their own radical understandings and methodologies of language, of activity, and of human life suggest, instead, that they are *being completed* by their synthesizers (which, of course, include Fred and myself). What ensues is a lovely intellectual dialogue in which Vygotsky and Wittgenstein complete each other—and us, their synthesizers. By the end of the session, they tell Braun they feel very enriched by the process.

REFERENCES

Baker, G. P. (1992). Some remarks on "language" and "grammar." *Gruzer Philosophische Studien* 42:107–131.

Bloom, L., et al. (1991). *Language development from two to three*, 261–289. New York: Cambridge University Press.

Cole, M., Hood, L., & McDermott, R. P. (1978). *Ecological niche-picking: Ecological invalidity as an axiom of experimental cognitive psychology*. New York: Rockefeller University, Laboratory of Comparative Human Cognition.

Hood, L., McDermott, R. P., & Cole, M. (1980). "Let's try to make it a good day"—Some not so simple ways. *Discourse Processes 3:*155–168.

Holzman, L. (1997). *Schools for growth: Radical alternatives to current educational models*. Mahwah, NJ: Lawrence Erlbaum.

Hood [Holzman], L., & Newman, F. (1979). *The practice of method. An introduction to the foundations of social therapy*. New York: New York Institute for Social Therapy and Research.

McDermott, R. P., & Hood, L. (1982). Institutional psychology and the ethnography of schooling. In *Children in and out of school: Ethnography and education*, eds. P. Gilmore and A. Glatthorn, 232–249. Washington, DC: Center for Applied Linguistics.

Monk, R. (1990). *Ludwig Wittgenstein: The duty of genius*. New York: Penguin.

Newman, F. (1968). *Explanation by description: An essay on historical methodology*. The Hague: Mouton.

Newman, F. (1996). *Performance of a lifetime: A practical-philosophical guide to the joyous life*. New York: Castillo International.

Newman, F. (1999). *Therapeutics as a way of life*. Talk given in New York City. October.

Newman, F., & Holzman, L. (1993). *Lev Vygotsky: Revolutionary scientist*. London: Routledge.

Newman, F., & Holzman, L. (1996). *Unscientific psychology: A cultural-performatory approach to understanding human life*. Westport, CT: Praeger.

Newman, F., & Holzman, L. (1997). *The end of knowing: A new developmental way of learning*. London: Routledge.

Nissen, M., Axel, E., & Jensen, T. B. (1999). The abstract zone of proximal development. *Theory & Psychology* 9(3):417–426.

Quine, W. V. O. (1963). *From a logical point of view*. New York: Harper & Row.

Shotter, J. (1996). Living in a Wittgensteinian world: Beyond theory to a poetics of practice. *Journal of the Theory of Social Behavior 26:*293–311.

Shotter, J. (2000). From within our lives together: Wittgenstein, Bahktin, and Voloshinov and the shift to a participatory stance in understanding understanding. In L. Holzman and J. Morss (eds.), *Postmodern psychologies, societal practice and political life*. 100–129. New York: Routledge.

Vygotsky, L. S. (1978). *Mind in society*. Cambridge, MA: Harvard University Press.

Vygotsky, L. S. (1987). *The collected works of L. S. Vygotsky, Vol. 1*. New York: Plenum.

Vygotsky, L. S. (1987). Thinking and speech. In *The collected works of L. S. Vygotsky, Vol. 1*, 39–241. New York: Plenum

Wittgenstein, L. (1965). *The blue and brown books*. New York: Harper.

Wittgenstein, L. (1967). *Zettel*. Oxford: Blackwell.

Wittgenstein, L. (1980). *Culture and value*. Oxford: Blackwell.

PART TWO

The Dialogues

Fred practices social therapy in New York City, in the 10,000-square-foot loft space that is the physical and spiritual center of a unique community building project. Over the last 25 years, the project has invited and supported thousands of people to participate in creating a new culture of human development. The loft space houses cultural and psychology-education projects that, while functionally distinct from each other, share in the continued process of creating the social therapeutic approach—that is, they are developmental, therapeutic, philosophical, and performatory (Newman & Holzman, 1996, pp. 151–161). It is an informal, open environment in which therapy, theater, and teaching activities intermingle.

One side of the loft is constructed for therapy and teaching activities—here are Fred's therapy practice, the East Side Center for Social Therapy (the largest of the 10 United States–based social therapy centers), and the East Side Institute for Short Term Psychotherapy, the research and training center that, among other things, offers training in social therapy. Separate rooms, with seating-in-the-round for up to 30 people, double as therapy and training spaces. The other side of the loft houses the All Stars Project and its performance programs—the 71-seat Castillo Theatre, the administrative headquarters of two youth development projects (the All Stars Talent Show Network and the Development School for Youth), and the large open "fundraising performance" space outfitted with round tables that provide seating and phones for 50 volunteer callers.

The space encourages freedom of movement and improvisational socializing. A rainbow-shaped, multicolored bench connects the two sides of the loft, serving not only to situate therapy as cultural and theater/performance as therapeutic, but also to "remind" therapists, trainees, and clients that they—and therapy—are in the world. People move about, sit on the rainbow bench, or make use of the various pieces of furniture (formerly theater props for Castillo productions) placed around the lobby/reception area to hold an impromptu meeting.

This openness and informality is, by design, coordinated with the encouragement of sophisticated dialogue, what we call the performance of philosophy. Fred's conviction that abstraction "is a critical developmental activity for the masses to engage in" and that "people must know how to philosophize" (this volume) is the methodological heart and spirit of the community and its activities.

This is the environment in which social therapy sessions and social therapy teaching-supervision takes place. Among all the community activities, it is in these social therapeutic settings that Fred most directly attempts to create a dialectical unity of ordinary discourse and philosophy, of informal everyday conversation and sophisticated philosophizing. The environment he strives for is one in which people just sit around, informally talking about personal things, and into which he can introduce sophisticated philosophical dialogue, thus transforming the conversation into one that is both personal and philosophical—and in that synthesis, emotionally/socially/morally developmental.

Having left academia in the late 1960s, the last thing Fred wanted to do was recreate the university. The East Side Institute, where Fred teaches and trains social therapists, is an anti-university or, as we said earlier, a "walls without a university"—meaning, of course, as free as possible from social–psychological– intellectual constraints of the institution. As teachers ourselves (both at the institute and within the university system), we know how difficult a task this is. Fred is a master at it. His teaching sessions are improvisational from beginning to end— in 25 years, we have never seen him refer to a note or a book in any teaching or speaking situation. He encourages people to participate with him to create a learning environment that is at once informal and intense, comfortable and unsettling, rigorous and playful, intellectually challenging and pointlessly silly, and lovingly accepting. His accessibility (he wanders around the loft space as much as anybody and talks to anyone who wants to talk to him about anything), the strong relationships he has with people he works with, and his sense of the comic and ridiculous all contribute, inviting people in to this activity—and more often than not, Fred and students do create a "school for growth."

Things happen to spoken words when they are set down on a page. They invariably lose their life, their particularity and nuance, their location within ongoing human discourse and relationship, their intimacy and their activity-ness. We have no illusions that this introduction to the social therapeutic learning environment will keep the words of the following dialogues alive. We do hope, however, that it helps readers be mindful that this kind of distortion, this deadening of language, is inevitably occurring.

All of the dialogues originated in dozens of Fred's training, teaching, and supervisory sessions held under the auspices of the East Side Institute for Short Term Psychotherapy. With a few exceptions they took place between 2000 and 2002. These sessions averaged 2 hours of free-flowing, open-ended conversation that often took a question-and-answer format. We worked from transcriptions of audiotapes, editing only for ease of reading. Also, we changed or deleted names and facts that might identify clients. We chose sections that we found particularly important, interesting, or in some way illustrative of social therapeutic method.

Initially, we thought to leave them unordered and untitled so as to preserve not only the process by which they came about but also the interconnectedness of their content. However, we realized that doing so would place an unnecessary burden on our readers by making it difficult, if not impossible, to find the content and create the order in which they want to read. So we chose to organize the dialogues around the following six topics: the core issues of social therapeutic practice; the social therapeutic group process; developing the social therapeutic relationship; therapeutic challenges: people and situations; social therapy integrated; and social therapy and philosophy (and politics). We also titled each dialogue with a phrase that captures its thematic as it relates to the general topic and to common practitioner concerns. The source of each dialogue is identified as colloquium, seminar, or supervisory session.

The dialogues vary greatly in length and detail. Some have a lecture quality to them; others are more informal and conversational. Many of the more substantial questions that begin dialogues were submitted in written form to be read at the monthly colloquia for trainees and graduates of the East Side Institute, staff of social therapy centers, and invited guests. Participants in these colloquia included professionals who came to social therapy with careers as social workers; clinical, counseling and organizational psychologists; doctors and nurses; alternative health and body workers; educators; and youth workers. Seminar participants were a varied group—social therapists, trainees, clients, professionals, nonprofessionals, and interested others from the broad Institute community. Participants in supervisory sessions were all practicing social therapists.

Speakers are identified as the generic *therapist-in-training* (a practitioner taking a social therapy course or someone enrolled in the Institute's therapist training program), *therapist* (a practicing social therapist), and *student* (a nonpractitioner participating in a workshop, institute, or class); *Fred* is Fred.

Lois Holzman
Rafael Mendez

Prelude

Dialogue 1. Therapy Is Like Writing a Song

Therapist 1: I recently observed one of Fred and Bette's groups. The experience was like watching a work of art. I was sort of overwhelmed by how well organized the environment was. It was the best listening environment I was ever in. Another thing I was very impacted by was that I didn't have the experience of Fred having these things to say and waiting for the opportunity to say them. As we were talking about that afterward, Fred said to me that his experience in doing group is that it's like writing a song. Something occurs to you, you see where it goes, and so on.

I was thinking about that in terms of my own limitations in doing therapy, in particular my work with C and the way that I feel I'm stuck in this place of my having something to say and waiting for the right time to say it. I'll have these moments when I'm walking down the street and I'll think to myself, "Damn, why didn't I say such and such in the session?" I think about what it is in my understanding of what I'm doing that prevents that from happening. An example of this with C is about her being very fragile emotionally, which she is defended against by her anger at how the world treats her. I feel like I haven't found a way to say what I have to say to her about this to help her to learn that about herself.

Therapist 2: I was expecting, after your opening remarks about how impacted you were by Fred thinking doing therapy is like writing a song, that you were going to relate your remarks about C to that.

Therapist 1: Yes, I think I was sort of expecting that also! Could you say more about how I might have raised this?

Therapist 2: I don't know. You might have said something like, "I was really struck by Fred saying it was like creating a song. I don't do therapy that way." Or, "What does that mean?" or, "Fred, I want to learn more about that"—especially given that you said it had a very big impact on you.

Therapist 1: I don't know. I think I might be scared or ambivalent about it, like that I wouldn't be doing my job or helping the person that way. Or that maybe I'm backing off from saying things that have to be said. I don't seem to be able to say hard things the way that Fred does.

Fred: I think the reason why you find things hard to say is because of what we understand our sayings to mean. I take it you don't mean it's hard to say the sentence or it's hard to pronounce the words. So you must mean something about what "saying" means in the context in which this other person and you speak. I think your sayings mean something different from my sayings. I don't think it's helpful to say that I say hard things and you don't say hard things. I say things that are on my mind and you say things that are on your mind. But I don't think my sayings mean the same thing as your sayings. It seems to me that's what you want to explore.

Therapist 1: I don't know. It seems to have something to do with the role I put myself in with patients—does that sound right?

Fred: You speak truth . . .

Therapist 1: Right . . .

Fred: I don't. That frees me up to say all kinds of things. I'm not even saying that people don't hear what I'm saying as truth—that's a different issue. But I don't speak it. That's their problem, not mine.

See, I think that people make a basic confusion here. I think that people sometimes think that they're not so invested in speaking truth because they're uncertain: "I couldn't be a truth speaker—I'm uncertain!"

Therapist 1: Yeah, they put it out tentatively by qualifying what they say.

Fred: Right. One has nothing to do with the other. I don't touch truth, but I'm enormously certain.

Therapist 3: There's certainty in the creative sense, like in painting. You're creating something, but there are laws that govern what it is that you're creating. There is a certainty.

Fred: To me, there's certainty—in painting, in creating music, in therapeutics—because there's nothing that it represents.

Therapist 3: It has its own internal rationale.

Fred: It's what I'm saying, painting, singing, whatever—call it what you like. When I say that I do therapy sessions like I write songs, I mean that absolutely literally. But I think that people here take it as a frivolous metaphor. Going back to [Therapist 2's] question to you, which I thought was very helpful, on the basis of our short conversation following the group, I guess I expected your question to be, "How do you write a song?" I would have thought that was an obvious direction to go in because, after all, I know how to write a song. You don't. So if you took that seriously, why wouldn't you inquire about it rather than treat it as a frivolous metaphor? I didn't mean it as a metaphor at all. I meant it literally.

Therapist 1: Okay. When you say that something occurs to you and you see where that goes, how do you decide, of the infinite number of things occurring to you all the time, which to go with?

Fred: See, I sit down at the piano, and I know the bare bones of playing the piano. I mean I know a little bit about it, like how to make harmonics, where to put my fingers down, I know not to put my nose on the keys. So I have minimal information of that kind, not a whole lot more. And now I make sounds. I make noises: You press these keys and they make sounds. Then I make other sounds. And what I try to do then is to step back from these sounds that I've made and see whether or not I can hear them speaking to each other—"Hey I think I could go with you"—or, "I think I should get the hell out of here," or "I don't think I sound very nice." And a lot of that goes nowhere. I keep doing that, almost by something resembling trial and error, though there is an ear—I don't know how to describe exactly how that ear works, but there is something going on. But it's a thoroughly noninterpretive process, and that's what I meant by saying therapy is like writing a song. When people speak I don't go to figuring out where to go from there off of some interpretation of what that means. Now, that's not saying there are no criteria, but I think the criteria, as I've said a thousand times, are much more aesthetic than they are interpretive or representational.

Therapist 1: I did think of therapeutics being like writing a song as metaphorical.

Fred: I don't want to simplify a very complex philosophical topic, but to me, *truth* is metaphor. And sometimes I think it's unkillable; I sometimes become skeptical that we can ever do it in.

Therapist 4: I guess I do hear your certainty as speaking the truth. What moves can I make to give that up?

Fred: Learn how to write a song! You see, you still persist in the thoroughly cognitive metaphor and modality of "I have to see it, understand it, before I can give it up." Why would you want this to be something that you see?

Therapist 4: Because I want to advance my skills as a practitioner.

Fred: But why is "advancing," to you, some kind of quasi-cognitive, quasi-perceptual seeing? There is one grouping of people who do something with relative certainty every day of the week and who have minimal commitment to truth. We call them mothers, raising young children. They are obliged to be certain, yet their relationship to truth is shockingly minimal. And children learn from that experience. Now, they don't always learn what you'd like them to learn, but they do learn. People need to put themselves through a similar, though not identical, experience to learn. It's not going to be learned through a cognitive perception. I think what you're raising is helpful, because part of the problem is that people want to learn this new thing in the old way. It's a contextual, societal arrogance. It's like saying to Beethoven, listen, could you please tell me how you do that? It's a misinformed question of a profound nature. It's to misunderstand the social therapeutic project.

from a supervisory session

CHAPTER ONE

The Core Issues of Social Therapeutic Practice

A. DEVELOPMENTAL ACTIVITY

Dialogue 2. Short-Term Therapy and Long-Term Growth

Therapist-in-training: I'm new to the program this year and am loving it. But I don't understand why the institute's name refers to "short term psychotherapy." From what I've seen, most of the therapy around here is what would be considered long term. Can you talk about the short-term-ness of social therapy?

Fred: I realize the answer I'm about to give might strike you or others as post hoc, like we had to come up with an answer to why we call it short term. But I actually think it's an accurate description of how we relate to and do therapy around here—and has deeper significance for how to understand the relationship between therapy and emotional growth.

What is typically meant by psychotherapy is people coming to a therapist with their presenting problems and trying to sort them out and deal with them. Typically, this consists of discussing and discovering how emotional problems are causally connected with events in their lives. In this sense of therapy, the therapeutic component of our work at the East Side Center and other social therapy centers is the individual work that people do before they come into group. That's the therapy. Typically, after some amount of therapy, the therapist will recommend to the client to go into group and have this positive group experience. Then, when they come into group, what actually happens is they give up therapy and go on to positive growth. Most clients leave individual therapy and come into group within months, so in that sense, most of our therapy is short term. When they come into group, I would argue, they're finished with what is traditionally known as therapy.

What you do after you've completed short-term therapy is you go on to then come to understand ways of looking at yourself and your growth needs which entail doing this extended work—perhaps even a lifetime of work—having completed therapy. So, the therapy per se is short term. The social therapeutic group, which is what you're referred to after you complete therapy, is best described as a bridge between the therapy you've now completed and the rest of your life. The group isn't the therapeutic activity—that we take care of relatively quickly. Now, it's important for some people to continue that process longer and that's always been fine with us; we've never told anyone not to do long-term therapy if that's what they decide. But the model is, effectively, a short-term one in that this introductory period of one month or two months or six months is what we count as the therapy.

Therapist-in-training: So it's short-term therapy and long-term growth?

Fred: Something like that which, taken together, is our therapeutic approach. But the long-term part of it is not therapy.

Therapist-in-training: You're not saying that the therapy part isn't social therapy, are you?

Fred: No. What's social therapeutic is the entirety of the process. The first part is much closer to traditional therapy in both its form and its content because people in an individuated form present their problems and the job of the therapist is to find out more about that. But all of that is preparatory to having this particular group experience. And that's transformative of what the first part is.

from a colloquium

Dialogue 3. The Improvisational Activity of Developing

Therapist-in-training: How is social therapy developmental?

Fred: From the point of view of development, I have come to believe that we are better off relating to life as continuous happenings, continuous emerging processes, complex social activity, rather than as things happening to things. Periodically we impose commodified forms on continuous emerging processes because it has a certain utility. For example, it's useful to know where things are on the kitchen shelf. The problem is that we leave ourselves vulnerable to coming to see the world in terms of what's on the kitchen shelf as opposed to the processes which got them there and which get them off.

I try to help people to take a look at what we do together. We engage in a certain human life process together, and the discovery of who we are is the discovery of what it is that we are continuously becoming. The notion that we discover who we are from getting a deeper look at the component parts that make us up is, in my opinion, a pernicious myth. We aren't who we are. We are what it is that we are continuously becoming.

It's very easy to hear this as completely intelligible, but as metaphorical. But metaphor is a relative term. After all, one person's metaphor is another culture's reality. Ours is a culture of commodified "being" in which "becoming" tends to be related to as a metaphor, at best. What I try to do in my therapeutic work is to help people to relate to becoming not as a metaphor, but as activity. Given our culture, what people tend to do, quite understandably, is to commodify activity itself, and to say, "I see, you mean by activity another kind of thing." But no, I don't mean another kind of thing, what I mean by activity is not a thing at all. What I mean by activity is the complex, ever-continuous social process that we are all continuously involved in; I mean by it life. Life is filled with things. But life itself is not a thing, although it is related to by all kinds of people, including the insurance companies, as a thing. You can understand why the insurance companies would relate to life as a thing. It's their business. That's fine. But I have no interest in living my life as if I were a thing, and I have no interest in relating to other people as if they were things.

To the extent that human beings come to recognize that life is the activity of living—and not the periodic identification of the components of our lives as certain things—they are helped to deal with the difficulties, the labels, the pains, the unhappiness, the distress, the emotional disorders that are inextricably related to the commodification of human life. This is what we have come to understand as we continue to practice and develop social therapy.

Therapist-in-training: Are there certain things that social therapy tries to develop?

Fred: For years, people have asked us, "Doesn't your concept of development, either explicitly or implicitly, include some kinds of particular things that you want to develop? Doesn't the notion of development have to have an end?" That characterization is a distortion of what it is that we're doing. We're trying to help people *develop*. To practice the art of development. To create with other people in their lives and to build their lives in the ways that they choose. I don't think we have some kind of hidden agenda. Yes, many of us in this room would agree on some things that would be good to develop. But people will have to creatively determine for themselves what is to be developed. This is a big improvisation; this is not a scripted play—not mine, yours, nor anybody else's. After all, you can learn something about acting and performing, but it doesn't mean for a moment that you're going to perform a beautiful play. Some of the most highly skilled actors perform terrible plays. Why? That's what they get paid for, that's where their tastes lie, who knows?

To me, it's analogous to democracy. I am deeply committed to the position that what needs to be created is an increasingly democratic society. Many people who call themselves progressives say to me, "Why are you pushing so hard for democracy? Don't you realize that if we had democracy the majority of the American people would support and enact positions that are antithetical to what is politically correct?" I frankly believe that we have to create a greater democracy and take our chances on that.

Likewise, I think we have to take our chances with development, which means that people might develop some things that you might not think are so nice. But the argument that you should stop development or steer it in a particular direction on the grounds that that might happen is ultimately elitist. That implies a certain power structure where some people give lip service to development and/or democracy but really hold to the position, "Here are the most valid kinds of decisions to be reached and goals to be set."

Therapist-in-training: There may be the alternative of combining development with certain kinds of goals.

Fred: You might be right, but my experience is that when people slip in goals then development gets shaped in such a way as to achieve those goals. Goals tend to be overdetermining. We haven't as a species taken this risk yet and we've gotten into big trouble anyhow. It's not as if the goal-oriented approaches have worked out beautifully! Maybe this is the essence of what I take postmodernism to be; maybe we're at a moment in history where we're going to have to take our chances with development. Maybe it's time to find out if we can get better and better at this stuff—and if we are going to destroy ourselves or not. Maybe the moment of truth is at hand and we should find it out once and for all, rather than just quietly murdering millions and millions of people in the name of good goals.

Therapist-in-training: I understand that you are against elitists, because they stifle development. But doesn't the existence of an elite class provide incentive to other people to join it to learn more? If everybody is equal in his or her development and learning, that's kind of like communism. Nobody's going to want to develop themselves, because there's no point.

Fred: It depends on what privileges go with that. I don't think we want to have a social arrangement in which people who have a capacity to teach or lead are not given a maximal chance of doing that. I just think it's problematic to give certain special privilege to people who make that contribution. I think you can create a community of people in which everyone is moti- vated to contribute the talent that they have and get the gratification of the total creation and their particular contribution without it having to be the case that what they get is some kind of caste-oriented privilege. That seems to me what holds human growth back.

Bringing this down to earth, in the therapy groups that I do, we talk about the "stars" in the group. They talk a lot; they lead things; people turn to them. But it doesn't follow from that that people who are not the stars are in any manner, shape, or form less privileged than the people who are the stars. Is that so easily effected? No. The culture in which we live is very verticalized. Someone asked me the other day what I mean by leadership. I answered that I'd like to introduce a new metaphor for leadership, which is not someone being in front of someone, but someone being alongside of someone. It is hierarchical verticalization that I am interested in breaking down, not different contributions from different people.

from a colloquium

Dialogue 4. The Politics of Being and Becoming

Therapist-in-training 1: I've been observing in one of your groups and recently you've been working to help people accept their limitations. I want to help people get rid of their limitations! From what I hear you saying, accepting our limitations is necessary for us to get help. But isn't developing going beyond your limitations?

Fred: That's an interesting question. And if I can add to it—"If what we're inter- ested in is becoming, then why is it that we urge that people not go beyond their limitations?" Well, it's precisely because we are interested in becom- ing that we want people to stay within their limitations, because if you don't stay within your limitations, if you don't function as who you are, then what comes out is not becoming but pretense. If it's genuinely becom- ing, there's got to be a dialectical struggle with the acceptance of who you are. Too many people and too much therapy try to get people to function off their fantasies—pretend you're a this, pick up another story—and there is no struggle involved. There is no recognition that what we're working with here is a very difficult dialectic.

A fundamental part of what we understand growth to be demands an acceptance of who you are in order to move beyond it. In my opinion, misusing the faculty of pretense and imagination and pretending you're something that you're not is one of the more non-growthful things we can do. Growth is a struggle, a dialectic, a recognition of our limitations so that we can build something off those limitations and in that process develop, go beyond them. The going beyond can't be some idealistic "I'll just make up a new story."

Pretending is a devil that we easily succumb to in big and small ways. We have a remarkable power to fool ourselves. There are few things we are better at as human beings than fooling ourselves. What's left out when we do that is the dialectical intensity of the relationship between learning and development. To be what is becoming is to go up against an intense force, namely, who you are. There has to be a recognition of this if there's going to be a successful process of growth. As a species, we have very serious natural, psychological, and cultural limitations and—here's the magic— despite the intensity of our limitations, we can grow. By any reasonable analysis, given the extent to which we are limited and determined, there should be no such thing as growth, either individual or social. Growth should be impossible. If you listen to much of what traditional psychology has taught us, you'll find growth inconsistent with it and this is a serious problem of psychology.

At the core of our whole theory is a political reality, which is how difficult the process of dialectics is. It's political in the sense that there has to be a recognition of the difficulty of changing anything, including you. It's not easy to change the world, even the little piece of it that happens to be you. It's difficult to grow. Sometimes after you see it, there's a tendency to pretend and mischaracterize it as easy because we easily forget how hard it was to accomplish it. After it's happened, we say, "Wow, that was a miracle," but what we're leaving out is the actual process that took place. We have a tendency to do that because we're all pretenders, even to ourselves. And I don't mean that negatively or critically. In any given situation, we're probably all doing some degree of pretending. Part of what socialization looks like is the capacity to know how to pretend. We pretend very well.

Therapist-in-training 1: So, performing is growthful but pretending isn't?

Fred: It's because we have the capacity to pretend that we can perform. Pretending is not performing, but our capacity to pretend is very related to our capacity to perform. To us, performing is—and I don't like using this word but I will—self-consciously pretending for the purpose of growth. Pretending doesn't necessarily have much to do with growth, although imitating, which is what children do even before they know how to self-consciously perform, is a kind of pretending in a zpd [zone of proximal development], that is, a context in which the pretending is a component of growth. We have imitation and we have pretense, both used in different kinds of ways in different contexts with different degrees of self-consciousness.

To us—and I think Vygotsky would agree—a zpd is a group particularly structured for growth. My job is to construct the zpd out of what people do so as to have an environment in which they can do things that are performances/pretenses for growth. Performances for growth require a certain environment. Hopefully on my best days, I help create that environment. That's what a therapist has to do. You work to help construct the environment so that what clients give to you and each other can turn out to be a developmental experience. That's your job.

Therapist-in-training 2: Is pretense the other side of the coin of adapting?

Fred: Much of traditional psychology is based in the belief that the highest form of change is adaptation, so I think it uses imitation and pretense to help achieve adaptation. I don't believe adaptation is the highest form of growth. I believe growth is the highest form of growth! I think people are capable of changing, of developing, of evolving. As I understand it, adaptation has none of the characteristics that I associate with qualitative change. To be sure, you could make out a strong argument that what they call behavioral adaptation or behavioral change is a whole lot easier to effect than doing something about a situation by changing the world. We think the way to deal with the problem is to change the entirety of the world. People think that's absurd, that if you do that you will never get anywhere. I think it's the other way around. I think that if what you accept as your idealized end is adaptation, there's no way you are going to go beyond what you start out with.

Of course, we have to deconstruct and analyze what changing the whole world means. That's no small part of what social therapeutic theory is about—not only what changing the world means but how it's done and why it's not as improbable as it might seem. I would argue that not only isn't it improbable, it's impossible not to do if you do any kind of growing at all. I don't think there is any room for growth absent transforming the entirety of what we have. I don't know where we would put the growth if it weren't transformative of everything we're doing. It might seem impossible, but I don't think it is. I think it's adaptation that's impossible.

The slightest change of a color in a painting is transformative of the entire painting. It seems to me metaphysical talk to say that you can do a thing so particularized that it only changes that particular point.

Therapist-in-training 3: But isn't the change in color a particular?

Fred: Don't be confused into thinking that because you call something a particular it doesn't have a complex interrelationship with everything else. The notion of particularity is what's at issue here. The dualism of particular/universal has been a staple of Western thought for thousands of years, but whether that holds up as a way of understanding from a developmental, growth point of view is the very question at issue in postmodern culture. Even if we've come this far with that distinction, it doesn't follow from that that we can go much further.

That's the fundamental contradiction of modernism, if you will. It's not clear how to account for genuinely new things, new conceptions, new comings-into-being under the, generally speaking, deterministic theory that modernism is. Now, adaptations have been made to the overall view of modernism so as to account for newness, but that raises the question of how adaptation can accomplish that. I don't think it can. I think modernism is self-contradictory on its own terms.

It's not easy to account for revolution given the overall deterministic way in which the world is viewed. And, indeed, revolution is hard, not only quantitatively hard but qualitatively hard, because of what's involved in the effort to develop and move beyond societally overdetermined and used-every-moment-of-every-day conceptions of nature, life, individuality, and so on. Those are unbelievably difficult concepts to move beyond. But, remarkably, they have been moved beyond in the history of modernism, not to mention premodernism. It's a remarkable phenomenon. To me there is no more remarkable phenomenon than revolution, and, as a corollary, none more difficult. That's why I love it so. It's fun to grapple with. It's slippery because we're all modernists. Why wouldn't we be? If we managed to exempt ourselves from it, that wouldn't be saying much about the power of modernism. That's our contradiction, that's the paradox that we have to move beyond, both in broad sweeping terms and in the therapy, and if you can't help your clients to do that, then you haven't helped them at all. That's what I'm getting at in seeing the patient as revolutionary. You have to relate to patients as revolutionary—not in the narrow, substantive, ideological sense of the word revolutionary—in order to help them to grow at all.

from a colloquium

Dialogue 5. What Develops? (Overcoming Individualism)

Therapist: In a recent group I was very aware that what was going on was that people were reacting and responding to individuals. I get drawn into people's stories and I found a lot of what people said interesting. But it seemed like a structurally competitive activity—people responding to each other. The liberals in the group tended to validate or identify with other people's stories, attempted to make them feel good, et cetera. The group has to do a qualitatively different activity to build the group, an activity that challenges this Enlightenment concept of liberalism. How does building the group challenge liberalism, and how is it therapeutic?

Fred: I think you answered the first part of the question. Given where you just characterized liberalism as coming from—its association with individualism and competitiveness—then insisting upon the fundamentality of the group as the unit of growth is de facto a critique of that Enlightenment conception, a conception that is fundamentally a notion of individual growth, individual competition, of the infinite capacity of the individual to learn more, know more, know better, to continuously grow so as to be more and more able to comprehend nature and to take advantage of it for personal gain of whatever sort, whether it's financial or emotional.

The very definition of growth that has come down to us from the Enlightenment is individual growth. The paradox is that there is no longer room for individual growth. Marx writes about the limits of growth of capital as an economic form and there is a similar argument to be constructed about psychological growth.

Therapist: And how is this challenge therapeutic?

Fred: I think it's therapeutic because it helps people to overcome in their own particular way the particular form of their frustration as individuals attempting to grow. It helps people to overcome it because it continually makes the point experientially that it can't be done. It's therapeutic in the way that trying to get someone to throw a ball 400 yards is therapeutic. When it becomes plain that you can't, you then have to consider what you can do, what's do-able, what's possible. It's therapeutic in the way that lots of things in life are therapeutic—they expose the limitations of what you're attempting to do, and if your own limitations are exposed, that's therapeutically helpful as part of the process of coming to more fully appreciate what you can create, what you can accomplish.

And then, if that's accepted and understood collectively, social therapy goes on to teach people how to do new things, which is to grow the group. And if you learn better how to grow the group then you can rekindle development. So that's how the social therapeutic process works: You first of all realize that you can't grow any more yourself, but that you can grow participating in the process of growing the groups in which you function, and 10, 20, 30 years later, there you are, all cured. Development in this sense is development by virtue of the group growing, by virtue of having learned the activity of how to makes groups grow. And that's completely antithetical to the Enlightenment conception of individual growth.

Therapist: And then you can apply this skill elsewhere?

Fred: Oh yes. You can do it everywhere that there's a group, which as far as I can tell is virtually everywhere. People have learned a new social skill and they practice it with varying degrees of success. Again, there's no guarantee that every effort to practice it is going to work; there's not even a guarantee that if you practice it perfectly well it will be effective because there are other factors in the world—you might be in the midst of practicing it and you get struck down by lightning.

People are at all the varying stages that you would expect in attempting to learn a new paradigm—a post-Enlightenment conception of who we are as human beings. It's exactly what you would expect. It's a different subject matter; something different is being taught. And it's a hard subject; it's difficult to learn. It's particularly difficult to learn because it's up against something that has been a structural part of the culture at the deepest level for a long time. It's not so easily overcome.

from a supervisory session

Dialogue 6. Radical Acceptance and Emotional Growth

Therapist-in-training: Could you help me understand better what is meant by radical acceptance and how it is important for emotional growth?

Fred: I was working with someone in group the other night who has been in therapy with me for a long time. She was saying, "What can I do to get over this? How can I stop being this way?" I said to her that she had to come to terms with the fact that this is where she was and that she had to reframe her question. I found myself telling her and the group a story that I had not told for 25 or 30 years. It just came to me.

Back in the 1960s, I was a very modest drug user. I occasionally inhaled. I was up in the country, at Woodstock. Some friends of mine brought out a whole tray of brownies that were filled with hash—but no one had told me. I ate them and I had a very bad trip. I was feeling very spaced out, paranoid, and so forth. What I finally found useful was to say to myself, "Well, this may be how you are now. Maybe this is it. Maybe there isn't any road back. Maybe this is the deal. You're going to have to figure out how to do things given this spaced out thing that's going on. In fact, maybe the concept of a 'road back' is what is exacerbating this experience, because you're giving so much energy to it." I was putting my energy into, "Can I undo this?" And nothing extends something more than focusing your energies on trying to undo it.

What I mean by radical acceptance is not a passive statement. It's not separated from the process of continuing development. It's a kind of serious looking in the mirror, not with the focus on "how do I make myself other than who I am?" but rather with the focus on the process of fully and radically accepting who I am. That is inextricably connected to going forward.

The person I was working with in group became, not surprisingly, very upset. The group is a very supportive, loving, and caring group, and I think we were then able to support her and help her see that it was important for her to come to terms with where she was, because she was profoundly upset that she was where she was. You can't grow from the denial of the starting point. That is not a growth step.

from a colloquium

Dialogue 7. Choosing to Grow

Therapist-in-training: How do I learn to get rid of my identity? And how do I, as a social therapist, help people who come to me learn to get rid of theirs?

Fred: I don't think it's something to learn—let's start with that assumption. I think it's something you do. It's a decision we all have to make. I think we have to face a certain moral issue—in all therapy, but I think particularly in social therapy. The moral issue is, do you want to be comfortable or do you want to grow? Who we are is unquestionably more comfortable. Growing is not altogether comfortable, particularly when you are older. It's not particularly comfortable for children, even physically it's not comfortable, but certainly for grownups, emotionally and in all kinds of ways, it's not particularly comfortable. It's a choice, a moral choice to decide to grow. It's a choice we can make at many times in our lives. I think you can continuously choose to take growth as your option.

What follows from that? That's hard to say because it's going to be what you do with it, and there are all kinds of things to do with it. I do think that certain things can be understood about it. I think it's going to involve not only a transformation for you, but for your environment and your world. I think it's going to mean reconsidering certain kinds of fundamentals, like giving and getting. I think it's going to take an ongoing examination in the aftermath of the choice. If flowers had to decide what they were going to look like as a function of growth, they would never grow. It isn't knowing what's going to come, it's knowing that you choose to participate in the process that you think increases the likelihood of this mysterious developmental phenomenon happening.

Development is mysterious, not in a way that makes it unscientific or religious but mysterious in the best sense of the word, in the sense that we fully engage in a process that we don't know the outcome of. That's an advance on modernism, it's an advance relative to premodern Aristotelianism. It's a great human change to accept the notion that much of what is happening in the universe is not happening because some person or some god knows where that process is going. We don't know where that process is going. And yet we participate in it. It's a choice.

Ultimately, the postmodern question is an ethical question. It's a question of choice. Will the people of the world make that choice or will they persist in what I would identify as an illusion or pretense—and it's that pretense, speaking ethically now, that gets the world in trouble because modernism has run its course. There is the pretense of knowing. Everyone is pretending to know. When I look at the situation in the Middle East, my first thought is, "How can we possibly go anywhere, or grow anything, or develop if everyone is so committed to the pretense of knowing what's going on?" We don't know what's going on. We don't know what's going on in this room and that's fine. I don't think that's a terrible moral dilemma. The moral dilemma, in my opinion, is knowing what's going on. So yeah, that's what it comes down to and again, it's a repeatable choice.

What happens in therapy, as I see it, is that one of the things I do as part of creating the environment is to continuously ask the people in group if they want to make that choice. It's not like it's a once in a lifetime choice; it's a choice you have to make repeatedly. I have to say, "Do you want to do this growing tonight or do you just want to talk with each other? That's fine, but it's a choice. I will persist in putting that choice before you, and you can persist in saying to me you don't want to do any growing tonight." That's the dynamic of the group work. I try to do it in creative and, some might say, seductive ways. I'm not neutral; I'm trying to get the group to do it. How often does the group do it? Not very often. More often than not, the group decides on not growing. Once in a while the group decides to grow and then you have the magic and people walk out and say, "What the hell was that?"

It's not a learning in any traditional sense of the word. It's a very hard choice. I have nothing but respect for people who go through social therapy. It's a very hard choice. It doesn't contribute to comfortability. It inspires me how many people choose it year after year after year.

from a colloquium

B. ENHANCING SOCIALITY/CHALLENGING INDIVIDUALISM

Dialogue 8. Creating Zones of Proximal Development

Therapist-in-training: I'd like to understand better the zpd in social therapy. I've been reading *Lev Vygotsky: Revolutionary Scientist* and learning the context in which Vygotsky introduced the term. In the book, you and Lois say,

> Central then to the discovery and use of the zpd is Vygotsky's concern with the character of the relationship between matured and maturing processes, and what seems plainly related, the relationship between what the child can do independently and in collaboration with others. While recognizing that a child can accomplish more with collaboration, help and support than he can alone, Vygotsky noted that the child's potential even with help is not unlimited. The view that imitation is a purely mechanical process and that therefore the child is capable of imitating virtually anything was according to Vygotsky incorrect. The child, and the rest of us for that matter, can only imitate what is in the range of what is in our developmental level. Studies of early language acquisition conducted in the 1970s gave further empirical evidence to Vygotsky's argument. It was found that the individual children not only varied in the amount they imitate from the language that they hear, but also that they are selective in what they imitate. Children do not imitate what they know well or what is far beyond their linguistic level. They imitate what they are in the process of learning. (Newman & Holzman, 1993)

Could you speak more about the zpd and your understanding of it in our social therapeutic method? What do we mean when we talk about evaluating the range of our development? And how does the therapist utilize this evaluation information to further the client's development?

Fred: Characteristically, people come into social therapy—as they come into all groups, characteristically—individuated. They want to grow the way they have been taught in the context of the broader society, that is, individually. They come in with that agenda and learning model. And that is understandable, since that is what they have been taught. So no small part of what we have to do in social therapy is to reeducate people on how to learn. We learn collectively and by our interrelationships with people at different learning levels. This is not easy to take in because the entirety of society speaks the opposite of that; it speaks to individual growth and learning.

Social therapy, in part, is an extended and complicated process of teaching people this new model of development and learning, and they have to be open to learning that model as a precondition for growth and development. It's an ongoing process; you don't just do that in one session. The teaching of this new model includes everyone coming together and learning the task of creating the group. It is an active process to build the group, and the group has to undertake that creative task over the long haul as a condition for learning anything.

Someone comes into group very upset, someone who has not participated in creating the group, and says, "I need help, I'm very emotional!" and everyone wants to help. I say, "The question before us is, can we help this person? Have the preconditions been established with this person as a member of the collective process? The issue is not merely does the person need help; I assume that everyone in the room needs help. The issue is whether we can give help." Some people think that raising this at that moment is cruel. I think it might be an occasion to reach this person to help her/him to see that we are not magicians. If people have not helped to create the group, they cannot be helped emotionally. So we have to constantly be attentive to the role that people are playing in the building of the group. By that, I don't mean whether the person talks or not. Some people do not talk but they are clearly functioning as builders of the group, and some people talk morning, noon, and night and they're not building the group.

There is a recognizable activity called building the group. It's as much a building activity as building a bridge. You have to help a grouping of people do that together as the creating of the conditions for their emotional growth. That is a Vygotskian concept. The creating of a zpd is best understood as a developmental rejection of individuated growth. It is saying, in effect, that people do not grow individually. They grow as a social unit. And so in social therapy we have to create the appropriate social unit for emotional growth. And if you fail in doing that you could be doing therapy for a thousand years and it will not make a difference.

That is why we have to keep coming back to building the group. It is not just a mantra that I created. No, it is fundamental to this work. We're social learners, social developers. And we have that ability. But in our culture we characteristically don't exercise it. Why? That is a complicated question. That is the history of Western civilization. But we don't. Take a look at some of the world's situations. Everything, maybe human civilization itself, turns on the capacity to function in a group, and people still don't do it. We haven't been socialized that way. That is the work that we are continuously doing in social therapy. My focus is not helping individuals with their individual problems. My focus is helping the group to understand the nature of what it means to grow, develop, and evolve and to create as best they can those kinds of situations in their lives out of this room.

So, does this derive exactly from Vygotsky? No. It's a creative use of Vygotsky. We learned some things ourselves. But I think our intellectual roots are surely identifiable with Vygotsky. We are creating zpds. And zpds create zpds. And zpds are very important things. They are necessary for human growth.

Therapist-in-training: Is human sociality self-conscious?

Fred: Some people treat self-consciousness as if it were a bonus. An add-on. I think that it's as fundamentally a part of the human activity as breathing. How are you defining self-consciousness?

Therapist-in-training: I mean, do people need to say to each other, "We are a team, so we're learning something together"—that kind of self-consciousness.

Fred: Are you asking if people have to say that in order to achieve what I'm talking about?

Therapist-in-training: Yes.

Fred: No. Does self-consciousness have to be present for us to go forward? Yes. But, I do not have a behavioral definition of self-consciousness. Which is how that sounds to me. I think that if people are learning together then they have, among other things, succeeded in creating a zpd.

from a colloquium

Dialogue 9. Engaging Alienation

Therapist-in-training: You've said that social therapy works by people's sociality being increased and that this occurs by dint of taking on the task of shaping the group.

Fred: Of being self-consciously social.

Therapist-in-training: Yes, so could one have predicted that enhancing sociality would produce development and cure? Could that have been known in advance? Or does it just happen to be the case?

Fred: *I* didn't know it. One of the great surprises of my life is that this social therapeutic approach actually helps people. For many years we used to say that our primary mission was to do a form of therapy that didn't hurt anybody. And then at some point, 15 years or so into it, it occurred to us that it was actually helping people.

It came as something of a shock. I have an understanding now of why that would be the case, but I didn't know it to begin with. I think it's fascinating and revealing that it does help, because what social therapy does, at its best, is engage—in very practical ways —the levels of alienation that dominate in our culture. Engaging alienation is a positive way of engaging people's emotional problems. I don't mean to imply that it is dealienating, because there are conditions of alienation that you can't overcome in a room for two hours on a Thursday night; there are other critical factors. But you can reduce alienation on a continuous basis and I think that makes a great difference in people's emotional lives. Alienation is a killer.

from a colloquium

Dialogue 10. Relational Awareness

Therapist-in-training: I came to social therapy with no meaning to my life, no reason for living, no desire to continue. Yet I did continue, and still do, for a host of reasons not having to do so much with "me" but with "me in the world." As I'm coming to the end of my formal training at the institute, I still—though very rarely—question the meaning, or should I say meaninglessness, of life.

I am the same yet different—same parts, different unknown outcome. I am loving the adventure most times and other times I think I'm going to sink. Your ideas go to places and see things in ways I never dreamed of before, and yet when you speak them they seem so obvious I wonder why I never did, and am delighted that I have the opportunity to hear you. If you can find something in what I'm saying that you would like to be responsive to, I, and I'm sure others, would find it growthful.

Fred: Here's the thought that occurs to me. I have the experience when I work with people that I take them to places they have never been before. And my understanding of that—the place they've never been to before—is *here*. Our culture is one in which people are socialized from very early on to be someplace else and not to be where they are. That's the very banal character of what I help people do. I'm able to help people to have a kind of experience of the activity that they're actually involved in, which is a strange "place" that most of us don't feel very familiar with. It's much easier, in an about-oriented culture, to see what we're thinking and doing as being about that thing over there or the depths of our minds. It leaves us in a permanently alienated state, always other than ourselves, in another place, another life. I try to help people have our life be here, wherever "here" turns out to be, to learn the simple yet extraordinarily complex activity of being where you are, learning to be who you are, learning to be what you are. Not from the vantage point of passively accepting all of that, but as a precondition for becoming other than all of that.

You can't go to the other place without going through who you are. But it's very tempting to want and to try to do that, given that people are understandably and justifiably unhappy with who they are. So the pull in our culture is to go someplace else. To avoid—even if it's not so conscious—being where we are. This is the journey that I have some skill to help people to take. It is the necessary though not sufficient condition for growth and development.

Therapist: What's the role of self-consciousness? And self-awareness?

Fred: I have no interest in self-consciousness. I have an interest in relational awareness, not self-awareness.

Therapist: What's the difference?

Fred: To me, the unit of our lives is our sociality. To have *self*-consciousness is a negation of that. There's no room in my way of understanding for self-consciousness because there's no room for a self. I think *self* is a deep-rooted cultural myth of Western civilization. It's an important myth because if you remove it what you remove is the most fundamental and oppressive myth of Western culture, namely, alienation. There's no alienation without self.

Therapist-in-training 2: What you just said kind of blows my mind. This phrase "self-conscious" is one I hear in social therapy all the time. Doesn't building relationally with people require that one is self-conscious about what one is doing?

Fred: How does it help?

Therapist-in-training 2: It helps by being aware of what's going on.

Fred: But what's going on is relational.

Therapist-in-training 2: Yes, but I could be relational and do things that I'm not mindful of.

Fred: Self-consciousness in that sense of the word—being mindful—seems perfectly harmless. Self-consciousness used in that way means something like being thoughtful, not being hurtful, nasty, abusive, and so on, and I don't have a particular problem with that— though I don't like the term because it is suggestive of some individualistic ontology of self. I think if one is relationally aware it would be a far better reason for not doing those kinds of things anyhow.

Therapist: So what we learn in social therapy is who we are relationally?

Fred: We learn *that* we are relational—that this is not a room made up of individuals who come together to form a group, but that this is a grouping of people. It's the group that's the unit.

from a colloquium

C. MUNDANE CREATIVITY

Dialogue 11. Creativity as a Collective Impulse

Therapist-in-training: Your concept of creativity as "not creating a product but creating the tool that gives rise to the product" has impacted my thinking of the therapist in a new way—as a toolmaker who helps patients to develop their own unique tool to give rise to new developments in their lives. The crisis in creativity that you talk about and that we are experiencing in this country is clearly apparent in the treatment of patients in clinics and hospitals. I don't have a specific question but I would appreciate your talking—as a toolmaker—about therapy.

Fred: You said it so eloquently. Yes, that is very much how I see group therapeutic work. I work overtime to make sure we don't reach resolution. In some ways I see that as my primary function. I want to help people to interrelate, to create, to build. We live in a culture, don't we, where we all want to insert into the social process some kind of leap to resolution, commodification, end product. I see my role in therapy as helping the group to create tools—not just once or twice but continuously, because it is a constant retooling process.

We are different people coming from different places; we are exceedingly individuated; everyone has had a different week and we come together as a group. The interesting and fascinating question is, what can we together create in order to make this therapy a creative and valuable event by our collective standards? What can we build? I think that many, many people in this culture are deeply deprived of that kind of experience. We function so much as if we know what the limits are that we are not sufficiently stretched to be creative in all kinds of ways, including emotionally. There are more emotions than were ever dreamt up and put in the *DSM–IV*. Emotionality is not simply reduced to nine standard emotions. It is a much more complex process than that. The beauty of emotionality is why I love doing therapy.

Therapist-in-training: I've heard you say that you see what your therapy groups do as creating a play.

Fred: Yes. In the last 20 years I have been doing a lot of theater work, including lots of directing. This has had an enormous influence on my therapy, and more and more I see myself doing theater in the therapeutic work that I am doing. I see it as people coming together on a weekly basis and creating a new play. Is each one connected to the previous plays? Well, yes, they are connected. Sometimes we look back and see that it's been a series, that what we thought were individual plays we now see as a 9-week family drama.

I try to work to help people create improvisationally. People are, of course, in all kinds of roles. The work is to see if we can find a use for those roles and not be locked into them. Do I make a different contribution than other people do? Yes. Do other people in the group make contributions different from each other? Of course they do. Are there some people who talk a great deal and are there some people who talk less, some people who talk for an extended period of time and then don't talk very much at all? Of course. Are there certain people who find they can't be open about certain topics? Yes. People are at different stages in their lives. It's all very fluid in that way.

But the uniform work is to create a performatory environment so as to give people an opportunity to be creative here. I think that is fundamental not only in therapy but in life. At Performance of a Lifetime [the training and consulting organization associated with the institute's approach] we even go into corporate situations and try to help people to see that some of the overbearing roles that corporate life locks people into can be troublesome even for productivity—not to mention for how people feel. These roles diminish people's creativity—and creativity is a good thing, a positive thing, a productive thing. In some ways, the social therapeutic experience is an experience in learning more about how to be creative, not by learning rules but by learning that activity. It's an exercise class in creativity. It's like going to a gym where people learn how to use different machines, get stronger and now can do certain things that they could not do before.

The same is true in social therapeutic work. People learn to create performances and if you have that available to you, then you have another thing you can do in life situations. People tell me—and this is what I feel so thrilled by—that they find themselves in situations at home with a loved one, a child, a husband, wife, mother, friends, and so on, and something comes up and the whole situation reads anger, and they are able to step back and say, "Can we recreate this performance? Can we do something else here?" even as they don't know what or how to do it. This is not a denial or repression of the anger—it's rather an opening for exercising the capacity to create new ways of doing things, given that anger is the emotional experience.

There is a tendency in our culture to think of emotions as natural, meaning something like, "If you feel it, you've got to express it in this prescribed sort of way." I think that myth has to be exploded. We can and will feel what we feel but we still have a huge range of possibilities of what we do with that experience. That is what we are trying to help people with in social therapy. We all know how destructive a limited repertoire of expressions can be.

Therapist-in-training: That is very helpful. Just using "creativity" and "therapy" in the same sentence opens things up. What's so difficult is how overdetermined people are by insisting on fixing the problem.

Fred: I think creativity is an enormously underused tool in the area of mental health. There is a whole repertoire of tools that we don't use, due in part to the unfortunate way in which the mental health paradigm has evolved to be problem and abnormality oriented. Certainly there are problems and abnormalities for which people need certain kinds of help, but even in those cases, creativity is a valuable tool. It's a valuable tool for everyone, no matter who you are and what pain you have been through.

What guides me, together with the people I'm working with, is a collective creative impulse. In some ways, therapy to me is very much like directing a play. It's not that I don't have some ideas of what I'm looking for when I am directing, but what dominates is the creative impulse of the cast, the technicians, and myself as director. By creative impulse, I mean a desire to take what we have collectively—the ideas, the talents, the presuppositions, the tastes, the energies—and to create something new with these inputs, something other than any or all of the inputs. I've come to see the therapeutic work I do as close to the theater work in this sense. I believe that we effect "cure" by creating something new together.

Performance language is the language that I've come to. The danger, as with all language, is that performance language can become overdetermining, which is why social therapy, as I try to practice it, is always tying to create new language—as much as possible, new forms of language—to further evolve and develop itself. In this respect, Wittgenstein is kind of a meta-director.

from a colloquium

Dialogue 12. The Limitations of Elitism

Therapist 1: I'd like to get some help with one of my groups. It's about a year old, it still feels new to me and I feel like I might be taking care of the group or substituting myself for the group. I know that it feels somewhat fragile. People have trickled in but it hasn't gotten bigger, which may be conservatizing me and making me overprotective. So concretely I think I may jump in too quickly to give direction to the group and maybe I should let the group flounder a bit. But I'm not sure; I don't have a good read on that. Given my liberalism, I know I can err on doing too much but I also think that given the relative newness of the people they may need strong direction from me.

In the last group, P started off by saying she didn't know how to begin the group, that she felt awkward. She said that elsewhere she feels competent, so this experience feels difficult. Other people related to that. Maybe about 8 minutes into the group, I asked whether they thought it was a problem that P felt incompetent. At some point I said that I supported her saying what she said, that that was a good move for her. So that's an example—I could have just let that go and see what the group did with that, and I thought about doing that—but I also thought it would be helpful for her and the group to open up the group experience of feeling awkward and incompetent, and to get help to not relate to it as an awful thing or a pathology. And it did produce some more dialogue. But I don't know whether I made the right move or not. Fred, what do you think about what I'm saying about the group?

Fred: Well, I think you probably should give it more room to get started before intervening. You said you gave it about 8 minutes?

Therapist 1: Yeah.

Fred: That doesn't seem to me to be enough. What's going on for you during those 8 minutes?

Therapist 1: I don't know. I was listening, observing, trying to pay attention to what was said.

Therapist 2: Weren't there any less-than-cognitive things that might have been going on for you?

Therapist 1: Well, I do feel somewhat nervous about the group. That it needs a lot of help or support or something.

Therapist 3: It does need a lot of help. Why should that make you nervous?

Therapist 1: I guess I'm nervous that it will fall apart. It's small, there aren't that many people in it. It still feels somewhat precarious in terms of continuing.

So I think that does make me feel conservative 'cause I'm frightened that the group might fall apart.

Therapist 2: Fred, is there a way to stop trying to make the group a "success"?

Fred: Well, you could let it be. From a distance it sounds to me that if you let it go this group will find its own way of failing. So you have to give it some room to do that.

Therapist 1: Are you saying that I'm being too much the busybody, that I need to let it fail more and then get more skilled at working with its failure? I suspect that I might be trying to prevent it from failing. Is that what you're picking up on?

Therapist 4: It seems that part of what's being raised here is having to deal with your insecurity. It might be helpful to take a look at whatever it is that goes on. I know from my experience it's hard to just sit there and let the group go through what it goes through and not try to fix it right away. That's part of the subjective challenge of social therapy from my experience, not to take the easy way out.

Therapist 1: I know that that's been an issue for me. We've talked about it before here. My history is that I'm more insecure than I need to be. I do find this really challenging. I love doing this group but I also feel like I don't know how to do it and that makes me nervous.

Fred: When you say "I don't know how to do this," I hear a subtext in that formulation—which is that somebody does; it just happens not to be you. Is that accurate?

Therapist 1: Yes, I think so.

Fred: It's a serious, serious problem; that misses the whole point.

Therapist 1: Uh huh.

Fred: I mean the point is, nobody knows how to do it—*it hasn't happened yet.* M doesn't know how to it, B doesn't know how to do it, I don't know how to do it, *nobody* knows how to do it. But you're not talking about it that way. Looking at it from the vantage point of "I don't know how to do it, but somebody does" or "I'll know how to do it some time in the future" is antithetical to social therapy. Where do you get that from?

Therapist 5: I have two thoughts. One is that I think we have a hard time believing that people can create something if we don't *do* something to make it happen. The other thought I had was, maybe we're not skilled enough at working with the group's resistance—which might be related to our resistance—to creating something together.

Therapist 1: I think I spend too much time worrying about myself, worrying that I'm not a creative person. So when you ask if we believe we can create things, I think I spend too much time in a degraded evaluation that, to say the least, I'm not as good at this as Fred or other therapists. It seems self-indulgent . . .

Fred: As good at what?

Therapist 1: At creating. I'm not skilled at that. Which is something, ironically, that I work on with my patients all the time. They are continuously comparing themselves with other people.

Fred: How creative do you have to be?

Therapist 1: More creative than me. There is no answer to that question. I think the question points up the absurdity of using this yardstick.

Fred: I think what the question points out is that you use "creative" as some kind of esoteric, abstract value term, as opposed to it having something to do with creating something, making something—making a table, making a meal. It sounds like you have this elitist, abstract conception of creativity.

Therapist 1: Well yeah, I think this is what I worry about—that I don't know what creativity is, that I'm no good at it.

Fred: What makes my therapy groups work is not how creative I am in your sense. In fact, that even stands in the way. What makes my groups work has to do with my understanding of what it means to make something—not to make something fantastic, something beautiful, something extraordinary, but just to make *something* with the elements you have to work with. Your notion of creativity is elitist; it stands above that. I don't think that you relate to the people you work with or yourself as the ingredients of an act of making something. That's what to create really means. The activity of social therapy is making what you can make given what you got.

Therapist 4: You're pretty good at creating in other aspects of your life. So I don't know if it's that you're not so good at this or whether it is that you really don't believe that it's collective creative activity that helps patients.

Therapist 1: Right. Not the result but the process. Yes, I think that's right.

Fred: This is not an esoteric therapy; it's a very simple therapy. Pam directs these young people in the All Stars [All Stars Talent Show Network, a supplemental education/youth development program utilizing the Institute's approach] to make a show, and it turns out that that's developmental. If you're in the woods and it's nighttime and getting cold, you need to make a fire. You use the materials that are available. You don't need to make a fire that's going to be extraordinary, that's not what creative means. You need to make a fire. Because if you make a fire it's going to be warmer. It's a mundane sense of making that we understand as creativity. It's not high falutin' or esoteric.

from a supervisory session

Dialogue 13. Creating Choices

Student: What role does making choices play in our development, culturally and individually?

Fred: I believe that we're in a potentially very nondevelopmental period in history because of the limitation in our capacity to make new kinds of creative choices. As a therapist, I try to teach people what it would mean not simply to pick this one or that one, but to create brand new emotional choices. I sometimes refer to it as helping people to create new emotions. Human beings have the capacity to create an infinitude of emotions; moreover, in the absence of doing so, we stop emotional development. I think no small part of what renders people emotionally paralyzed is their inability to continue the process of creating emotion.

    The limitations on what you're allowed to create in America today are shocking. Look at politics, look at schools, look at art, look at theater, and so on. I am very concerned with the impact of our being so limited in what we are allowed to and able to create.

from a seminar

Dialogue 14. Creating Meaning

Student: What is meaning? And has the power to make meaning come to an end?

Fred: Wittgenstein discusses this. He quotes a passage from St. Augustine that he says encapsulates what has come to be the popular view of meaning—the naming theory of meaning. In this view, words and sentences gain meaning by virtue of what they are about. Words are like pictures, pictures of aspects of the world. To understand meaning is to understand what they are pictures of. This theory and its general acceptance tend to stultify development. Wittgenstein says that it's all wrong. Language, he argues, can be used to denote something, to describe and to name, but its complexity lies in the fact that it has an infinitude of uses—in poetry, as commands, for the sharing of emotions, to mention a few. Many misunderstand Wittgenstein to be saying that the meaning of what we say is to be found in the use that we make of a particular text, sentence or words or speech pattern.

    Vico [Giambattista Vico, the 17–18th-century Italian philosopher] talks about the origins of meaning. He gives an example. Imagine a tribe of people before language. There is a horrendous storm. They gasp collectively. When they remember the storm, they remember the gasp. The gasp is not the name of the storm, but a response that goes with the storm. It is not a picture of it. Meaning is thus understood as a subjective activity that has, not a naming relationship, but an interconnect to other aspects of the world. The collective reactions gain a currency, because they function as a reminder of a process, which includes that storm. It's not the storm but it's connected historically with the storm.

Meaning making is not the use of the language, but the creative capacity to include a subjective component in the complicated natural life of our world. The meaning of language is not the use, but the companion activity to a phenomenon as it unfolds. We learn language by babbling in a social process and creating meaning, not by meaning being imposed by others as denotative. The child learns that there is such a thing as meaning, that is, when people are speaking there is something going on to attend to. That is a participatory activity that teaches not only the particularity of what the specific words mean, but that there is such a thing as meaning and meaning making. We learn that socially by participation in a social activity.

Once words start getting used, they become transformed into commodities. Speaking becomes the skillful use of commodities (placing them together). Language becomes enormously useable but loses its creative origins. The process of creating meaning is stopped. Yes, I think we are losing the creative power of meaning making, the power to transform things by creating new meanings. For example, pathology is defined in terms of a few emotions. But what if the commodified understanding of emotions is a profound ontological misunderstanding, inconsistent with what any of us would wish to call human development?

Social therapy challenges the notion that all we can do is relate to emotions in a commodified fashion. As therapists we deal with emotional problems by relocating, defetishizing, or decommodifying them. We have to create something different because problems vanish by virtue of their relocation in a creative understanding. We have to exercise our capacity to give a new meaning to what we identify as the problem, by virtue of an activity that transforms its ontology. Naming has become so pervasive that the inner workings in our life have come to be even more overdetermined by labeling than the physical world. We have come to believe in the existence of all kinds of things going on in our minds that nobody "in their right mind" would ever countenance. The force of a commodified understanding applied to the human mind creates an inner world that is untouchable. This is a universal malaise that limits our ability to make meaning.

Social therapy helps people to participate with other people to create new meanings. People come into therapy with pain and problems and they speak the commodified language of emotionality. The effort in social therapy is to help people see that what they are saying to each other has no meaning. It has meaning only in terms of the commodified conceptions of meaning, which are individuated and alienated. What has to happen, if this joint activity of people in therapy is to have some meaning, is for these people to create the meaning that it has: "What would it mean for us to exercise our collective capacity to determine what all of what we're saying means?"

We decide what it means. How do we do that? It's very hard to do. We have to begin by opening that up as a possibility. None of us knows what we mean. We don't know what we are talking about. That doesn't mean we can't navigate within a commodified society but it does mean we're not able to participate in development, because development is a creative process. We are trying to teach people how to create meaning, which makes it possible to exercise the power of creativity required for developmental transformation. And that isn't done short of stripping away the commodification that overdetermines how we see things and our understanding of meaning.

from a seminar

D. PERFORMANCE

Dialogue 15. Performance in/and Therapy

Therapist-in-training: I am brand new in the training program and I'm fascinated by the idea of therapy as performing. But I don't understand how that helps people solve their problems.

Fred: People come into therapy and, understandably, they want to know what's wrong with them. They feel bad. They're upset. They're hurting. They're anxious. They're panicked. They're fearful. They're distressed. They're depressed. They can't sleep. They can't eat. They eat too much. They eat too little. They're having terrible fights. They're in emotional pain, or worse than that. They've been diagnosed. They've been labeled. All kinds of things have happened to them. Some of the people have felt improvement from things they've already done. Others don't feel that at all. They come to me, as they've come to others of you who are therapists, and they, quite reasonably and understandably, ask if we can make them better, and it seems to me that the only honest answer that one can give to that question is "No." We can't make anybody better. It seems to me that what we can do to help people who come to us in all of this pain and distress is to help them to live. We can help them to create something new. We can help them to be who they're not. We can help them to perform.

Therapist-in-training: Aren't they, though, coming to therapy and asking to be who they're not, even if they don't mean "perform"?

Fred: Many people say, "I can't stand what's going on in my life, I'm desperately unhappy. I want to find something inside of me. I want to discover who I am so as to be able to overcome this terrible pain." And I say something to the effect, "Sadly, what I think we have to recognize as a starting point of this process is that you are the person who's in this terrible pain. That *is* who you are. The problematic is that who you are has turned out to be inconsistent, for whatever reasons, with your becoming anything other than that." But many people want to hear that that's not really who they are, and that there's something that we can do to transform the inside, some kind of surgical transformation, to discover that this upset, anxious, hurting person is not really who they are.

   To me, what is fundamental to helping someone to deal with the terrible pain they are in is to help them to see their capacity to exercise their power to be someone other than who they are. We have the human capacity to be other than who we are, and we simply, for the most part, don't make use of it. Now what is the term that we give to the human capacity to be other than who we are? We perform. We each have the human capacity to get up on a stage and to be King Lear or Lady Macbeth or whoever, to tell a bad joke, to stick out our tongues, to wiggle our nose, to jump in the air. We are capable of performing. We are capable of becoming who we are not. "Wait a minute," you might say, "that's just on a stage. That kind of thing is institutionally validated by virtue of being on a stage." "But look here," I say, "this stage wasn't always here. I remember when we built this stage and put it up. We created this stage." We have the capacity to create environments in which we can perform. We can create stages anywhere. We are performers. It's a wonderful talent that we have. The performatory talent is the exercise of our capacity to be other than who we are.

   When people come to therapy, I try to help them be other than who they are. I'm not looking to get to the deeper interpretive inside of who a human being is. What I try to do is see if I can get a grouping of people to perform, to create a performance, to play a game. Some people react to this as trivializing human life. I think therapy as traditionally practiced trivializes human life; for me, the exercise of the capacity to perform other than who we are is the glorification of human life. We don't have to be who we are, we don't have to accept someone else telling us who we are, and most importantly, we don't have to accept ourselves telling ourselves who we are. We don't have to sit back and say, "I can't do that or I can't do this because that's not who I am." That's the wonder of life.

   But within our culture, being who you are has been transformed into the glorious statement, "I know who I am!" Well, big deal. "I know what makes me tick." The same people also say, "And by the way, I'm miserable. I've spent thirty-three years in analysis and I know precisely what's going on during every single depressed moment of every day of my life." Well, that works nicely at cocktail parties and all that, but it leaves people fundamentally depressed.

I know this is provocative and offensive to some people, and indeed, it's provocative and offensive to me. Over 30 years ago I first went into therapy myself and it was one of the great discoveries of my life, it was transformative for me. Over the years I have come to see that what was transformative was being with another human being—in this case, a very wonderful person—and being in group therapy eventually with other wonderful people, going through a process of coming to see that I didn't have to be who I was emotionally. Who I was emotionally was nothing to be glorified. So, people come to therapy, and what I try to help them to do is to perform.

Therapist-in-training: Do you mean that literally?

Fred: Well, it's hard to say, because I don't know what literally means. The therapy I do is some kind of complex dialectic that goes back and forth between people performing as other than who they are and people insisting on being who they are. The interesting paradox is that we never stop being who we are even as we become something totally different.

Therapist-in-training: What happens to your pain and problems when you're becoming something totally different even as you're still who you are?

Fred: What is developmentally transformative is helping people to grow and develop so as to change the gestalt in which those painful problems and difficulties are located. You don't get rid of the pain or problem by way of removing it; it doesn't go away in some surgical sense. In Wittgenstein's language, the problem "vanishes" by virtue of continuously creating something so that the relationship between this problem, this pain, this difficulty and who you are is continually evolving and transforming. I love Wittgenstein's metaphor "making the problem vanish." I think he is saying that there is a kind of magic in the philosophical play that helps us recognize the limitation of language and of our conceptions. There is not a clearcut cause or moment of outcome. You do the work and suddenly—it seems—the problem disappears. I find that metaphor useful in social therapy. The group engages in the process of creating the environment and "magically" it transforms.

from a colloquium

Dialogue 16. Performance and Behavior

Student: What is performance relative to behavior? It seems to me that performance is more creative behavior.

Fred: Performance is the addition, or completion, that we have brought to Vygotsky's work, a contemporary modification that, we believe, is consistent with what Vygotsky is talking about. Often people mistakenly think that by performance we mean something that one does over and above normal behavior. That's not what we mean at all. We are trying to identify that we are a performatory species. We are constantly engaging in all kinds of performances. Performance is not so much a special category of behavior as it is a substitute for the concept of behavior.

The notion of human beings as forever engaged in behavior, while probably trivially true, is ontologically unsatisfactory, mainly because it introduces a mystical and inaccurate understanding of human activity. So what we are substituting for behavior, as it is traditionally used in psychology, is the notion of performance.

We are a performing species. It's difficult to say what that means. Part of what it means is that there is a conscious component to all of human activity (whatever consciousness is). The understanding that everything is performance is part and parcel of the claim that all human activity is social. The behaviorist notion of behavior is tied to an individuated characterization of human beings. Vygotsky didn't accept that notion and neither do we. We take all human behavior to be social, not just social in its origins, but social in its expression on a minute-to-minute practical basis. What we are denying—and here we extend not only Vygotsky, but Wittgenstein—is the notion of private activity. In our culture, the preeminent kind of activity is identified as private activity. However, with sociality as part of our contention, whatever it is we are doing includes this conscious component of the performatory.

We use performance in a broad way to mean a whole range of performances. Some are very rehearsed, some very improvisational, some a mixture of those things, some wonderful and fascinating, some uninteresting, dull, boring. It's not a term that we use in a glorifying way, as in "If you perform that's doing something wonderful." No, we are all performing all the time. Performing is far more than a couple of actors speaking words to each other. The people who have no lines in the play are performers nonetheless. They are performing, and contributing by virtue of the very slightest nuance of the movement that they make.

Performance is a dramaturgical concept. We are taking it over from theater. It's a useful way of looking at how we operate in life. We operate as part of a very complicated, multifaceted play. Creating a play, even for the stage, doesn't derive from an act of imagination, in the sense of creating it out of my mind. It's simply adding a level of self-consciousness to what is standard human behavior. By and large, that is how come plays work. Even the most absurdist plays work by virtue of the fact that they play off what we are doing all the time. If they didn't, if the plays were so far removed from what human beings are doing all the time, my philosophical sense is that we wouldn't be able to discern them at all. Theater is profoundly different from normal life, but it also derives from something that we do all the time in normal life, which is perform. The performance on the stage is a variation of what we do all the time. The significance of that is that we have a vastly greater capacity to creatively affect how we perform life than we tend to think.

The culture tends to teach us that there are very limited areas of creativity. Maybe you can perform on the stage or in certain ritualistic moments, or maybe people can sometimes come together and make up something new. But much of life, in the traditional view, is seen as behavioral more than as performatory. If you open that door just a little bit, it changes everything. It changes what we mean by growth, development, emotional cure, et cetera, because if we accept, even subtextually, the behavioral view with a small *b* and all that tends to go with it, then we are profoundly limited in our capacity for development and for creative transformation.

So when we say, at social therapy centers, that development is the cure, we mean that it is the creative act of performance that has the capacity to transform social behavior, social activity, social existence, to creatively change the entire context in which we carry out what we carry out, including our emotionality.

from a seminar

Dialogue 17. *Improvisational Learning*

Therapist-in-training 1: I'm not sure how to ask this question or if it is a question—what are your thoughts, comments, reactions, et cetera, on improvisation, therapy, and life?

Fred: I now think that life is much more improvisational than I once thought. I think improvisation is something we can learn and that it helps us live our lives better. My picture of the culture in which we live is that it tends to be very role over-determined. I don't mean that as a moral critique. We teach people to be who they are, to adjust to society, by putting them in roles—

and we do this in a way that we think is positive. We try to help them see their roles. That can be of value; I think it is important, in some sense, to learn who we are. On the other hand, so much of life is lived between the cracks, in the subjective nuances of how we deal with each other.

As for therapeutics, I think it's too bad that psychotherapy has been so associated with abnormality. That this is changing is a very good thing. Emotional/developmental skills are an important part of what we need to learn everywhere—in schools and families and so on. Maybe we are heading toward a time where therapy is part of life and maybe it will not be called therapy.

People can become very much better at emotional interaction; it is something you can learn. There is still a tendency to believe that normal emotionality is simply picked up automatically. I don't agree. I think it is unfortunate that we don't learn how to touch each other, how to relate to each other, how to be with each other, how to give, how to create social environments. Will the day come? It probably will not happen in my lifetime or in most of our lifetimes.

Therapist-in-training 1: I'm not sure what you mean by improvisation.

Fred: For me improvisation is the skill of creating something unexpected, outside of the boundaries of role-governed activity. You've seen those puzzles in which you are supposed to connect the dots and the only way you can do that is to go outside an imposed box? I think that improvisation is going outside of the socially imposed boxes that we all live our lives in.

Sometimes there is nothing better than being in a role; I don't think that people should improvise when they are crossing the streets in New York City. There I support role-governed, rule-governed behavior 100 percent. On the other hand, there are so many life situations in which it would be wonderful and developmental to be able to not be constrained by that—for example, when relating to a loved one to be able to continue to grow the relationship, to consciously try new things, even at the dinner table. Even if we choose not to do something different, it would be nice to have that option. We can be a very conservative, overdetermined species, but we also have the capacity for choosing to step out of the box.

Going back to your question, I was slightly shocked how the media and the Democratic Party handled the Nader campaign. That level of demonization. I mean, my God, he simply wanted to run for President! It is supposed to be a free country. He was turned into this ogre. It really is a constraining attitude. I think people should be freer—not only Ralph Nader but anybody—to do different kinds of things. We can learn how to break out of the box and improvise.

It is hard to break out of a set of socially accepted expectations, not only that others impose on us but what we impose on ourselves. We have a school that teaches improvisation [Performance of a Lifetime]. People come in and they sit petrified at first and say, "What am I going to do; what is going to happen?" We say, "We would like you to improvise." And they say, "How do I do that?" We say, "Go up on the stage and take 1 minute and improvise the story of your life." And they say, "You must be mad." And we say, "Yes, but that's not the issue. The issue is whether you will learn to improvise." And they go up on stage and they do unbelievable performances. Because all of us have the capacity to improvise; we are all creative.

Sometimes contexts do not allow us to create. We send children off to school scribbling outside the lines, doing beautiful and wonderful stuff. They go to the first grade and someone—not a bad person but somebody who is working as part of some kind of arrangement—says, "Now you have to draw inside the lines." Sometimes that can be a little hard to understand—"How come I was wonderfully creative yesterday and now I get an F for it? One day and what happened? What did I do?" So, not to negate a lot of what's done in terms of cognitive learning, there are other things that need to be stressed for a culturally developmental lifestyle.

Therapist-in-training 2: I definitely agree with your answer about what improvisation is. As I'm learning and teaching improvisation, I'm working out of the box and doing something different. I think what is beautiful about improvisation is that it is a social activity that reorients people to work to create something with somebody else.

Fred: There is another person outside that box. Once you go outside the box you bump into other people.

Therapist-in-training 2: What is hard about doing improv training is helping people see that improvisation is a social activity. Often when people create an improvised scene they feel very connected to you there in that performance. But other times they experience what they are doing as an individual and are consumed with how they look on stage. I don't know if you have any thoughts about how hard it is for people to grasp that improvisation is social and that what is paramount is what the group can create. A lot of people I'm working with in business don't get that, which is connected to how difficult it is to break out of the individual, right? I do experience improvisation as therapeutic for the teams I work with, yet I struggle with understanding and conveying this group piece.

Fred: What I think is important to share with people is that the learning we do as children is profoundly social; it takes place in what Vygotsky identified as zones of proximal development [zpds] between people of different locations—older people, younger people, peers, nonpeers. Not only do we learn in that way, but we learn in a particular kind of way in that way. It is the kind of learning I identify as creative; it is not the learning that takes place often later in life, which is much more associated with role-governed and rule-governed behavior.

We have to go back to the kind of things that took place when we were all children, when we didn't just follow rules and roles, but created them. We need to build on that capacity we had as children and now, as adults, create an environment where people can allow themselves to do some of the childlike things we all recognize because we have them as part of our history. We have this childhood as part of our history. As an example, the movement work in the beginning of the Performance of a Lifetime program is important because it helps people to move differently with each other. A lot of how we learn as small children has to do with changing our position and our perspective. We have to find more and more ways to support people in doing that.

from a colloquium

E. WHAT'S WRONG WITH TRUTH TALK?

Dialogue 18. Description as Truth Telling

Therapist-in-training: If society is built on the paradigm of truth—a phenomenon that takes on enormous, almost godlike, proportions—then engaging in conversations about truth and truth telling seems to be the work of social therapy. Could you speak to whether or not you think that the paradigm of locating internal truths might serve to keep individuals from developing? Internal truths, for example, such as one saying to oneself, "That's just the way I am" or "I can't do that, I've never been any good at driving, math, cooking, et cetera." Could internal truths keep us from working harder; could they allow underdeveloped activity to continue and result in a type of internal private alienation from others? I'm worried about truth!

Fred: I agree. The standard form of dialogue in our culture is rooted in a truth paradigm, which is inseparable from the descriptive paradigm. What it means for a description to be successful is that it is a true characterization of an inner state of affairs or an outer state of affairs. I think psychology's major failure is that it insists on being descriptive. Descriptive conversation is not what I think is most valuable or useful in the process of helping people develop and become socialized. There is an excessive focus on descriptive conversation in our culture and psychology buys in on that. It's the wrong mode for dealing with emotionality.

What we're doing in social therapy is working in different ways to keep away from the paradigm of truth and to focus on activity and performance. We want to help people to focus on the relational activity of their interaction, to see that it is a relational activity. It isn't simply one individual giving her or his description of what she or he takes to be the case, followed by another individual giving her or his characterization of what she or he takes to be the case, and trying to convince each other or even to agree on something. We are trying to come up with an understanding that is not descriptive at all. We're not looking to help people to get better at describing.

I am always trying to help people break out of this descriptive truth-telling paradigm in favor of an activity-theoretic paradigm—to relate to what's going on as the activity of what's going on, and not as the truth of what's being said. I'm not the least bit interested in the truth of what's being said. Generally speaking, I don't think it's very developmental.

And it's not easy. I think it's especially difficult for those who were traditionally trained before becoming social therapists. They find it difficult to break out of the descriptive mode because that's pretty much all they learned in their traditional training. They tell me they sometimes have the feeling, "If I don't do that, what in God's name will I do?" I find it helpful in teaching to say that it is important to relate to your clients in the way that we, perhaps at our best, relate to children at play. Hopefully, on our best days we don't stand around watching children play and describing everything they are doing and, at a certain point say, "Hey, wait a second, I know what you are up to now . . ." But that is what psychologists actually do, and many therapists do, too—they relate to their clients in the role of an adult who describes what children are doing

Fortunately, there are other ways we relate to children playing. We help them play better, participate, create together. You can help children to enjoy the activity of play, to enhance the activity of play, to grow further off the activity of play. Describing what they are doing, on the other hand, is a fundamentally alienating activity. It's the bread and butter of traditional therapy but it's not what we do in social therapy at our best. At our worst that's what we lapse into because we are only human. Our therapists think, "Oh my God, I have to say something!" and they offer up some description or interpretation. You can get away with it because you have this big old chair underneath you and you can get away with all kinds of things when you're a therapist—which is unfortunate, but that's life. But I think we have to keep challenging ourselves as well as the people we are working with to not fall into descriptive psychology. This is just my opinion on how to best help people.

from a colloquium

Dialogue 19. Moving Forward Without Knowing

Therapist-in-training: When we talk about "a nonepistemological practice of method" what do we mean?

Fred: In ordinary language, it simply means a practice that doesn't rest on the assumption of knowledge, of being able to know. I think that's a dangerous assumption in our culture, one that is dying—and I don't regret it. It might be a good historical moment to get beyond knowing. It's gotten us into more trouble than it's done us good. One could make out a strong case that knowing—individuated knowing, which is the general form of knowing— had its heyday in the heyday of science. I think there's ample reason—both within science and within other fields too—to consider giving it up and to try to create a methodologically based approach, as opposed to an episte- mologically based approach. What that means roughly is that the task is not to discover what's true, the task is to discover the method for moving further. Leave truth out as much as possible as we leave knowledge out. The general consensus is that knowledge is true belief, so if we get rid of knowledge we get rid of truth as well. "Good riddance," I say, "to both of them. High time!" That's what we mean by methodologically based.

We work to create methodological environments, to create the mean- ing, the construct, whatever, for moving forward with the conversation, with the discovery, with the therapy, with whatever it is. What do we have to construct to go on? What do we have to construct to get from where we are to someplace else? The question is a locomotive question, not a reli- gious or epistemological question. The issue is not to discover the truth so somehow we'll be able to go forward. No, let's go directly at this point in the process to have human beings collectively figure out how to go forward from here to wherever we choose to go, not mediated by some kind of appeal to truth or to knowledge.

from a colloquium

Dialogue 20. Don't Share Knowledge

Therapist: In our supervision we've been talking about how sharing knowledge in therapy can be distancing. We all agreed that we didn't want to distance our clients and wondered how we could share with them while remaining close to them. My question, then, is, can you share knowledge with clients without distancing them? If so, how and when?

Fred: Don't share knowledge. Share performance. The problematic word in your question is knowledge, not sharing. Sharing is fine. Share a performance.

You have words to speak; you have things to say and passions to express. Do that. Don't be a knower. Sharing knowledge is, in my opinion, an alienating activity. Because—and forgive me if I'm being too traditionally philosophical—from Plato down to the present, the definition of knowledge includes, as a critical component, truth. Knowledge is identified, generally speaking, within philosophical circles as true opinion. So, it is very hard to share knowledge. That doesn't mean that you can't say what is on your mind. It doesn't mean you can't perform. It doesn't mean you can't give.

You know me well enough to know that I can talk incessantly. In many groups, I talk a lot. But I work very hard to do it as pure performance. I don't do it as an interpretive truth. I do it as performance and I try to help the group with directorial moves. What I am doing is in some ways an effort at an exemplary performance to help them to further perform. Not to articulate truth. Not to articulate knowledge. I tell groups stories. In some ways that's my major contribution. I tell a good story. Is it true? I don't intend for it to be true but it's a good story and it helps people tell each other their stories and, moreover, create new stories together. The activity of people creating stories together is, in my opinion, an extraordinarily useful developmental process that we don't exercise sufficiently. We are a creative species that doesn't get ample opportunity to create. The kind of creativity I'm talking about tends to be stopped when someone is about 4 years old. From 4 on out we no longer are allowed this kind of creativity; that's roughly the age when truth takes over. "Stop telling stories. Stop making up stories. Now you're a little bit grown up, you're going to school, let's start hearing the truth."

So, yes, don't share knowledge. Share performance. Be a performer for your clients. And, of course, they will interpret what you are saying as truth. So, you have to do another performance that disabuses them of that idea. "Didn't you just say . . . ?" "I did. I said those words. You took that to be truth? What are you talking about? Because it came out of this [the therapist's] chair, my body, my voice, you think it's truth? It's not truth. It's no more truth than what you say is truth." We can still create together. We can make very beautiful things together. We don't have to take everything we say as truth.

Therapist: Then why would people come to you for therapy?

Fred: Why do people come to plays? The people on the stage aren't telling the truth. People love to see a good performance. We learn and we grow from good performance. We learn more from performance than we do from truth, otherwise kids would never learn. They don't know what the hell truth is. They learn from watching their parents.

Therapist: I'm taking what you are saying tonight as truth.

Fred: That's the very problem I'm talking to.

Therapist: I think that we in the group learn something from you. But I guess it's not from the truth you are saying but from what we are doing together.

Fred: Yes. That's what I'm saying. And I think insofar as you are growing in that group it is because you are performing differently and better. I don't think the things you are saying now are any more truthful than the things you were saying a few months ago. I don't think truth has anything to do with it.

Therapist: Intellectually I get it but I find it very difficult emotionally.

Fred: Intellectually it's easy because you can take it to be true! I know that trick. We're very truth overdetermined. And as you say, intellectually it is very easy to say, "I've abandoned truth" and the next thing you're saying is— "This is the real deal." It's very hard to change our practice in a culture so imbued with truth. You are quite right, it is very hard to do, but I'm personally convinced that this commitment to truth is the source of what's called human pathology. There are, of course, other factors, but I don't think we can deny the need to engage the overall sociocultural context in which pathology comes into existence. A lot of people say, "That's the context, let the sociologists deal with it. We'll simply deal with the symptoms—we'll give them pills or interpretations." I don't accept that because part of what we have to cure in curing people of emotional pain are the cultural biases that give rise to them.

from a colloquium

F. PROBLEMS

Dialogue 21. The Language of Problems

Therapist-in-training: In a particular group, I saw the therapist as helping someone with a problem. When I brought this up in supervision, the therapist said that she wasn't helping the individual with her problem, she was helping build the group. What does she mean by this? Can a group be built without problems? Would such a group look different, or does building happen whether or not there is a problem?

Fred: People talk the language of problems and since the group is a noncoercive environment, people bring in whatever they want and they talk however they choose. The issue is whether or not we carry on the group based on problems and efforts to resolve them. That's the question—not what people bring in. People will bring in whatever they bring in, and moreover, you can characterize what people bring in in a thousand different ways. There's no fixed way. It's a truism in philosophy of language that any phenomenon can be described in an infinite number of ways. If you want to describe things as a problem, you can.

The point is that what we're doing is not resolving or attempting to resolve problems, either individual problems or the group's problems. What we're doing is attempting to build something. We're attempting to build a certain kind of environment in which people can converse in certain kinds of ways with each other. An environment for helping us to go forward—or go in a direction that the group decides it wants to go in.

It's a methodological task. A grouping of people can collectively make a determination as to what they want to do, including solving problems. Sometimes my groups decide that they want to solve problems. This is not under my advice, but they decide anyway. They don't really care about my advice 85 to 95 percent of the time—which is good and healthy. But they decide what they wish to do and then engage the issue of what you have to do to get there. How do we accomplish that? How do you talk about it? What kind of language do you use? Why do we use that kind of language? How do we relate to each other? How do individuals relate to each other? Do individuals relate to each other? Does the group talk all at once? Does the group dance? Does the group jump up and down? Does the group go to the window? There is an infinitude of things that a grouping of people have to do in an effort to go from where they are to where they have collectively determined they want to go. That's what it is that I'm eager to help people to do therapeutically. I'm not looking to find the answer. I'm not looking to resolve the problem. I'm not looking to have me or anyone else in the room utter what they know. If they choose to, that's fine, but that's not what I'm looking to do. The group has a right to do what they choose; it doesn't follow that what they choose will be most helpful for people to grow. That's true of every group, not just social therapy. But we're working to help people with the method of moving forward, of advancing—not with getting the right answer, not with resolving the problem.

I don't know the right answer. Sometimes individuals think they know the right answer. That's their right to say they know the right answer. Sometimes the group is satisfied with that. Sometimes it isn't. If I had my way, it isn't. I rarely have my way, but I try.

from a colloquium

Dialogue 22. Making the Problem Vanish

Therapist-in-training: When you say, "Let's build the group," you are talking about something beyond the group, that the group is more than the sum of its parts. Group members bring their problems and the group builds relational activity with them. What is the role of the therapist?

Fred: Let me begin to answer that by talking about problems. My understanding of what I am doing as a social therapist is—to paraphrase one of my favorite quotes from Wittgenstein—working to make problems vanish. We're not looking to solve or resolve problems. As you point out, people come into therapy talking about their emotional problems. It makes perfectly good sense. I have no critique of that. It's as legitimate a thing to talk about as anything. What's important in therapy is what it is that the grouping of people who come together do with what they share with each other. It's the next level of activity—what you do with that kind of dialogue. What we are working on is how people create, develop, and build off what it is people do bring in. That seems to me to be the activity of the group.

When people present their emotional problems, I think it mainly manifests their commitment to their individuated identity. The problem presentation is highly individualistic, not just in its language but in its concept—"I have this problem." It's not relational. What we're trying to do with the group is to take all these inputs and say, "There's a way we can relate to this which is not simply the sum total of those individuated inputs." Insofar as the group is identifiable qua group, its activity is figuring out the method by which it can relate to the presentation of problems so as to create a certain kind of environment. As we've said for a very long time, social therapy is a practice of method. It isn't concerned with this individual's problem or that individual's problem. It's concerned with a grouping of people discovering and creating a method for them to relate to each other, to create a method of relatedness.

How are we to talk to each other? What are our assumptions as to how people typically talk to each other? Week after week the group tries to throw out, as much as possible, all of those assumptions in favor of the group engaging in the creative process of focusing on the activity of the dialogue, not the content of the dialogue. Is the content of the dialogue completely unimportant? I think so. I don't expect in my lifetime that we will reach the point where people will come into therapy and talk about nuclear physics. I suspect people will keep coming in and talking about their emotional problems because there is a broader institution known as therapy and people are impacted on by that and not simply by what we do here. But from my vantage point and the work that I do—they could just as well talk about nuclear physics. I could work every bit as effectively.

from a colloquium

Dialogue 23. There Are No Answers

Therapist-in-training: I decided to give up psychology as a science before I moved to the United States and before I entered social therapy, but I didn't know it wouldn't be easy. Recently in one of our evening groups, I realized that we are all "little" psychologists. We all have our stories, our theories about something in our lives that we are trying to explain, to understand, to justify. As a psychologist in my country, I knew a few "big stories"—theories that I used while I was working with my patients. I found them narrow and insufficient for understanding how we human beings live our lives, but still useful as a "referential rug," as you say.

    Then one day in a one-to-one session with a patient, I found myself stuck. Paradoxically, instead of being more human, I am more blocked. I don't feel. I don't know what to say. I am blank. I tell myself to perform active listening, perform conversation. I am like a child who is learning how to walk. Make more demands, don't smooth over things, engage conflict. All of a sudden, I saw what my alienation was. It was not a matter of feelings. I didn't feel like I was alone. I have family and friends who care for me. I saw that I was involved in an alienated, individualistic, product-oriented, and knowledge-oriented activity, determined by psychology. No wonder I felt guilty when my country fell apart and I/we did not do anything to prevent it.

    In social therapy, I found that to look at my activity—doing therapy and living in day-to-day life—as performance is extremely helpful. It feels freeing and nondeterministic and helps me to take myself and others less seriously. It leaves more space for play, creativity, change, and development. I feel more alive.

    Where is my problem? I am trying to write about my personal and professional transformation for my dear colleagues, the clinical psychologists back home. I do not want to deny them. And I do not want to deny myself before I came to social therapy; being a clinical psychologist who was experiencing the limits of psychology in helping people brought me to social therapy. I need some help in growing further by building from who I was and still am without denying it.

Fred: That is a bona fide graduate school level question. It is very impressive. Let me see if I can give you something resembling an answer about what you *haven't* given up. There is this meta-methodological pull in thinking about something, that somehow or other we are going to come closer to getting "the right answer." Even if we deny rightness and deny answers, there is still the meta-methodological pull. We think that we will be, in some sense, better off for doing it this way, that we will come closer. And that to me is the hardest thing to give up.

We have to appreciate that as human beings we have an enormous capacity for stimulation. Endless things impinge upon us—internal things, external things, emotive things, cognitive things—and we have an extremely limited capacity to put all those things together to figure out what the hell is going on. We are very limited. The myth of the last 50 or 60 years of the cybernetic age is that the human machine is the machine extraordinaire. I don't think we are the machine extraordinaire. I think we are a third-rate machine relative to all the impingements that come in. So, most of the time the issue in therapy is not to discover "the answer" or even an answer, but rather to help someone see that there is nothing that should be regarded as, nothing resembling, an answer. That is what is therapeutically valuable.

Social therapeutics does not bring you one iota closer to the answer. I think that is hard to come to terms with. It is hard because, as you are saying, you are sitting there in that chair and the person across from you is expecting you to have an answer—maybe not a right answer, but something that is more of an answer then what she or he has. The hardest part of the social therapeutic approach is to convey to the person you are working with that you don't have an answer.

Going back to Wittgenstein's model of language, in some ways this is at the core of making the problem vanish. What makes a problem vanish is not that we overcome the problem. It is that, in some sense, we don't accept the framework or conception of "problem" inquiry. What you said in your marvelous question goes a long way, and I think you have come a long way. You were coming a long way before you got here. Maybe this is useful as a characterization of another step that you and others have to take together in abandoning psychology.

As Lois and I have written again and again, psychology is an extraordinary claim. Psychology might well be the most pretentious activity that this species of ours, which is well known for its pretentiousness, has ever come up with. It is going to take a pretty overwhelming set of personal acts to come anywhere near giving it up. Anyway, it is a very lovely question. I really appreciate it.

from a colloquium

G. IDENTITIES AND IDENTITY

Dialogue 24. The Oppression of Identity

Therapist-in-training: I have been wondering how a person's social location might
affect the way that they come to be engaged in social therapy. By social
location, I mean the set of overdetermining factors, such as race, ethnicity,
sexual orientation, gender, et cetera, that compose a person's identity or
sense of themselves, especially in relation to others. In my group facilita-
tion work, I notice that social location often influences the participation of
group members. Because identity in our culture is a hegemonic construct,
with certain reference groups privileged over others, certain group members have described feeling "disempowered" from participating as much as
others in the group and, consequently, feel alienated. How does one address these issues as they arise in the context of the social therapy group?

Fred: In some respects, that is pretty much all we address in social therapy. We
certainly don't address people's emotional problems. We much more address those constructs and how they function. As you point out, in some
ways they function socially to privilege certain people over others. Psychologically, they function to keep people locked into their identity locations, which often makes it very difficult for people to grow. Many people,
by virtue of their identities, won't even come into therapy; it's simply not
within their frame of reference. They aren't ready to accept the public image that is associated with being in therapy.

Identity is hurtful as a sociological construct, and it's also inhibiting
as a psychological construct. It's oppressive in both ways. In both our practice and theoretical writings what we regularly engage is not simply particular identities, but the whole concept of identity and why we need, how
we use, and how we've been imposed upon by an identity understanding of
self. It's fundamental to our work of reinitiating growth.

One of the ways that we try to deal with the identity understanding of
self is to work hard to do what we call "building the group." The reason the
building of the group is so important in social therapy is that it is the counter
force to breaking down individuated identity. You can't simply work in a
deconstructive way to break down identities; people clutch them too dearly.
But what we have seen in practice over many years is that working together
to create a social construct—namely, the group—is a way for people to
take a look at, engage, and reconsider—not simply intellectually but in
practice—the isolation of their own private identity, whatever that identity
might be.

Now, along the way lots of people are, in varying ways, resistant to
that. They either want to hold onto the privilege of their identity or—not

surprisingly, but in some sense paradoxically—they want to hold onto the victimization of their identity. Both things happen all the time. People cling to identity on both sides of the social spectrum. We're all acculturated to hold onto our identities, much the way we're acculturated to a glorified sense of self. The social therapeutic approach attempts to deconstruct the sense of self in favor of a concept of social relationship, which we think comes, not from some abstract ideological commitment, but from a participatory process in which people actually construct something together— namely, the group. The key focus is building the group.

A lot of people think that the way to deal with social problems is to work on the problems as part of building community. We feel it's exactly the other way around. We think you build community, and in creating that community, you deal with social differences and social problems. In our work, we are always oriented toward creating the social environment as part of the complex dialectic of breaking down the individuated self-identity. We've found that makes a huge difference in people's ability to deal with their emotional difficulties. It's a fascinating irony. My experience has been that the more people participate in the creation of group, the deeper is their understanding of who they are individually—not the other way around. Creating the group curiously enhances who they are individually. Part of what keeps us so unable to know who we are is that we're too close to ourselves. We're so intimate with ourselves that we often don't know what we're about. As we participate in the process of creating something bigger than ourselves, we actually come to get a view of who we are and what we're about—even as we transform. That's the general framework. It's right at the core of what the social therapeutic activity is about. It's an engagement of identity.

from a colloquium

Dialogue 25. Particularity, Not Identity

Therapist-in-training 1: When working with gay clients who, of course, have special experiences, concerns, and perspectives, what kind of adjustments should the therapist make?

Fred: Generally speaking, I don't think in terms of special concerns. I think in terms of particular concerns. I think that "special concerns" introduces a category that stands in the way of you and your client. I think there are particular things that happen in the lives of gay people, in the lives of women, in the lives of Black people, in the lives of older people, et cetera, and the focus needs to be on the particularity of the people you are working with. I don't think this is just a semantic distinction; I think it's a different conception of what human beings are. I rebel in general at the identity characterization of people. Yes, I think that some people are oppressed in special ways but when that comes to take our focus off the particularity of people and to get us into categories, I think that's bad stuff. I think it stands in the way of helping people. I find it, generally speaking, harmful. I try to avoid it. I don't like it in politics. I don't like it in therapy. I think the focus needs to be on our capacity to attend to who people are in particular, not what categories they fit into.

Therapist-in-training 2: Do you think that programs that focus on bringing together people with the same identities get in the way of people getting help?

Fred: I have a bias against homogeneous groupings. The 1960s promoted that kind of thinking but I didn't like it then and I don't like it now. I don't see how it holds up theoretically or practically, so I've gone quite the other way. I try to have groupings I work with be as heterogeneous as possible. There is a whole literature on how helpful it is to be with people with the same problems—I happen to think that a totally heterogeneous grouping is a grouping of people with the same problems! Problems may vary in particularity, but I've never met anyone in 30 years of doing therapy to whom I couldn't say, "Oh, I understand that, I get that." I don't think I'm unusual in this way. You just have to be open to hearing what a person is talking about.

from a colloquium

Dialogue 26. Culture and Assumptions

Therapist-in-training: This is a question about culture and identity. In my work as a physician and community organizer, I learned a great deal about the cultures of different peoples and how they impact on behavior. For example, I learned how poor people can be victimized and how that is expressed in how they relate to me and others. Given that I have learned a lot about groups of people, I find myself all too frequently relating to people that I'm working with—residents, patients, et cetera—as members of a cultural group and not as the unique people they are.

Yesterday one of my Indian woman residents, who is pregnant, asked me to give her a lighter assignment than the others in the group. I felt her request was picky and petty and got annoyed and went to a place of thinking things like, "Indian women complain a lot and are overly reactive in making petty distinctions in tasks, et cetera. Given the sexism of the culture, it is probably a way that they can get a little for themselves." I told her I would look into the situation. My assessment of where she was coming from was accurate but I felt that my relating to her as who she was culturally was not a very developmental experience for either of us.

My question is this: How do you relate/respond to people as the unique people they are but also take into consideration everything you know about them culturally, historically, and socially? Do you have any assumptions about people when you respond to them? Or do you respond to them completely based upon what you are doing with them in the particular conversation you are having with them?

Fred: Let's start with assumptions. Do I have assumptions? I have endless assumptions. The issue is not whether we have assumptions; it is what we do with those assumptions. Are we willing to include, as part of coming closer to a person, exposing those assumptions? Are we willing to include a consideration of our assumptions and a consideration of the other's assumptions, and how those assumptions—ours and theirs—stand in the way of intimacy and development?

No one is assumption free. But I think you can do something with assumptions. What is troublesome in your formulation is not that you had assumptions, but that you went through that process privately.

We have to learn how to say in a caring, loving, and giving way, "Where does this resistance come from? Is this coming from your cultural background? Who are you? *You tell me* who you are, rather than me imposing my assumptions on you. I want to learn more from you about where this is coming from."

The imposition of assumptions substitutes for learning who the person is and using that process to give room for you and the other person to create something new. You have to create something together—which is not assumption free, but is free of the imposition of assumptions. You have to create a context, a relationship, in which you can discover more of who you are. That is part of the process of becoming something else.

We only learn who somebody is retrospectively, including ourselves. A lot of people think that you have to know who you are to figure out what you are going to do. Wrong. You've got to do something and then go and figure out who you are. We all have to go some place in order to see where we came from. The question "Where are we right now?" is meaningless. Who the hell knows where we are right now? How can we possibly know where we are right now?

Children don't look back at childhood because they are living it. We are living adulthood, and need to be as "constantly becoming" as children are—in order to know where we are coming from. Adults have this illusion that we can somehow figure out where we're at. Nobody knows where they're at. How could you know? And why would you want to?

Therapist-in-training: Does this involve sharing your assumptions?

Fred: Yes. Part of working with another person is to create the environment for sharing your assumptions: "Tell me more about yourself. Tell me more where this is coming from. I want to understand this. I have some assumptions, but I don't want to impose them." In that process, you are trying to create something new with this person. We have to break out of boundaries in order to better understand who we are. Tradition teaches that you have to learn the boundaries. I don't think so. I think you have to break the boundaries. You have to be creative to learn who you are. You have to become who you are not in order to learn who you are.

Therapist-in-training: Isn't putting out what your assumptions are saying where you are at?

Fred: I don't think so, unless what you are saying is, "Here are my assumptions and that is the deal." If you put out your assumptions in the spirit of using them to build something, then you are not so much saying where you're at as laying out the material for creating something. Yes, some people do say, "Here's who I am, and here are my assumptions of you—period, end of sentence." That can be troublesome. It is another thing to put out your assumptions about another person in the spirit of taking that as the material of becoming something other than who you are.

from a colloquium

Dialogue 27. The Paradoxicality of the Other

Therapist-in-training: In your recent workshop [Lovers and Other Strangers: The Paradox of Relationship] you spoke of the challenges of reaching out to and creating with people who might seem, from an identity standpoint, extremely different from you. You made the point that even though we perceive the other to be so vastly different, *we are the other.* You didn't say "We complete the other" or "We and the other are continuous in history." And that has me pondering. I want to know why you used the construction you did. Even with my closest friends or those I'm involved with in a unified team effort, I would never say, "I am you." But I don't think you were being metaphorical in saying, "We are the other." I believe you were making a statement about what is. Can you speak more about this? Is it an identity relationship? Does it say something about the inseparability or continuity of self and other? What bearing does it have on our understanding of class, race, nationality, gender, and so on?

Fred: I am being very literal in that formulation. I try to be as literal as one can be, because I think that raises the greatest degree of paradoxicality. For me, literalness is most intriguing and enticing.

Let's do a minor piece of deconstruction by way of question and answer. When I say, "You are the other," who do you think "the other" is? If there's going to be "me" and "other," then what we have is a world in which we have other-ness as well as me-ness. But there's no one available to be other except us. We're all other to somebody. To say that we are the other is not to make an identity claim about me and, say, John. We're not the same people. No one is exactly like anybody, but we are the other. Otherness is one of our ongoing social roles.

People might say, "Isn't that semantic? Isn't that trivial?" I don't think so. Sometimes we get so preoccupied with self that we forget that not only are we who we are, but for other people, we are other. It's important to periodically recognize our sociality by appreciating that there is nobody else available to be other than us.

What is the point of that? The point is to engage the notion of a "me-centered" universe—a picture that so many of us have in our culture. There's me, and then who else is there? The others. But that is not the world. The fact is that it's not me and the others. We are all interchangeably self and other. That is an important thing to realize because it changes how we relate.

To me, it's like moving away from an earth-centered universe to a Copernican understanding of the universe. That happened hundreds of years ago, but we haven't moved away from a "me-centered" universe. The me-centered universe still dominates, but we are not—any of us, individually—the center of the psychological universe. I don't know that there is a center to the psychological universe, but I feel confident that it isn't me. And I feel fairly confident that it isn't you—and so on and so forth. In fact, the notion of having to have a universe that is centered has been very important in our culture's psychological understanding, and it needs to be questioned. In psychological terms, there isn't a universal center. We have to come to understand that in order to fully break out of the constraining notions of identity that contribute so substantially to our emotional alienation.

from a colloquium

CHAPTER TWO

The Social Therapeutic
Group Process

Dialogue 28. Beginning a New Social Therapy Group

Therapist-in-training: How does a brand new social therapy group begin?

Fred: What I say to the group to begin it is, "Listen, what I want us to do to-gether—and I'll help you with this—is to collectively create an environ-ment that could be used—but not necessarily is used—to help people with their emotional problems." That's the start.

Therapist-in-training: And what happens?

Fred: Often, silence. And then people might start asking me some questions, such as "Well, how do I do that?" and "I have a problem, could I work on it?" I say [something like], "No. What we're going to work on together is creat-ing the environment in which you and others could get help. In other words, it's the creating of a therapeutic environment, not the using of a therapeutic environment. And each therapeutic environment is going to look a little bit different depending on the grouping of people. You create yours. I'll help you create yours. That's our task. That's what we're going to do together. We're not going to work on anyone's emotional problems—unless that's useful to do in the name of accomplishing what it is I just I set out as our task." That's the starting point.

from a colloquium

Dialogue 29. Talking to the Group

Therapist-in-training 1: I want to learn more about how the social therapy group functions. Does the group work in a different way from an individual?

Fred: To talk about the characteristics of groups, it's important to go to the obvious first. A group speaks with many voices. Sometimes individuals do that, but we regard them as weird or strange when they do. A group has many eyes. It can simultaneously turn left and right. It can stand and sit simultaneously. It can leave the room and go to the bathroom and still be there. These are all things that individuals, generally speaking, can't do. A group can engage in a whole host of what would appear to be contradictory activities were it predicated on an individual.

Groups have the characteristics of groups and individuals have the characteristics of individuals. It's ill advised to turn to metaphor to make the distinction. The distinction could be made and should be made in literal terms.

Therapist-in-training 2: It seems that, qualitatively, the emotional life of a group and of an individual would be different. I'd like to know if there is a difference, and how you understand/see that.

Fred: The first thing that comes to mind is that groups are far less patient than individuals. Individuals are remarkably patient with themselves. They'll go on and on and on and on. And they think everything they say is interesting. Groups are not like that. As a matter of fact, they tend to be impatient. I think that's a virtue therapeutically. Individuals are far too patient with themselves. Groups are, generally speaking—it varies from group to group—more volatile than individuals.

Freud took that to be their biggest problem. Freud disliked groups. Freud thought groups were the ugliest thing in town. I don't think so. I'm inclined to think that individuals are more of a problem than groups. Individuals have too much control of the emotive situation so—even Freud noted—you have to spend years getting over resistance. The beauty of groups is that you don't have years of resistance, because groups don't behave that way. They're more volatile.

Therapist-in-training 1: Are you saying groups are less resistant to change?

Fred: I didn't say that, but yes, I agree with that. Again, there's variation between group and group, and individual and individual, but in general by being more volatile the group is more open to some degree of transformation. Individuals are very conservative. I don't mean in the political sense, but in the emotional sense. Individuals tend to be quite conservative.

Therapist-in-training 3: I was wondering how you see the role of the therapist as organizer of the group—organizing the individuals to build the group. People can be asked to be more giving to the therapist, to follow the therapist's leadership in building the group. I was wondering if you agreed with that— is that a primary way of building the group?

Fred: I pretty much won't work with the group unless they're building the group, because that's the function of our therapy. That's how the therapy works. With very few exceptions that's all I'll participate in. That's my method for organizing. I make that as plain as I can in every way that I can. I don't stop people from doing what they want. I just convey that if they do something other than what we're there to do, I won't participate.

Therapist-in-training 3: How do you participate with others to build the group?

Fred: I speak to the group. The way that I work with others to organize the group is that the entity to whom I relate is the group. If people are doing something other than that, then I'm not conversing with them. That's my primary way of organizing the group. People aren't used to being related to in groups; they're used to being related to much more individually, particularly relative to the kinds of issues that we characteristically relate to in therapy.

I don't have to do anything special. I don't have to do a magic trick. All I have to do is persist in relating only to the group and, by doing that, I create a useful tension because the members of the group want to relate to me as individuals. I don't do it, and then all kinds of things come off of that. They get pissed off at me. They get competitive with me. Sometimes they just ignore me. Which is fine. They can ignore me for long periods of time because they want to talk to each other as individuals.

Therapist-in-training 4: You might be talking to an individual in the group, but you're talking to the group, right?

Fred: My response to you saying that I'm talking to an individual is that I'm also talking to the chairs in the room. In other words, all kinds of things—if they can hear—can hear me, including individuals. That doesn't mean that's who I'm talking to.

Therapist-in-training 4: It's a helpful distinction, thinking that any word that's coming out of your mouth is talking to the group.

Fred: Yes, almost without exception. Occasionally, under certain circumstances, I'll talk to an individual, and it's conspicuous when I do.

from a colloquium

Dialogue 30. Seeing the Group

Therapist-in-training: In the last colloquium you mentioned that you look for the therapist's ability to see the group. Since then, we've been working on "seeing the group" and talking about it in the training program. In our last meeting, it was pointed out that we tend to see individuals and not the group, and that groups have personalities. As cotherapist, what do I look

for when I am looking at the group? Am I looking for the group's personality, attitude, how it's working? All of these? None? And are these the
things that I need to bring to supervision?

Fred: The answer to most of those questions is, "I haven't the foggiest idea." The
seeing of groups has become increasingly important to me over the years.
I've become more convinced that the group, or the relationship, or the interactive unit, is the socially critical—and, therefore, in my opinion, the
psychologically critical—unit. I've become better at doing that, although I
don't know how I got better. I just practiced it; I didn't make any kind of
theoretical or practical breakthrough. I've done a lot of hours of group
therapy, so I've gotten better.

This is a big issue, because we're all socialized to see individualistically. I am reminded of that every session I do, because most of the people
I work with not only see that way but insist on practicing that form of
seeing in group, so among the various dialectics in the group is the fight
that goes on between members of the group and me over what unit we're
going to work with. I have groups in which people do individual seeing
from beginning to end and somewhere toward the end they ask me what I
think and I tell them that I think this is fine but it's not very developmental.
Yes, people are socialized as individuals, not just in a moral and legal sense,
but in a perceptual sense. Not only do we not see groupings of people, we
don't see processes very well. Perceptually, we tend see groupings as collections of individuals.

from a colloquium

Dialogue 31. *Freedom and Participation*

Therapist-in-training 1: In social therapy we speak of "building community." My
question is why the use of a mechanistic, physically oriented word like
"building" to talk about nonmechanistic activities?

Fred: You can spin the metaphor "building community" different ways. When
you spin it as mechanistic, I can see your point. However, I'm partial to the
term. I see it as a nice working-class metaphor. I like the concreteness of it.
I like to build off the more concrete metaphors into more qualitative metaphors. Building, after all, is not so mechanical as it seems. Looked at less
functionalistically, building is more qualitative than strikes the eye.

I talk about my groups as being work groups—not affinity groups, not
friendship groups. The point is not for people to fall in love with each
other, but rather for people to learn how to work together to create something. It's in that sense that I use the term "building." You build a play. You

build a house. Building a house doesn't just reduce to the mechanical steps of putting x numbers of nails in; there is a qualitative process going on. Also, given my politics, I'm very prone toward working and building and those kinds of metaphors. I think they are rich. I don't see them as being mechanical. I actually see them as generating new quality and making use of that quality in an ongoing process. In that sense I feel very comfortable with the building metaphor. I'm drawn to it.

In raising my daughter, a major part of what I would do is not be critical, not be negative, not be condemning if I could avoid it—mostly I could—but to simply make plain to my daughter that she has a right to do what she wants to do, but if she wants to do certain kinds of things that were agreed upon in working together, then there's got to be a way that she participates. I work with people that way. I'm very much a libertarian about people not having to do things that they don't want to do. But if they agree to do them, then they have to recognize that they now have a group and they have to participate in a group. It's perfectly fine for the people in the group to do what they want to do. It's even fine for the group to decide that they want to do the group without me. I have no problem with that. But if they want me to participate, this is what I will be doing. That's very central to how I organize with groups.

I'm devoted to libertarianism. I think individuals have every right—and so do groups have every right—to do what they choose to do. It comes out in my political work in electoral politics. I just don't favor disciplining groups. What I do favor is everybody agreeing that if we decide to do this with (as) the group, then that's what we should be doing. I feel very strongly about that. If we don't decide that, then people should do whatever the hell they want. It's sort of a radical position, somewhat fanatical, but I don't favor organizing through gradualistic means. I'm not a gradualist as an organizer. I very strongly convey the message—"If you want to do this with a bunch of people, then that's what you should be doing. If you don't, then don't." I don't see very much room in between. In fact, the room in between those two—which some people think of as a good thing and a compromising thing—I see as nondevelopmental.

Following Vygotsky, I think the zpd works, but half a zpd doesn't work. What "room for both" does is deny both individuated libertarian thrusts and what you learn from working together as a group. I believe that groups have to be voluntarily disciplined in that way. I don't see much room for compromise with that. Compromise simply relates to the group as if it were an individual, and if you want to do that, why not just have individuals? This isn't a moral position for me. It's just that I don't see the point from a constructionist point of view. To use very simple language—I think people gain an enormous amount from learning how to work together. Some people resist that on the grounds that it impinges on individual freedom. I don't think it does. You have to make your decision about individual freedom before you enter into the group arrangement. That's where the freedom lies. You have the freedom to agree to participate or not. But you don't have the freedom to participate and then not do what the group is doing. I don't support that. I don't know if that is an extremist position or sounds that way to you, but that's how I operate.

I'm guided by that principle in my work, and it's been very effective. I think the people in my groups have the sense that they have a great deal of freedom in working with me. I think I'm much less imposing than most therapists are, but very demanding in terms of the work that I'm doing with people in the group. This is an agreed upon activity. I accept that even with people who aren't "doing very much" in some traditional sense.

People sometimes say to me, why don't you get individual members to do more? My response is that being there is a statement from them that they are participating, and I will honor that and respect that even if they don't do things that other members of the group, or even I, think they should be doing. I don't have a reactive response to people who don't talk. Some therapists do. Some therapists try to get people who don't talk to talk. Generally speaking, I don't do that. Some people think that's not nice of me. But I think people are participating in the group whether they talk or not. I don't go on the assumption that they're not. How do I know they're participating? They are there. They've come to group. How do people properly participate? That's not for me to say. I can help the group. I'm not there, however, to get people to participate. I don't see that as my function.

Therapist-in-training 2: Do you think people who are critical of you for doing that are intolerant of silence?

Fred: I think they have an idealized sense of the way that people should be. It's not as if most of us don't have that. I just don't think it's appropriate for me as a developmentalist to impose it. People I've worked with for years who say virtually nothing have told me—and I believe them—that this has been the most developmental experience they've been through in their life. I have a lot of other people who never stop talking and one could raise some questions as to how much this is helping them. Therapy is a qualitative experience. A full range of things goes on. It's very difficult to reduce it to some modes of behavior.

Once again, from my point of view, the most developmental thing going on is the creation and development of the group. So if the group develops, everyone benefits. It is sometimes the case that one person is far and away more active in helping the group to develop, but I think everyone in the group benefits and grows. It doesn't reduce to some kind of democratic notion of equal participation, or even certain kinds of participation. Groups go through all kinds of changes in this regard.

Some of the most successful group therapy work I've ever done was in a group where we spent a year and a half working with just one person week after week. The group grew dramatically working with this single person. And the group was conscious of the fact that they were growing. Yes, there were some issues of resistance when it first began. Some members would say, "How come we're always talking about so and so?" And I would say, "Talk about whatever you want." And that's what the group decided to talk about, week after week after week after week.

I often say to my group that I can work with the group talking about anything—as long as they do it as a group. Some people think I'm kidding about that. Every once in a while I'm tested. And I often prefer the topics that come up when we're being ridiculous than when we're being normal. It doesn't make much of a difference what you talk about. It's not a major factor. *How* you are talking about it is certainly a major factor.

from a colloquium

Dialogue 32. *Creating a Shared Experience*

Therapist-in-training: Last month, we talked about the group building through the use of silly, ridiculous, outrageous questions. Could you say more about that? As well, could you talk about how question asking can build the group as "greater than its individual parts"?

Fred: What we are always working on in social therapy is what the group is doing. Concretely, that means that we have to discern how the group responds to what people bring in, all of which is individualistic. You might ask, "Don't people bring in a problem and then we work on it?" No. People bring in whatever they bring in—their histories, their wants, what's on their minds, whatever. And then what we have to do as practitioners is to see how the group responds to all of that. If the group simply tries to solve somebody's problem, it is resisting engaging in the activity of responding as a group to whatever it is that's going on. The group has to do something together in order for us to know what the group is doing. As long as people are going around and talking about themselves individually—how their week was, how their Uncle Charlie is, how they have the same problem as so-and-so—the group is resisting responding to the activity taking place in the room. The activity taking place in the room is shared by virtue of the situation. You can identify with something an individual says, but you can't share in that. The shared activity is what we all de facto do together in the room. And sometimes people don't want to do that. That's their prerogative.

In social therapy we're always looking for what the group is doing and the way you discover that is by the group doing something together. I don't care what it is; it doesn't make a difference what inputs you start out with. It's the collective reaction to those inputs that is the subject matter of social therapeutic work. That's when you have the beginning of meaning making, of collective development, of growth. People have this idea that some people are good at bringing in good subjects. I think if people more carefully studied the actual history of a social therapeutic group they would discover, strangely enough, that it's the people whom they identify as not being very good at therapy who invariably determine what the group is going to react to, because those people typically say something preposterous. And the "Oh my God" response becomes the subject of the group. So people who say seemingly dumb stuff are very helpful in that kind of way. And when people resist doing that because they want to be seen as being smart, then we're in trouble. Then people sit around making individualistic remarks and everybody else is making strange faces, which are really judgments at how bad the remarks are. And that can go on all night.

The social therapeutic group begins with a kind of group upheaval over the stupidity of what someone in the group has been free enough to say. And by the way, as John Shotter points out, you can make out the case that that's the way language begins as a social activity, anthropologically speaking. It doesn't start out with people being wholly rational machines who start introducing the laws of Chomskyian syntax. No, it begins in chaos. And then there is a group collective effort to order that chaos. Social therapy replicates what I take to be that anthropological fact of life.

You see this with children. You don't give them a grammar book and ask them to talk. If that's how it was done nobody would ever learn how to talk. It begins with a mess. Children make strange sounds; adults make even stranger sounds back at them. Language is not learned in a way that looks anything like the finished product. If you try to make it look too much like the finished product no one ever learns it.

So that's why these "silly" questions are of enormous value. They trigger responses that introduce a shared experience, which we can then work with. You never work with simply "what people bring in."

from a colloquium

Dialogue 33. Bringing Someone Into Group

Fred: [Responding to a therapist's description of a difficult group session] If you believe that you're in a dangerous or frightening situation with someone, then you can't do therapy with that person. Then your job would be to tell him that you can't work with him. I don't know if you're prepared to make that play, but you can't help somebody if you're afraid of him.

Therapist 1: I brought him into the group fairly early in his therapy, and that went well. We were initially able to do therapy together. Later on he became more antagonistic.

Fred: The purpose of group therapy is to help people to grow and mature and deal with their emotional problems in something closely resembling "the real world." Given that, the dichotomy that you're making is a strange one. Everything you've been saying is connected with your relationship to him and his relationship to you, rather than his coming into the group being the occasion for continuing the work with him by virtue of creating a group which is going to function in relation to him, to you, and to others in a more developmental way. I don't see any of that in how you're talking. The ring of what you're talking about is that group therapy is being related to as individual therapy: "I could do this with him"; "At first I was scared of him, now I'm not so scared." It seems very filled with egocentricity—yours. At a minimum, why wouldn't you be raising questions about why you brought him into the group prematurely?

Therapist 1: I thought I had answered that. I thought that his coming into the group when he did and how he initially related to the group was fine.

Fred: But that's the claim that I can't understand. How could you say it was fine consistent with how you describe the women in the group responding to him? What's fine about that? I take it you must mean fine for you in your relationship with him. But how could that be fine?

Therapist 1: Okay, I understand what you're saying. I think that how I under-stood it was that the group was functioning well earlier on and that it wasn't a problem.

Fred: How could it not be a problem if this is how the women have wound up in their relationship to this person? How did that happen? I mean there must have been a problem or the women wouldn't have wound up where they are now.

Therapist 1: I don't know.

Fred: See, I don't even know what you mean by saying you don't know, because on the basis of this discussion I think that you would say that you do know, we have found out.

Therapist 1: That I was oriented to this individual relationship with him.

Fred: Right, and you had worked out your relationship to this person, but you hadn't helped the women in the group work out their relationship to him; you substituted your relationship with him for their relationship with him.

So if that's what's going on everything can look fine for a period of time. But eventually it won't look fine. Given how it's turned out, then retrospectively you might want to look back and say, "Gee, maybe I didn't do enough work with him before bringing him into group."

When you bring somebody into group, what you have to be ready for is continuing to do what you have to do *as a group therapist*, given that this person is now in the group. The major issue to think about in deciding whether someone's ready for a group is the impact that's going to have on the group, not the impact it's going to have on the person. I think the really hard question here in terms of bringing people into group is not even whether or not you or the group can handle this new person. It's whether the group is going to *grow* with this new person. Whether it's going to be a positive thing for the group. That's got to be your focus and your concern.

Therapist 1:   Could you say more about how you think about that—how the group can grow from this person?

Fred: It's an appraisal of who's in the group, who this individual is, what you've taught him or her. I don't think there's a formula, but that's the nature of the judgment you have to make.

Therapist 3:   To say the obvious, there's a million ways we can slip into doing individual therapy when doing group. In terms of just how we think about bringing somebody into the group—will the group grow from this? How will it grow? Can I help the group grow bringing this person in?

from a supervisory session

Dialogue 34. Listening

Therapist-in-training 1:   I have a question about people who don't talk in group. Even though my experience working with large communities (not therapeutically) is that some of the people who don't talk are the best workers, my bias is that if people don't talk in group, then they are not building the group, because the medium of building is talking.

Fred: No. The medium of building is listening. People come together and form a collectivity and a capacity to be more intimate. Insofar as language is involved at all, I think it comes mainly from people's capacity to hear each other, not from the capacity of individuals to say things. Listening is an enormously intimate activity. Talking is not. Our ability to make sounds realizes only a modest degree our capacity for intimacy.

Therapist-in-training 1:   Well, not everybody who is not talking is listening.

Fred: Well, now you're raising a different issue. If you're saying to me—would I try to do something about people who come in and stuff their ears and hide under the chairs, yes, I would probably respond to that. But to infer that people are not listening because they are not speaking is insulting to people. It might mean that they are not, but that's a different matter. I think those people who are doing the "you gotta talk, you gotta talk, you gotta talk" stuff are really saying "you gotta be like me, you gotta be like me, you gotta be like me." It's very rare that people will even make inquiries about whether people are hearing. I presume that people are listening. I find that people who don't talk are some of the best listeners and contribute their listening to the group. And it's a great contribution.

Therapist-in-training 2: You've said it's not important what the group is talking about. If the group is babbling and not talking about anything, then what would the group be listening to?

Fred: The nonsense. Children do that all the time and they become very intimate. There is a bias toward the notion of propositional listening—listening *to* something. But listening is an auditory activity. It's something that you just do. We hear sounds. We hear voices. We hear other people. The notion of listening is so adult biased. You think listening is sitting there and discerning the meaning of the terms used. That might be part of what happens in some listening, but a lot of listening is literally the response to hearing another human being making roughly recognizable sounds and noises. We are the only species that talks, presumably. We're not the only species that listens. There are lots of listening species.

from a colloquium

Dialogue 35. Contributing

Student: Can you help me understand how contributing to what is going on— even, or especially, when you think you have nothing to contribute—changes how you feel? I find this especially when I'm angry at people for urging me to contribute, and then when I do, their response gives me so much encouragement. I begin to think that my "mental blocks" can be overcome.

Fred: When someone says, "I have nothing to contribute," people typically respond, "Yes, you do"—and, typically, they mean it. I say, "You *are* contributing. The problem is that you aren't getting gratification; you aren't self-consciously creating and determining what you are going to contribute." Growth involves saying, "Given that I am contributing, I would like to be more self-conscious of how it is that I am doing this contributing.

What can we come together and create out of a conscious, collective effort to contribute and create in ways that we want to and choose to?" We can contribute and create whatever we want. That is obscured in a culture that is so over-determined by knowing and authority. Knowing is fine in its place, but it is not creative growth or development.

I don't know that the answer is to simply overcome that anger. One has to become creative in ways that add to one's life, and not necessarily simply overcome the anger. We don't overcome things by going directly at them. We overcome them by creating larger pictures, larger stories in which that stuff is located. That's my idea of helping people to grow. People ask, "Are you going to help me get rid of this anger?" I say, "No, but if we can creatively add on to your life, then that experience has a different location. If you change the overall picture, you change the relative strength of some of these experiences."

from a seminar

Dialogue 36 Group Understanding

Therapist-in-training: What is understanding, as opposed to knowing?

Fred: People often use the language of "I understand this because I know the truth of the matter." But one doesn't have to speak of understanding in that kind of way. In general, Lois and I use the notion of understanding as a much broader category than knowing because knowing makes a more direct appeal to truth than understanding does. It seems reasonable to say that people can understand things without making an appeal to truth. Understanding can be a practice, an activity, an agreement. An understanding can be some sense that we're able now to move forward without an epistemic appeal to truth.

Knowing emerged from about the 16th century as having a relationship to reality: "I know this because it's true. It's true because that's how the world really is." That scientific paradigm has dominated epistemically for centuries now. There are often moments of consensus in the group when everyone seems to agree with what it is that we've determined to do that night. I don't think that we need an appeal to truth. My perception is that an appeal to truth is made when the group is breaking down into argumentation. It's no longer understanding and consensus, it's "I know what's right," says this individual over here, and this one over there says, "I know what's right and it doesn't happen to be that." At least that's how I see it.

Therapist-in-training: When the group comes to consensus or breaks down, are those moments usually self-conscious?

Fred: I don't know about self-conscious, because we're not too big on the notion of self, but they might be group-conscious. There is a feeling in the group, and an attitude and a method, that seems to be operative that suggests, at least to me, that we're now heading in the same direction and moving in the same way. Borrowing from Wittgenstein, imagine two or three or four people walking down a road, and at some point, some of them do what someone looking at them might call diversion, but it might not be diversion. It might just be that one person is going to move about and then come back to the road, but they are still walking together down a road.

There is no decision procedure for determining if we've established an absolute consensus. On the other hand, for practical purposes—and this is all about practical purposes—when you are walking down the road, if someone were to stop and go the other way or to hop into a car and drive off, the things that people might do in a practical sense might lead the group to understand that what was happening was someone leaving the group. Could you be certain of that? No. But can we reach that degree of understanding in the group? Often. Some nights we never do. Some nights as I look about the room I see 26 different people all of whom seem to be going to a different place in a different way—and that's life. There you are. I try to suggest, hopefully in a noncoercive way, that we might want to consider what we're doing here if we want to do something together tonight. And perhaps we don't. After all, the group's prerogative just might be to simply not do social therapy tonight. They have every right—it's their group. But I will try to at least suggest that they might give some consideration to figuring out where they are going and how they might want to get there. Sometimes I succeed and sometimes not.

In my view, there isn't a procedure for deciding when we achieve that understanding. I think we have to move on without that. I just wrote a paper called "Undecideable Emotions." I think emotionality is as undecideable as mathematics and in roughly the same way. I think one can say—I don't know if you can prove this in the way that it's proven in mathematics, but this isn't mathematics, it's psychology—that we can't come up with a decision procedure for correctly characterizing group (or indeed, individual, but I'm not much concerned with that) emotionality. It remains open and undecideable. But we go forward. We go forward in mathematics despite the fact that it's undecideable. We go forward in lots of areas of understanding despite the fact that they are undecideable. And emotions are, it seems to me, unusually undecideable as we go forward in life. Some people in the group will persist in looking for a decision procedure. They want to know the right answer. And they have every right to want to know that. I have no capacity to assist them in that because I don't think it can be discerned.

Therapist-in-training: What do I look for when I am looking at the group, then?

Fred: Look at what they have decided to do and look at how they have decided to try to do it. And stay focused on that. In a way, the question that you neurotically repeat in your head over and over again is, what are these people up to tonight, and what are they doing to get there? And periodically you say it—every therapist needs to say it, but how much of a need they have varies. Some people say it all the time. I'm about a 20-minute person myself. I can go about 20 minutes and then I have a compulsive need to say, "What in God's name are you doing?" Some therapists say it every 2 minutes. Some people never do it at all.

That's what you are constantly focused on—the method. What is the group (not the individual) attempting to do and how are they attempting to do it? That's what you're there to help them to do—if they so choose, if they reach a consensus on whether they want help with that. Often they can't because it is a group of regular human beings, individualistically overdetermined—as we all are—and they want to do individualistically what they want to do. But they find themselves in this room where the focus is on group and that has an impact over weeks, months, and years. That's what you, the therapist, are always focused on. That's how you never lose sight of the group.

Do we ever focus on the individual? Yes. There are occasions when people are in some very great crisis and what I do is to stop doing social therapy and help someone who is in great pain. I don't do that very often. After a while, people don't request it very much, because that's not what we're doing in this therapy. Sometimes it happens in any event and I feel a human need to respond to it. Sometimes I respond to individuals—and people think I'm doing it in the name of rejecting social therapy, but I'm not—I'm responding sometimes to an individual because I think that will be a means of helping the group reach consensus.

from a colloquium

Dialogue 37. Abandoning the Group

Therapist-in-training: My skills as a supervisee are quite underdeveloped, and therefore I'm not able to work well at creating the supervisory environment. What do you, as supervisor, find helpful in creating a developmental supervisory environment? Although you have not supervised me personally, can you suggest anything that I can do? When you have encountered an undeveloped supervisee, what have you asked that they work on, perform differently, et cetera?

Fred: My general advice on how to be a good supervisee? To be as ruthlessly honest as you can be and be ready to make a fool of yourself. Say what you did as honestly as you can and not be afraid of how people will respond. I think we all have the capacity to be more ruthless with ourselves than we tend to be. That's the second most important thing. The first is to get yourself a good supervisor.

Therapist-in-training: When you're doing supervision, what kinds of things are you looking for?

Fred: I look for whatever there is to be seen, but what I'm focused on is the very strong tendency in group therapy to focus on the individual members of the group at the expense of the group. The major issue of what therapists raise when things don't work out is that somehow they got seduced into helping an individual member and took their eye off the group as a totality. That's what I'm trying to teach because I think that's what group social therapy is largely about, and yet the strongest seduction is to focus on individuals. You can't give into it. You have to learn how not to cave in to it. It's the group that is paying me. It's the group that's hired me. It's the group that I'm working for. Individuals will, of course, come in there and say, "Can you help ME out tonight?" I say, "No, I can't help you tonight except insofar as the helping of the group and the development of the group helps you. That's the vehicle for helping you. That's the understanding of social therapy."

That's mostly what supervision looks like. I help the therapists look at why they abandoned the group. "Well, this person seemed to be in deep, deep trouble." Well, the deeper the trouble, the deeper should be your commitment to not abandoning the group. I don't say that critically. We've all been organized in a modernist psychological environment. I respond to individuals saying they're in trouble by helping the group. My experience over the last 30 years is that that is the most effective way to help individuals to grow. People grow as part of groups. They don't grow individually.

from a colloquium

CHAPTER THREE

Developing the Social Therapeutic Relationship

Dialogue 38. Responding to Individuals While Building the Group

Therapist 1: Fred, you made a move in one of your groups this week that I'd like to better understand. It was a move with M, who raised how he feels like a failure all the time. He gets up in the morning and second guesses everything he's doing: "That's not good enough," "I'm going to fail," and so on. You invited him to work with you in the group by way of supporting you. At one point he said he wasn't sure how to help the group, and you replied, "*I* help the group—*you* help me." And then someone said that that might make him feel like a sap, because he wouldn't be saying "his own smart thing." This referred back to the week before when you had raised with the group people's resistance (men's in particular) to being a "sap," to being giving to people they love in ways that they might perceive as unmanly.

      I have over the years imitated you in this—organizing people to work with me to build the group. And leaders of your groups will step out and support you in this specific way. I know this is central to how you build the group, and I guess, though I understand and follow it at one level, I want to understand better what you're doing when you make a move like that.

Fred: What I'm struck by is that you make it seem as if this was a move that came from the top down. You talk about it as if I make a move to make a statement about what social therapy is. In my experience, it comes from the bottom up. In this situation, this particular move with M came out his saying that he didn't know how to get close to me. So my direction to him was an attempt to answer that question. And I think that's important because I don't do what you interpretively see me as doing. Generally speaking, I can't remember ever saying anything in therapy out of some idealization of what social therapy is. Even your describing it as a "move" makes the hair on the back of my neck stiffen a bit. I don't "make moves" in therapy.

"Move" suggests a calculation based on some notion of what social therapy is. Now, that might be an accurate characterization based on what you see, but it's not what goes on for me at all. So I'd be interested in knowing why that would be your experience of this, given how thoroughly foreign it is to my subjective experience.

Therapist 2: So this was a move that M could make that would bring him closer to you and help the group.

Fred: See, I think it would be good for the group for M to do that but I didn't ask him to do it in the name of doing something good for the group. How come you see it that way? I think it would be interesting to explore. There is a strange dissonance between my subjective experience of what I'm doing and your characterization.

Therapist 1: I definitely began to think about it this way after the group and when I was thinking about asking you a question about it here in supervision. I think I almost immediately create distance. Even in my asking you this question now I didn't raise or think about the interaction with you when M said he wanted to be closer to you. That was important in what was going on. Also, I've worked with M for a long time, and I'm close to him. I know a lot about his relationship with you and that how you talk with him is very meaningful to him. But I went in to this mode of "Oh, I've seen Fred make this move before." And so I began to think about it as "a move."

Therapist 3: [who is a member of the group being discussed] Fred, your emotional prescription for M relative to his fear of failing was to seek to fail. That then became a topic of discussion and a theme for the group as a whole. And in the ensuing discussions over the next couple of weeks it got divorced from M in particular as it became a "topic." I'm not sure what I'm saying about this, but I can see where, after a while, you may not remember that the topic came from there. I wonder sometimes if the group is generalizing too much off of what Fred says very specifically to somebody. It does create very productive discussion, because you can always relate to something on some level. But I wonder sometimes if the issue loses its particularity and gets divorced from its historical origins in the group.

Therapist 1: It seems to me what Fred is raising is that that's not what he's doing. You can characterize it that way but that isn't what's going on.

Fred: Let's try to raise this discussion out of the vaguely theoretical. Say you are close to someone or getting close to someone; you may say something to that person, and you can be aware as you are doing it that doing it will enhance the relationship. But it makes no sense at all to say that you are doing it *in order to* enhance the relationship. Indeed, were you to do it for that reason you would be disingenuous. And it probably wouldn't work.

It is that very ordinary dynamic that I'm talking about here. It's part of the human contradiction. You can have an awareness of what you might call a generalization even as you are articulating a particular thing. Of course, you have to be careful not to confuse these two things. That is why I find this slightly startling. I find it very interesting, because I think—and I could be wrong—that I work overtime in therapy to say what I'm saying by virtue of what I want to say, by virtue of increasing the relationship with this person or whatever. And to be sure, those things can be turned into subjects, not by virtue of what I do, although maybe I enhance that happening by virtue of who I am, but just by virtue of human language and human discourse.

Therapist 1: Yes.

Fred: Every particularized statement between two people can be generalizable. Sometimes we do that self-consciously. But we all work to not lose our authenticity by transforming the motivation for what we're saying from the particularity of an interaction to the potential generalized outcome. Unless you are Woody Allen, you won't typically say "Gee, I really like your hair, doesn't *that* really help our relationship." It's a Woody Allen standard joke form, but most of us don't do that because that would be undermining of the very statement that we made. Which is neurotic and what makes it funny when he does it. I think that I work particularly hard at making these kinds of particularly intimate statements. You're watching it and seeing the other side of the dialectic as dominant. It's fascinating that that's your view of it. In some ways I'm not surprised since that's part of what happens in the viewing. Viewing does that to things.

Therapist 1: I watch you and I then characterize what it is that you are doing.

Fred: It's characterizing generalized forms. It's like my saying, "How are you feeling today," and you responding, "Wasn't that a smart thing to say!" That might well be the case, but you don't typically lump them together in discourse unless you want to be funny.

Perhaps you think that because I am so fixated on building the group I violate the existential particular. But I don't. That's the very contradiction of social therapy that one has to grasp. The creation of the group is what is fundamental, but it is not the case that anyone does anything in the name of creating the group. I think that people have a hard time understanding that, but it's how social therapy does "replication of life" at its best. I think that is the paradoxicality of life—you produce certain results but, by and large, you don't do what you are doing in the name of producing those results. Which is not to say you are not conscious that it might or should or would produce those results, but that is not the reason for doing them.

Therapist 3: Are you saying that you're not result oriented at all, that building the group is not just the wrong result, but that it's the activity, the ongoing process and not the result that's important?

Fred: Our responsiveness to life situations is best understood as separated from a recognized result of doing the things that we do. Though a recognized result may be there and we can even know that it's there, from a developmental point of view that doesn't turn out to be a healthy reason for doing it, because it's a dehumanizing and alienating way for people to relate to each other.

Therapist 3:   At a certain moment in the group you said to W [another group member] that he has done wonderful work week after week and that he could go further and be more focused on the activity of building the group. That was not a move with the goal to help W or to help build the group. It was just a move . . . I don't know how to describe it for what it is, but it was neither one of those things.

Fred: Exactly. We need a way of formulating it that has nothing to do with making it sound as if it was a move made to accomplish something. It was a responsiveness to W in the face of the role that he plays in the group. It was an existential responsiveness to him as a person given what he has done. I wanted to give him something. I want to have an emotional connection to him. Do I know that that will have a certain positive consequence? Is that likely for him or us? Yes. But that is not the answer to the question "Why am I doing it?" I don't do things like that. I don't believe in that.

Therapist 3:   I think the group produces topics when a discussion ensues in which many people are identifying with and building off the discussion. And I often see it as teleological in the sense that on some level this is what you wanted to have happen. Now obviously, you are saying that it is not true. But this is what I ascribe to you.

Fred: The interesting part about what you are saying, as I see it and hear it, is that while I think it's accurate that I turn those things into topics, which we then do work with, this phenomenon that you are talking about is present everywhere in everything that everyone does. I think that it goes on all the time in interactions. I think it's there all the time, but it happens so quickly that it is kind of unnoticed, and then I think part of what gets produced is the understandable feeling of inauthenticity in human interaction.

We interact with someone as an existential need to be giving, to be intimate, to be closer, but a component of the interaction, for both the speaker and the hearer, is some recognition of what the result might be, and that comes to substitute—almost instantaneously and unself-consciously—for the articulation of the existential need, for the interaction. What's lost is something of the particularity and the intimacy and what it is that you are saying to each other. We see this with children. A child says something and grownups say, "Isn't that cute?" making it seem as if the child said it to be cute. What they are doing is teaching that very thing that they will want to smack the child for a few days down the road.

Therapist 1: Stop showing off.

Fred: It's that syndrome that is operative here that is distressing.

Therapist 1: See, I think I'm drawn to social therapy precisely because you don't do what I described. I've made a lot advances in my therapy and training work, but I think it's still an emotional problem of mine that I am not dealing well with this human paradoxicality.

Fred: I think social therapy should be taught as an art form, not as a science. And art can be taught. People go to art school all the time, and they learn something about how to be an artist. I think that social therapeutics is an art form.

Therapist 1: I'm trying to engage the distinction between teaching social therapy as a scientific form and an art form. In a way, that was where I was coming from in my question, and I am glad that I exposed it.

Therapist 4: Talking to people in a way that builds the group is something I don't do very well. So I try to imitate you and other people who know how to do that better. And sometimes that gets turned into doing what you are saying, turning it into "moves." But I also agree with what you're saying, I know that you work that way—that you respond in this existential particularistic way, not "in order to" build the group. I believe you, but still it seems to me that responding in a particularistic way is better in terms of building the group.

Therapist 1: Are you saying you have to learn this scientifically and not as an art form?

Therapist 4: Maybe.

Fred: The curious feature of learning art, learning how to be a better artist, is that you learn endless techniques, but you do it all for the purpose of being *not* like what you are imitating. In fact, if you turn out to be just like the person that you are imitating you failed the course. That's how it works. In science it is quite the opposite. The purpose is to do it exactly the same way. So when you say you imitate me, everything turns on the meaning of the word "imitate." I think what you have to do to learn the art of social therapy is to internalize, in as accurate a way as possible, what I do in order to not do therapy the way that I do it at all. That's the paradox of learning an art form.

from a supervisory session

Dialogue 39. Relating to Stories

Therapist 1: [Referring to a prior supervision in which the group worked with a woman on enduring traumas from stemming from her childhood abuse] What's been very helpful in Fred's work with A is to see how the stories that people tell need not be related to as just a reference to the past. The critical thing, from our point of view, is how that story is playing in the group. This has helped me to understand that in a creative activity, an artistic activity, you don't know what something is until you create with it. So in A's case you don't know what the abuse is until you create with it and keep creating with it. The root of our pathology is the inability to actively create and reorganize life off of the events and circumstances that happen. In group we are constantly helping people to do that, to create the group and to create a new history.

I went back to Fred and Lois's *Beyond Narrative to Performed Conversation*, in which they talk about the confusion of the narrative therapists—their insistence that human beings need stories in order to understand life and, thus, the dualism between life and stories. For us, what's important is our ability to continue to create stories, not to use the story to understand something. I think many narrativists would respond to A by equating her story with life and then helping her to reinterpret that life experience in order to come up with a more empowering story—to "reauthor" her story to one that is more positive. Which is different from using the story to help create the group.

Coming now to the group I want us to talk about, it started out with B saying she had a burning issue to raise, namely, that the previous group's work with A had really upset her. She then had a story, which was that sometimes when her partner touches her and wants to have sex when she doesn't want to, she gets crazy. And that it reminds her that it's just like with her father, who sexually abused her. People were trying to respond to that in the group; one member became defensive and upset and started to dispute the notion that if you were sexually molested you were "wounded," that it determined your whole life, that sexual abuse is often used to define people—you get stuck into a role. The group took up this issue about how people's stories lock them into roles; it went around and around with people debating with each other about that, not particularly asking Fred much. There was a real combativeness in the group about this issue of stories.

B had become quieter and quieter; she sort of withdrew from the group. At one point she got very upset and said that the whole dialogue was making her feel like a foreigner, that she was completely alienated by what was going on. She was pretty angry and rejecting of the group. At that point Fred said that that was an example of her not wanting to do what others want to do. In doing so Fred brought into the room the very issue she had raised—that when her partner wants to do something, in this case sex, and she doesn't want to do it, she gets crazy. And that when the group wanted her to do something, to get involved and participate, and she didn't want to do it, she "got crazy," she said "I can't do this," "I'm a foreigner," et cetera.

I thought that was such a good example of Fred breaking out of the need to separate things—past and present, for example—it was a moment of clarity for me. And it was very helpful to the group. People started raising with B why she has to be a foreigner, why she couldn't just disagree with what was going on in the group, and why she doesn't just become a fellow disagree-er, like everyone else in the group.

Fred: I think the *creation* of stories is beautiful; I think the referential aspect of stories is troublesome. A's story about what happened when she was young is as much her history as whatever it is that happened when she was young. Do people understand that point?

Therapist 2: I think that history is something that people create, so that A telling us that story is history that we are creating now.

Fred: Are you making the distinction between history being created and not being created?

Therapist 2: I'm not trying to make that distinction.

Fred: I guess I don't understand what you man by "creating history." What do you mean by that?

Therapist 2: People produce things together, and that's part of creating history together.

Fred: In a way I agree with you, but I have a slight problem with the formulation. Because when you speak of creating history, you make it seem as if there is something called the activity of creating history and then there's something else called what it is that's created when we are creating history. It seems to me that you introduce another dualism. But there isn't any separation between what we do, what we make, and history. This is it. History is continuous. This is the ongoing activity of people talking, picking their noses, saying hello—this is the historical process. So yes, you can formulate that as "people creating history," and that seems perfectly fine except if you look slightly more closely at it, it can be slightly misleading. There's only one thing; this is the whole story!

Therapist 1: This is the move you made in the group with B, when you said, "Oh, is this what you do when you don't want to do something?" It was a move to organize that continuousness by breaking down this notion that A had too, that "I'm upset and have difficulty *because* I was abused."

Fred: Yes. You don't have to tell us what you're like when you don't want to have sex with this person. We know what it's like when you don't want to have sex with people—you don't want to have sex with us right now! Why do we have to learn it from a story that you tell us?

Therapist 3: Is that a critique of people telling stories in group?

Fred: No, it's not a critique of her telling us a story. But her telling us the story comes complete with her belief that doing it is an effective way of getting help; it is done to maintain her distance. We don't need that distance because we have an immediate experience of that exact same thing. So I have no problem with your saying, "I'm here sitting in this room right now." If that's what you choose to say that's fine. But I would say, "Gee, you really don't have to tell me that. I know that. I know that because I can see you and hear you." Redundancy is an unfortunate characteristic of the way that people speak to each other, as a way, I think, of keeping their distance from the actual experience that everyone is having collectively. People prefer to tell stories because stories give you better control. Because stories are *about* something, they give you control over what you're talking about in ways that you think can leave you unassailable, as it were, by the people who you're participating with. Stories can be perfectly wonderful things; I love stories, they're good things. But they have their downside.

  So people should of course say whatever they want to say in group. What's problematic is the illusion that that way of communicating is more fundamental than the shared performatory mode that comes out of our creating the group together. And people insist upon that—"You don't really know who I am." There's a subtextual message in that—"I have control over telling you who I am." People prefer to tell stories, because stories give you better control.

  To put it another way, A thinks that her story is just a way to say what *really* happened, that it's what the story is "about" that counts, as opposed to the story being another element of the continuous process of what happened, the activity of telling it contributing to the overall process of the group. What she and the group are doing is as much historical as anything that happened anyplace else, anywhere, any other time. But we insist upon having this distance between the subjective capacity to articulate our story and what happened. But there's no distance between the two. They might be other than each other in some sense, but they're not two different categories of ontological being. The story is not a problem; the story is a problem because it is introduced as a dichotomy between what happened and the telling of what happened. That distinction doesn't hold up. It might work out for God. Theologically speaking, God and only God alone has the capacity to be both where he or she is and at a sufficient distance from her or him to discern what is happening.

Therapist 1: We have the capacity to continuously overthrow paradigms.

Fred: Right, but that capacity has to come hand in glove with the recognition that there is no absolute.

from a supervisory session

Dialogue 40. *Creating, Not Invoking, New Ways of Seeing*

Therapist: I'd like to get help with my group. D, who's very fat, came in looking down and sad and someone asked her how she's doing. She said she didn't want to talk about it. So group members asked her why, and she said that it was something she couldn't get help with in group, that it was her burden and hers alone. So people asked why she felt that way, said that they cared about her and wanted to help, et cetera. This went on about 25 minutes. I decided then to say something. I said to D, how come you're talking about this as your problem, as opposed to *our* problem, that you're upset and preoccupied? So people asked me more about this, they didn't quite get it. And we talked about it for awhile.

Up until that point no one was talking about the problem. So I said to D, "Presumably the problem you're talking about is that you feel fat and disgusting and overwhelmed by that"—we had talked about that previously. So D said yes, that was what the problem was. So I asked how come she or the group isn't talking about this concretely. I forget what the group said, but she replied that she feels hopeless about this, that she feels like she can't get help from the group. I asked, "How come your feelings dictate how you perform in group? Because you have a feeling doesn't mean you have to act a particular way." At some point in the ensuing discussion D said, "What if I am obese and I *feel* obese?" I said, "Let's take a look at what it means to say I am obese and I feel obese. That has a quality of defining yourself. Does that mean that's all of who you are?" And she said, "No, I'm a great cartoonist, I'm funny, caring and a whole bunch of other things." I said that was true, she's all of these things, so why does she (and other people) talk about herself in this definitional way?

Fred: You had no idea what the answer might be when you asked her that?

Therapist: Well, no, actually I know a fair amount about her in this regard. About a month ago she had been vaguely alluding to this problem, and I said, "What's bothering you and what you won't talk about is that you feel fat and disgusting—you and I have talked about it in our individual work." And she said, yes, and the group did some work on it but in a limited way.

Fred: So wouldn't it have been more precise to ask her a different question based on the fact that you already knew the answer to this one? I would be inclined to ask her a question about her performance in the group. So you might ask her, "Given what you've said about how you've grown when you work with us, how come you won't talk with us today?"

Therapist (cotherapist in the group): When we previously worked with her some people were saying, "Oh, you're not so fat, I don't know why you're talking like that" and things like that.

Fred: So what she should have been saying is, "I don't know if I can get help from you because you're a bunch of bullshit artists." That would have been closer to the real deal, yes? I think that's a common feeling—"Why should I go through this if you're just going to bullshit me?"—for people who have issues like being overweight. They're very used to people saying, "Oh, don't worry about it; I don't see you that way." But you might have gotten to this point more quickly if you had done what I'm suggesting, if you had engaged more literally what she was saying in her performance, rather than making some abstract point about defining herself in a certain way. I don't know what value that has, except to lead the discussion down some path where you could guarantee that you would have something smart to say. That's the way it reads to me. I don't see any therapeutic reason for doing that. In effect, you're doing the same thing the group is doing; in effect you're telling her, "Don't look at it that way."

Therapist: "That way" means what?

Fred: "That way" means looking at it as her problem rather than our problem. That's the "that way" that you're pushing. The group is saying, "We don't see you as fat; why should you see you as fat?" Like the group, you're also going to another—albeit somewhat different—way of "seeing it." I don't think that giving someone another way of seeing things is particularly helpful.

Now at this point you're supposed to say, "That's weird! I thought that was the basis of our whole approach!" And my response to that is, "No, our approach is about *creating* new ways of seeing things, not giving people new ways of looking at things." There's a difference between creating a new paradigm and simply invoking a new paradigm. If you say to somebody, "Oh, just look at it this way," they're going to respond to you by saying you're full of shit. Because that doesn't make a bit of difference. New paradigms are a *creative* act, not just a trick. "Look at it this way" is bad therapy.

from a supervisory session

Dialogue 41. Radically Improvising

Student: Talk about tool-and-result and tool for result. How they are different? What can we do to make tool-and-result?

Fred: Tool for result is confined to finding a tool to obtain a fixed result, a particular end. With tool-and-result, you are continuously obliged to reconsider the totality of what you are doing. There is a continuous consideration of what it is you are attempting to create, and the tools are created in the context of that examination and reexamination.

Some of the improvisational work I've done recently is radically tool-and-result. We improvised knowing nothing, creating not just the approach to a comic outcome, but the entirety of the process. The tools emerged from what it is we were creating. We didn't identify where we wanted to go, and then figure out what had to be done to get there. We had no idea where we were going. There is humor in watching people going somewhere without knowing where they're going. A principle of improvisation is to always pursue where someone is going. In this work, we violated that principle, not negating but doing something other than what the other person did—going someplace else.

That methodology is exactly what I have been doing in social therapy. We work very hard not to negate where anyone is going, but frequently one person says something, and another says, "That reminds me of something." Then someone else will say something else. And someone will say, "What does that have to do with what we are talking about?" And the answer is, "Nothing." Our work is to create what it has to do with what we are talking about, not to presuppose that it does. Some say this makes the discussion chaotic. Well, maybe. We work on what we can create from the chaotic input and we grow from that in an emotional sense. Emotional life is chaotic—except when it is dull. We have to challenge the criterion of relevancy or consistency of emotions that we have imposed on ourselves.

People say, "I am angry," and then say why they are angry. I ask, "How do you connect those? Why do you believe that what you just described made you angry?" We have a linear understanding of emotionality and impose it on how we operate emotionally. That's unhealthy. How would I be better off by knowing or understanding where my emotion came from? We overwork what we think we get from knowing. I am against knowing, and for creativity.

Student: How do you manage to be creative with people in group who over and over say really stupid things?

Fred: I don't know what what they've said is going to become. I don't want to respond to what something is. We tend to short change creativity by insisting that what we are going to operate with as we relate to each other is what is. That leaves out the beauty of becoming. We don't know where things are going. When we predict or respond, we very quickly run out of space. It becomes: "That's stupid." "No, it's not," et cetera. Such morality discourse limits what you can do. You limit your creativity when you respond as if you know what is going on. We don't know what is going on, *because we haven't created it yet.*

I'm not interested in what is going on now. I don't trust now. There is no such thing. "Now" imposes a stoppage on an ongoing process so as to have the illusion that you have an understanding of it. As a therapist I reject an understanding that involves me saying, "Stop, take this picture, this is what is happening and I am the person who knows what is happening." It stops growth. It's stultifying.

from a seminar

Dialogue 42. *Learning to Be Intimate*

Therapist-in-training: I returned to social therapy 2 years ago after a 10-year period, and last year I joined the therapist training program and it has changed everything. When I would be in a meeting—it wouldn't matter what kind of meeting—I always felt like I had to say something. I was compelled to say something. I always thought I had something to say. That is no longer the case.

Fred: Those three are probably in the reverse order. I think this whole problematic scenario starts with thinking that you have something to say.

Therapist-in-training: Okay, yes. In my work with my staff, I am letting people do their work. I'm letting go more in a way that seems to my team and me that I am providing more leadership. I'm slowing down and getting more work done. We're working harder and smarter. The work with the young people and the young adults is more intimate and demanding. Other people, friends, coworkers, tell me often how I and we are developing.

What am I learning in the therapist training program? I don't know. I still find it easier to ask a room full of Black and Latino young people if they want to get close to me than I do with my White women patients in individual sessions. Do you think that I find this easier just because I have been working with young people a lot longer? In a group setting I think that I would be able to do this better. The potential intimacy is intimidating. I think that I am afraid to be rejected. Could you share any thoughts that you might have about this?

Fred: It's easier with the young people. Let's go back to classical therapeutics. Clients come to therapy for help and they need help and we have to be caring. But don't be confused about this. The client or patient will no sooner get there than he or she will begin to discover every resistance possible to keep you the hell away from them.

And if you happen to be Black and they are White that will be close to the top of the list. I guarantee it. So you are right. That is going to happen. The kids in your program are not doing that; they are doing other things. But a patient will do that and one has to appreciate and understand that that is a critical part of the therapeutic process. If you aren't tough enough to handle that you should not be doing therapy. I don't think that means that you should never draw some lines, but you can't be thinking about drawing lines. You have to go into it with an attitude of "I will find a way of helping people to understand as we get through this." You have to incorporate their responses as part of the developmental process, which includes your growth as a therapist.

Doing therapy is an enormously growthful activity because you start to learn very deeply what you have to do to be intimate with people who aren't looking to be intimate with you. They may be looking to control you or possess you, but they're not looking to be intimate with you. That is what makes it hard. I think it's wonderful that you are taking on that challenge.

I've been doing therapy for a long time, and I have developed some extraordinary relationships with groups of people, but I don't think I've ever done a session where someone has not implied in how they responded to me, "How the hell do you come off thinking that you know anything about me?" This happens with people that I've known for years. I think that people do see it as I have a lot of nerve and I understand that—in some ways it is a lot of nerve. I've had success with it, but it doesn't mean that people are going to stop thinking that it is a lot of nerve to suppose that you know more about what is going on for them than they do.

The patients have to work on their relationship with you in your way, and that's what they resent. People don't object to working on relationships; in fact, they tend to want to seduce you, so they are perfectly willing to do the relationship in their way. What they find out is that you think that you know better than they do the way to do the relationship. They might even be right, but that is neither here nor there. You can start keeping notes right now on the book you are going to write on racism and sexism in therapy: *The 500 Nastiest Remarks Ever Made to Me as a Black Therapist.*

from a colloquium

Dialogue 43. Challenging Assumptions

Therapist-in-training: In our seminar 2 weeks ago, we discussed and wrote down answers to the question, "What is a group?" Then we picked out a few of the statements we wrote and tried to find their underlying assumptions. I realized I wasn't very good at discovering them. How do you think about assumptions and how do you search for them?

Fred: I think discovering assumptions and making them explicit is a valuable enterprise in doing therapy; it's often a helpful part of the process of helping people. Sometimes you can feel these assumptions even if you can't point them out. For example, a family is fighting and the teenager says to the father, "Oh yeah, this is what always happens. You say this or this because you assume that you're always right!" And the kid is right; that is the assumption. Pointing it out might not get the person to change, but it might at least get people to see what the structural arrangements are that lead people to do what they do.

This happens in therapy all the time. People come in and start talking and you realize that what they're saying rests on something other than what they're explicitly saying. So someone might say to them, "You don't know what you're talking about," and they might be right, but you might say to them that their saying that is not based on what that other person is saying but on their assumptions of who that person is. One thing you notice in all groups, as in life, is that some people have certain status. Whenever they say something people nod in agreement. Another person can make a perfectly brilliant observation and people say, "That's bullshit, let's move on." People quickly evaluate what someone is saying not on the merits of what's being said—that's one big assumption—but on who said it. So it is useful in doing therapy to have the skill to be able to separate yourself from some of those assumptions and be able to point them out to people.

Frequently what happens in the group is that some of the most useful stuff to work with is said by someone who's not one of the big honchos. And sometimes the reverse is true—because a honcho said something it's taken to be a valuable direction. That's true for everybody—including me. Sometimes the stupidest stuff in group is said by me. And it won't get picked up on. I'm reasonably good at not pursuing something if it doesn't go anywhere; part of what it means to reexamine your assumptions is to be continuously ready to reconsider what you've said and what you've done. It may not be that you abandon it forever, but that you come to the recognition that you don't have to stay with that—you can go elsewhere. There is an infinitude of ways of reaching people. And you have to discover that.

from a colloquium

Dialogue 44. Being Demanding

Therapist-in-training: Creating an environment seems like it needs more than one person to do. I have been thinking that somehow I have to set it up, that it's up to me.

Fred: Why?

Therapist-in-training: I don't know how to bring the other person in to it.

Fred: Maybe they know. Maybe you have to make that demand. Maybe you are not demanding enough, and that is something you have to work on. I think that the hardest part of helping people—whether it is verbal therapeutics or physical things—is learning how to be caring, giving, loving, and demanding. And if you are saying that you have to set up an environment, that means to me that you are not being demanding enough. The two of you have to create the environment.

Finding your way of being demanding is difficult. I think I make an enormous demand on my groups in therapy. Sometimes there are long periods of time, particularly in the early phase of group, that I don't do anything at all. The message I'm sending out—implicitly and sometimes explicitly—is "If you (the group) don't create the proper environment, I can't work. I need you to create the environment. I won't create it. You've got to create it. You want me in there? You create the environment."

You have to learn to make that demand. You're too nice. You can't be only nice and help people therapeutically. Nice is wonderful if it comes as a part of the process of being demanding. But if nice substitutes for demanding, then you become less effective. It's hard to be demanding, because people are in pain and they have needs and you want to be giving to them.

Therapist-in-training: That is not really true. I want to tell them, "Stop being a jerk."

Fred: "Stop being a jerk" is a giving thing to say if it is said in a caring and loving way. That is being demanding. Maybe you've got to tell a lot of people that they are being jerks. You have to say that they can't do things this way and expect to feel anything but isolated.

from a colloquium

Dialogue 45. Sharing "I Don't Understand"

Therapist-in-training: Sometimes when I'm doing therapy and something doesn't seem quite right, I say, "I don't understand." Should I include that with what I am doing with my patient?

Fred: I was struck by your formulation. Let me share my reaction. Here's what
      you said, "Sometimes this happens . . . and I don't quite understand." The
      word I have trouble with is "quite." That seems to me to be a hedge. Be-
      cause I think the implication there is that there is something problematic in
      what they said. I think *you* need to take on the full responsibility for not
      understanding. And that seems to me to put the focus on activity. "I don't
      understand" is something you need to share, but it's not to be shared as if
      they are doing something wrong, like not being clear enough or not saying
      the right thing. Rather, "I don't understand" is a subjective report that's
      necessary for the continuation of this activity with this other human being.
      In our culture it's very hard to say, "I don't understand" in a way that is
      nonjudgmental. But you have to find a way to do it. So, again, "quite" is
      the troublesome word for me. Drop the "quite" and you'll be fine.

from a colloquium

Dialogue 46. Being Adored

Therapist-in-training: Bette [the Institute's director of training] recently stated in
      a class that to do good work with people they must adore you. What does
      adore mean to you? Is it important to your work? What is it like to be
      adored? What does it require? How do you stay on track? I wonder about
      power, trust, and betrayal. Do you adore the individuals that adore you? Or
      is it something else that you adore? I have a lot of reactions to this adora-
      tion stuff. Is adoration something an ordinary person can and wants to en-
      gage in? Or am I being completely off the wall? What about adoration and
      worship? Is adoration worship?

Fred: I have a love/hate relationship with adoration. I detest what it is about in
      our culture. I think adoration can lead to oppression and worship, which
      inhibits creativity. On the other hand, there is something wonderful and
      positive about it.
          Children sure as hell adore their parents. There must be something in
      that, and I don't think adoring is a negative phenomenon. I adore a lot of
      people. To me, the adoring relationship is one in which we're creating some-
      thing together. I'm not out in front; I'm with you. We are going to
      coparticipate in the glory and excitement of "doing together." When people
      you're working with in therapy feel—as they no doubt will—that this is
      too hard, too extreme, too "something," that is when the adoration comes
      in. It's then that they'll be able to say, "I'll go over that next hill with this
      guy. I'll go with him." It's like a child having sufficient trust in this person,
      a mother or father, to go to a place that they're apprehensive of. The thera-
      peutic process takes people to some very hard places, and I think they have
      to adore you to go with you.

It is not an adoring that turns into worship. I don't experience it as worship. I experience it as people saying, "I love what you are doing. I want to do it with you. I'm afraid to do it. It frightens me, but I'll go with you, side by side. We will both go down that road together. I think I can trust you. I'll trust you enough to go with you." I take that trust very, very seriously. To be responsive to people's trust is in the singular highest value in my life. I sometimes fail at that. I have let people down. Those are failures and mistakes. But trust is the value that I operate with and I give enormous energy to that in my therapy.

There has to be adoration when somebody thinks, "Why in God's name do I put myself in this torture?" And they are right. It is torturous. Going beyond ourselves, going to becoming, trying to overcome societal norms, our ego, our id, our this, our that—that is a painful process. I think people need something that motivates them, something that helps them say, "I'm going to go with that person." That kind of friendship is what I mean by adoration. I love the people in my groups. I have a passionate relationship with them. I often find it hard at the end of the group to go home. I just want to be with them. It's like theater. In creating a play with people, you produce a closeness that is best described as a kind of adoration. You adore each other in this way that you come to by collectively creating something new. This is your joint product. In a way, it is something connected with families at their best. You create it.

I adore this community. Some people don't know this about me, but I love to hear the most minute details of what people have accomplished. I have an insatiable appetite for all the wonderful things that the people in this community do and I love to hear about that. I love the creativity that comes out of that collective adoration. I don't think this is a cult. I think it is an adoring community. If people don't agree with that . . . well, I can live with that.

This is a love community. Historically, it comes from an effort to create community completely unlike the love communities of the 1960s. It is a love rooted in creativity, not in sentimentality. I have no problem with sentimentality when it is combined with growth and creativity. Maybe we're postmodern love children.

from a colloquium

Dialogue 47. Being Intuitive

Therapist-in-training: When I'm with my patients, in my roles as social therapist and nurse, I sometimes find myself feeling like something's not right, something's not sitting well with what's going on at that moment and I wonder, should I go with my instinct . . . with what my intuition is telling me? Could you speak about intuition and insight—and instinct? Do they have a place in social therapy? Do you listen to them? Can they be useful?

Fred: We have a nervous system that seems to produce certain instinctive responses. I think there is a big distinction between instinct understood that
way and intuitions. Intuitions seem more conceptual and mentalistic in their
origins. The concept of an intuition suggests the idea of particularizing, of
separating it out from the complex gestalt of our whole cognitive, attitudi-
nal activity. It's one thing to be intuitive and it's another thing to think you
can identify certain things called intuitions. The process of thinking, feeling, emoting, believing . . . this whole set of complicated physical, mental
processes that makes it what it is to be a human being is so continuous that
I find it difficult to even talk the language that would suggest that one
could separate out the various elements of it.

   If intuition means something like "going with something that is not
fully rooted in a completely explanatory or cognitive process but is rather
some kind of quasi feeling, cognition, whatever and it pulls you in a certain
direction"—then yes, I think that's part of what it is to be human and,
therefore, part of what it is to be a therapist. I think it's important to demystify
intuitions; they are as much a part of the complexity of who we are as
everything else. I don't think they are necessarily less reliable than empirically verified laws or theses. In some contexts what takes precedence are
things that are empirically verifiable but in other contexts we have other
kinds of ways of responding to things in life.

   Sometimes my experience as a therapist is that my response seems
shockingly emotional in some "pure" sense of the word. It doesn't seem to
be rooted in empirics or in understanding. But then in the very next moment my response can be unbelievably intellectual. I don't get particularly
caught up in the inconsistency of that—there are multiple things going on
all the time for all of us. We're simultaneously lots of different kinds of
ways. Intuitive is one of those ways. My understanding of it is, at best,
intuitive.

from a colloquium

Dialogue 48. Don't Be a Helper

Therapist in-training: I have a question for you regarding a young woman I've
been seeing for awhile. A is very isolated and originally came to therapy to
get help with her frequent fits of anger. [Therapist gives background
material.]

   In therapy, A usually begins by telling me about what she saw on TV
the day before. She talks about the shows, the actors, the commercials. I

am learning to stay present with her in the conversation. I am continuing to work on the relationship. A is bright and interesting and I've learned a great deal from her about the history of dolls, other toys, and the history of children's games. When I respond to what she's telling me, she often ignores me and my attempts to build the relationship or bring the conversation into the room. She will change topics or not respond to me, or say, "I'm confused, that is interesting, or huh?" I respond by asking things like, "What is confusing?" et cetera. And she will twist the conversation back to TV.

A is about to begin group where I am the cotherapist. She is eager to begin and meet new people. She does share some of her concerns with me, like her sister's behavior, which is very upsetting to her. She's made comments that she wants to hurt her or kill herself if she does not change. I asked her why are those the only two options she could think of and suggested that there may be other things to think of and create in response—and we go back to TV.

Fred, I need help. My rear end is sitting in a chair as a traditional therapist. My heart and head are longing to do the work of social therapy. I want to get lovingly tough and more demanding of A and feel less frustrated by her pushing me away. How do I support her in changing the totality of her life without needing to help her or solve her problems?

Fred: Let me act like a therapist and ask you a question in response. How would A respond to hearing this? What would she say if you read her this piece?

Therapist-in-training: I think she would say, "Really?" I think she would be surprised.

Fred: From what I hear in your question, you have a hard time surprising her. Wouldn't surprising her be a positive thing?

With a situation like this, let the person know what your problems working with them are; see whether or not they are open to being responsive to your difficulties. What you are saying, in effect, is, "I'm open to being responsive to your difficulties, but I find that very hard to do. It might be helpful if you started helping me. I think that may be a big step forward in my capacity to help you."

Therapeutic work is a dynamical process—whether it is individual therapy or group therapy, and you, as the therapist, need to constantly look to the person or people you are working with to give you the help you need to be of help to them. That doesn't mean talking about your sex life or your family problems. It does mean talking about emotional difficulties that are brought up for you in the context of the therapeutic relationship with them. That is totally legitimate and I think it is quite a positive thing to be share.

While there are many causes for our turmoil and difficulties, I am convinced that a component of them is that people don't understand how the world is behaving relative to them. They don't have an understanding of how they are viewed. One of the things you do in therapy is be honest—in a principled, caring, and loving way—with the person with whom you are working.

The person is there because she or he wants to get help. Beyond that, it is reasonable to presume that she or he has no idea what that means. Sometimes, therapists get into thinking that they and the client are talking the same language. In general, my supposition goes quite the other way. A lot of therapeutic work is an effort in radical translation. Yes, there is some common ground, but working to create a common language works much better than thinking that we have a common language. That is more of a give and take than what I am hearing in your description.

Sometimes it is important to break out of the roles of the helper and helped in order to be helpful, because "helper–helped" assumes a number of things that may not be true—for example, that you are speaking the same language. Sometimes somebody will raise something in group and be talking, then another person in group will say, "Well, wait a second, last week (or just before, or yesterday) you said that and that and that . . . how come you are saying this and this and this now?" It's one of my most frustrating moments in therapy. I want to say, "Now listen, if you want to be that consistent and rational, you may not want to be in therapy."

Therapy, in some ways, is about irrationality. It is about inconsistency. That's not just a feature of therapy, but rather its subject matter. So, you may have to be more open and share this question you asked me with A. The first threshold in therapy is to get to the place where it isn't just helper and helped, but rather both of you working on the same side, working together to create something. It is easy to leave that step out. You can have that for a moment and then lose it, and you have to go back again and reconsider what your clients are doing there and what you are doing in being there to help them. You have to find ways of articulating this which are not filled with judgments and do not put people off. As I understand it, this has to be constantly reengaged.

This might be a moment to engage that with A. Often the form of the conversation in the therapeutic process is for you to say, "I've got a problem. You are not my problem. I want to be here and to do this with you and help you, but I have a problem. And I want to know if you want to help me with this problem. I want to help you to help me with my problem." Does that seem helpful at all?

Therapist-in-training: Yes, it helps me understand how judgmental I've been. That has made it hard—and frustrating—to understand her.

Fred: The most judgmental aspect of the helper-helped model is the assumption of the helper that she/he knows what the other person is talking about. It's not particularly useful in helping people therapeutically. Creating some kind of common language, a kind of radical translation in both directions, has to go on. It's my sense in the years that I have been doing therapy that you have to do that again and again with absolutely everybody. You have to keep creating a common language. If you get stuck in that helper–helped model, there is a tendency to think that you should or do have an understanding of what the other person is saying.

And, of course, the presumption of the person coming to you for help is that you are going to be of help. That is a fair presumption. But I don't think it follows that you have to know more than you could possibly know as a way of giving that help. But there is the pull to say: "If I am the helper, then I have to have a certain kind of knowledge." And you may have, but I don't think you necessarily have any kind of knowledge of this other human being. So when the pull to know extends over that boundary, then I think you are substituting some generalizations that you think are useful for the difficult process of understanding who that other person is. The generalizations and information you have might be of value in the context of mutual discovery, but not as a substitute for it.

I understand, though, the pull to use the tools that you have available when you are on the spot and want to be helpful. Going back to Vygotsky, however, I think you have to create tools. You have to make some tools that are specifically constructed for this relationship and that is a different task from using tools you already have. I don't suggest that you give up using those tools. Just don't substitute them for the harder job of creating specific tools. That is classical "tool-and-result." This may give you an idea of what it is that I think you need to do.

from a colloquium

CHAPTER FOUR

Therapeutic Challenges: People and Situations

Dialogue 49. Women, Men, and Sexism

Therapist 1: I've been observing one of your groups for a few months now. I wanted to talk in particular about your work with the men in the group. I think you're showing people who men are, how they function in the group, how they function in the world. And it's not psychology. It's how the world works. You said in the group a couple of weeks ago that the men have nothing to give there, in that particular context. Is that right?

Fred: I think the formulation was that we didn't need the men.

Therapist 1: Yes, and I think the point you were making was that it's not that the men are withholding, it's that they just don't have much to give. One of the men was enraged by that and said he felt like he has a lot to give but he just has trouble giving it. And there was some dialogue off of that. I'd like to try to understand better what you were saying, and maybe one piece of this is the distinction you just made between what I remembered you saying— that the men have nothing to give—and what in fact you said, that the men aren't needed.

Fred: I take it to be almost unquestionably true that everybody has something to give. Whether or not someone is needed for the continuous building of the group is another question. That's the distinction I'm making.

Therapist 1: I feel like I work with the group to not be reactive to what a particular man is doing.

Fred: See, I work with the women to *be reactive* to what the men are doing, and try to work with the men to *not be reactive* to what the women are doing in reaction to them. That's where I'm coming from.

Therapist 1: And why is that? Why do you want the women to be reactive to the men? I think I try to cool that out, to not be determined by the men.

Fred: Because I think that that's how the world is. Women are, generally speaking, profoundly underreactive to men. There are social reasons why that's the case—it's somewhat dangerous in many contexts, it may not be in their self-interest, et cetera. So I don't know why one would want to in any way repress what is already profoundly repressed. Now, I don't think being reactive has to mean being nasty or hurtful or violent, but I think it's a very healthy thing for women to have a place where they can give expression to their reactions to men.

Therapist 1: I think of women as being very reactive to men. I feel like the women in my group become reactive and in some ways stop building the group; they just kind of get into what a jerk this guy is.

Fred: It seems to me a good thing to create an environment where women can say to men, in a way that supports the building of the group and therefore is helpful to everyone—including and probably most especially to the men— things they don't ordinarily say. And it is a good thing to help men to say the kinds of things that for a variety of reasons they tend to repress in their relationships with women, as well as with other men. I think that often the group tries to suppress reactions. I virtually never do. I think if people take the risk of saying something, they're entitled to get a reaction. I don't see the logical basis of telling people to participate if we're not going to give them that. So I think that the women in most of my groups carry the group. What I urge them to do is to respond, to react. I think that if women are being very strong that's a good thing. Sometimes it goes over the line, but I think you have to take that chance. You can do something about it. But it's a small price to pay to create a helpful and supportive environment.

Therapist 2 [cotherapist in Therapist 1's group]: In the group, the way that the women react to this particular man, there is a certain impotency in terms of building the group. They'll be really pissed at him as individuals and stop working together.

Therapist 1: Yes, and I'll try to build with what he says, but sometimes the women want me to shut him up. I mean I have said to him at times that he's being nasty or stupid or whatever.

Fred: Don't you think it's a problem that *they* don't say it to him and so you're forced to say it to him?

Therapist 1: But I find the way they say that to him to be impotent and abandoning the group in some way so I end up not supporting it.

Fred: I hear that as you competing with the women in the group over who can have the proper reaction to this guy. They don't do it right; you do it right.

The work of the social therapist is to as much as possible stay out of reacting—in this case, to this man—so that you can mediate those reactions. In that situation I think you have to work with the women at getting better at this so you don't have to be in that role.

Therapist 1: I want to return to you saying to the group that the men weren't needed to build the group. I know that I wouldn't have said that to the group.

Fred: Perhaps you and others hear that sentence differently than I do. If I were to say, "We don't need the women in the room right now to carry the chairs out," I think that's accurate, in the sense that the men could handle it. It isn't a moral judgment to me. I think anyone who looked at the dynamic of my group and said, "Wow, the men are really needed in here to do what we're doing," would be lying. Could they do that, would it be wonderful if they did? Well, yes. But they don't. Who makes the group move are, with few exceptions, the women. It's a factual claim, not a moral claim. But it sounds like you're responding to it as a moral claim. Do you think the men play a much-needed role in the development of that group?

Therapist 1: No.

Fred: Then why wouldn't you say it? I mean, not provocatively, but in the proper context, why wouldn't you say it?

Therapist 1: Well, I think because of the potential of the men to be enraged by that—that's one thing. And I think the women aren't going to agree with it. And I think it was a big statement that you were making, not just about the group.

Fred: Yes, I think that's fair. Men are characteristically less needed in emotional situations because typically they don't contribute very much to them. I was talking about the men in the group but I did say it in a tone of voice that suggested that it was a more general phenomenon. Men don't carry their burden in most emotional work. They carry their burden in other areas—they carry their burden often intellectually, they carry their burden physically—but they don't very typically carry their burden emotionally.

Therapist 1: I think as a woman saying that to men that it would invoke greater rage. I feel like you can say that to men but that I can't. They'd rip me apart.

Therapist 3: Okay, so they'd get really angry at you. What's the problem with that? What would your response be?

Therapist 1: Well, it seems like it goes back to my relationship with the women in the group.

Fred: I don't feel in a position to disagree with you, because I'm not you, I'm not a woman. But my inclination is to say that your seemingly victimized characterization is nowhere near accurate. In the context you're describing, if you said that to the men I don't think they would rip you apart. I think that's a serious misunderstanding of how men operate. Again, I'm talking in general right now because I don't know the particular man and I'm talking from my vantage point because I'm not you. I'm not denying your subjective feeling about it, but if I examine the relationship between your subjective feeling and what I think would go on, given my understanding of how men operate, I think you're way off the mark.

Therapist 1: What's your understanding of how men operate?

Fred: Most men that I know? They'd try to work overtime to get themselves needed by you. That's how men operate with women.

Therapist 1: That's what you're teaching in the group, that men do relationships based on their being needed?

Fred: Right.

Therapist 4: How might that look in this group given that they're not needed emotionally?

Fred: They'd look to say a correct line so that the women would respond differently to them. They'd try to find some way to change how they say things. And some women might buy it; that happens often in our groups. But if a woman were to say that to one of the men in my groups I don't think the men would get up ready to slug. Occasionally one of the men gets furious. But to be perfectly frank, more typically the men get furious at me when I say it than when women say it.

Therapist 1: Why do you think?

Fred: Because men are not so heavily invested in being needed by me; they're invested in being needed by the women.

from a supervisory session

Dialogue 50. Men Who Act Violent

Therapist-in-training: I am a social worker working with men convicted of battering their intimate partners. The participants are mandated to a 26-week educational course. The course, taught from a feminist perspective, looks at oppression, racism, sexism, and how people of color and women (and particularly women of color) are invisible, objectified, and devalued in society. The course also asks men to be accountable for their choices with regard to violence within their homes.

I continually find myself in the conflicted position of teaching the curriculum yet I recognize—and the men make it clear—that they do not know how to change, in their relationships and in their community. These men do not want to repeat the behavior that got them into this situation in the first place. Some men really express the desire to change.

I teach concepts like oppression and then, in response to their questions and reactions, I not altogether kiddingly suggest that the men "make the revolution outside our classroom." I am wondering how, within the room, my co-instructor, myself, and these men can collaborate in an activity that enables them to feel more empowered. To some degree, I can model an equitable relationship between myself and my male coleader. I am respectful of the men and do not see their violent behavior as being the totality of their experience. But these seem like limited and fairly instrumental responses.

On a larger level, in the activity of doing something different in relationship to their partners and also with their children, families, and communities, the curriculum seems inadequate. Although the agency addresses issues of choice and personal accountability, it sees itself as a community response to the domestic violence crisis. How do I answer their questions as to how they can change their behavior? The agency response of "Give up the aggressive, violent behavior" seems inadequate, especially given that their communities are violent, and dealing with that violence is part of how they survive as poor Black or Latino men. What can they do differently and what would their new, developmental performance look like in their homes or communities?

Fred: That's a very interesting question, a helpful question. I think the problematic in what you are raising is reflected in the core question of what you're asking. There is, of course, within all of psychology and certainly here in your description, what I take to be a bias that goes like this: You can't accomplish anything unless you know how to do it. That's a rock bottom bias, a cognitive bias—somehow you have to know something to effect developmental change.

I think that needs to be carefully explored. Obviously, the most profound developmental moments in our lives occur when it couldn't possibly be the case that we knew anything at all of what was going on—namely, when we are very young. The evidence suggests that development of the most intense kind, quantitatively and qualitatively, occurs when we are least cognitively conscious of what it is that is going on. But strangely enough, what happens as we get older is that the model inverts itself and now it turns out, for complex societal reasons that would take the next 50 years to spell out, that a precondition for development is that you have to have some cognitive awareness of what you are doing.

That's the first thing that has to be challenged. That's not easy for many reasons, not the least of which is that the institutional bias is so strongly cognitive that if you try to get a grant passed through, you'll have people making X's all over the proposal asking, "Well, how does this work? How does this work? How does that work?" because you haven't spelled out yet what it is that one understands cognitively in order to produce the developmental change. And if you say, "Well, I want to challenge that . . ." well, forget about the grant.

To answer this question that you are raising so eloquently, we have to find some other social activity that is not specifically cognitive and that can be the basis of developmental transformation. And here we come to performance. Performance, as we understand it, is not specifically cognitive at all. It's useful to look at what happens in the theater. Actors and actresses perform. Sometimes some of them do this by an actual cognitive process. They think of some image; they think of another person; they think of characteristics; they look at their own inner life and they try to find resources there. But not everyone performs that way. Some people perform by simply allowing themselves to be other than themselves. In my own life experience as a director, writer, and theater person, I've seen that some of the most wonderful performers carry out performance in this way. That is, they don't specifically have another conception or image that they choose to be or imitate. They just have the capacity—in the stage setting, in rehearsals—to be other than themselves, to experiment, to be, as Vygotsky says, a head taller than who they are. To be dedicated to being other than who they are and to seeing what happens by being other than who they are—not because the other is necessarily wonderful or so great in itself or in the finished product, but because the exercise of performance, the exercise of doing other things, is critical for development.

It's not easy, as we see with our improvisational trainings at Performance of a Lifetime. You're up there on a stage and someone says, "Okay, do something other than you've ever done before. Do a brand new thing." And people freeze and say, "I can't think of a brand new thing." And yet, it can be done. Just as people freeze in that situation, they thaw out—with support, with help, with some direction that helps them to see that we can creatively do other than what we typically do. You see that people learn to do strange and weird things. I think what is learned in this is not so much from the content of the weird performance, but we learn *that we are able to do weird performances*. The learning of that is profound and important.

The work with performance is a very important challenge to the cognitive bias. I think you're quite right in saying that if the message is simply "Stop being that way," it's not going to go very far. I'm sure everyone in this room agrees that these men should stop doing hurtful, destructive things. Presumably they are there in part because they agree with that. But I don't think we can grow very much off of that negative cognitive statement or proposition. I actually think that what these men have to learn—this might sound utterly strange—is that they can be weird, that they can do weird and unusual and different things.

You are right in asking that if they learn how to do just those kinds of things, how does that fit in with their existence within a macho community, within a violent community. There is a way in which the answer to that is, "It doesn't." But I don't think it follows from the fact that it doesn't fit in that people can't learn how to do it for themselves, to give social expression to their weirdness.

There are situations in which we value being different and weird. I think about the All Stars Talent Show Network [a youth development, supplemental education program that utilizes the social therapeutic approach]. The young people have done such an extraordinary job with it. Part of the challenge of the All Stars was helping the young people to do weird things, to create shows, to not simply stay locked into the stereotypical relationships that are characteristic of their communities. We took something the young people love, performance, and we turned it into kind of a springboard for weird behavior. Performing is something they already feel close to in life; watching it, doing it themselves, being on stage, they get great gratification from it. We said, "Let's use this as a motivating basis and have you do something which is actually quite weird—have you create your own entire show, the whole thing." Now, that's beyond their sense of normalcy. Their notion of a normal life activity might include going to a talent show or doing something in class where someone else has set it up and structured it, but it never would include being the people who actually created that production. That's the weird act that they engage in. It actually gets a rather positive response from their peers. It's a cool thing to do; other kids relate to it as a cool thing to do, and so it tends to substitute for other, more destructive, cool behavior.

Weird can't mean something that is so far out that people are looked at as if they are completely ridiculous. On the other hand, I think there is a way in which human beings are responsive to and like to see people doing weird things. People are amused if the weirdness is combined with a coolness, an acceptability, an accomplishment, a gratification. The All Stars is a weird challenge to a whole lot of the social structures that are characteristic of some of our inner city communities—gangs, for example. It's not a matter of putting gangs down. Gangs are cool. It's totally understandable why kids wind up in gangs. Forget whether you think it's good or bad. It's totally understandable. The All Stars creates something that has some similarity in structural form, but is not a gang at all. But it's weird, and the weirdness of it is what sells it.

I don't know exactly what form this might take with these men, but the approach would have to be, from this vantage point, performatory and positive. Maybe they have to do something totally different in the environment that you are in together. Maybe they have to create some theater in that group. Maybe they have to do something that doesn't look like psychology at all. Again, I'm not talking about just performing roles—which is one thing they can certainly do—but maybe they have to create new plays that they can participate in. Maybe they have to have the experience of what it feels like to not give their usual response to a situation that cries out for it.

In the play that we're currently doing at the Castillo Theatre, there's one point where the character Mayor D—obviously a takeoff on former Mayor Dinkins—is talking about Blacks and Jews, Blacks and Jews, Blacks and Jews, and he says something like, "How much of that is hate is hard to say. Maybe it's hate. Maybe it's habit." That's a profound statement, because I think a lot of what we do with each other is habit, in the deepest sense of habit. We just don't know another thing to say, or another way to be. There are deeper emotional things, there's fear, there's all kinds of complex social things, but often what young people—and not so young people—do is what we have done before. And the accounting for how come we're doing it is in part that it's what we've always done and it's the only thing that we know how to do. Sometimes it's enormously useful to help people to say and to do some things that they couldn't ever imagine coming out of their mouths.

Part of what is exciting about performance is you create a situation in which you say, "All right, let's try another line. I want you to see and realize that you could say this and you will get another human response off of it. You won't get that same response. It might feel uncomfortable; it might not feel natural. But we have to do some things that are unnatural. If we're not going to do unnatural things, then what are we doing in the program in the first place? If we're going to change anything, we're going to have to be different."

Performance is where I would go to with these men. Again, I have no idea what that might look like. I'm sure that you and people you're working with can do something creative, you can figure it out. But supporting them to do a different performance is the place you want to go to, rather than accepting the cognitive bias that says you have to know. I don't think you *can* know what to do. The stuff we're talking about here runs much deeper than cognition.

Why don't they make plays? That might be the future of psychology. That's my hope at least—people all over this country and all over the world making plays. That's my own personal dream of what psychology turns into.

from a colloquium

Dialogue 51. The Fragile Client

Therapist 1: I wanted to get some help about a young woman I've begun to see. She's quite depressed and spends most of the day in bed. She attributes her depression to the near death in an accident of a good friend and her guilt over not doing enough, though she also acknowledges having been depressed since childhood. She's not very verbal and in sessions she speaks with a whine, in pretty short, repetitive sentences; it seems to be an effort to just get sentences out. She has been a heavy drinker and attends AA and Al-Anon meetings occasionally, although she says she hasn't been to one for over a year. She is on medication, which is prescribed by a psychiatrist whom she sees occasionally. Her father takes her to the sessions—she says she has fears about going outside. She calls them panic attacks, feels overwhelmed and starts to cry, though when she describes this it sounds more like desperation. I don't think she's ready for group at this point. She is wanting to find some kind of activity to participate in; she used to volunteer with an after school program.

I find myself in the sessions not knowing what to say to her, or how to be with her. When she speaks I don't have a sense that she's trying to have a conversation with me; she seems to be saying the kinds of things she has learned to say from prior therapies. She strains to speak. I don't know how to relate to that kind of emotionality. Whether it's a way she's learned to get attention, self-protective in a way, or whether she's always had real difficulties in having any kind of interpersonal relationship—how crazy is she? Every once in a while I get a glimpse that what she's saying makes no sense, for example, that she remembers being abused by her father when she was an infant.

Therapist 2: Did you ask her about that?

Therapist 1: I did. I said something like, "Did somebody tell you about that?" She said no, she had a clear memory of it.

Therapist 3: How are you with her?

Therapist 1: I'm very cautious; she presents herself as so fragile.

Fred: Have you asked her how fragile she is?

Therapist 1: Not in that direct a way. I implied it. In one of our first sessions I said something about the work of our therapy. After a long pause she cried and said that nobody sees how hard she's working, that people don't realize how hard it is to go out and so on. I felt like she was saying, "Don't make any demands." But no, I didn't say it directly.

Fred: I think you should raise that question. You need to engage that directly, so you can find out how to relate to her. And part of that involves finding out how fragile she is. There are things you can do to be helpful to her, but if she's that fragile you probably won't do them. But you have to discover that, and the only way of discovering it is by talking to her.

I'm also a little struck by a kind of a contradiction in what you've been saying. On the one hand you relate to the question of her coming to group—in the tone of your voice and your words—as being out of the question. But you describe her as volunteering in the past, looking to do so again, going to Al-Anon, and that seems to me something of a contradiction. I wonder what you think about that.

Therapist 1: I guess I thought I wanted to have a stronger relationship with her therapeutically before inviting her into group.

Fred: But your description of the individual therapy doesn't sound to me like you strongly pursuing and deepening your relationship to her.

Therapist 1: I think that's what I don't know how to do with her, and your suggestion of asking how fragile she is sounds like a step in the right direction.

Therapist 4: It sounds like you've made a lot of assumptions already—about how fragile she is, what she can handle, et cetera. Actually, *you* sound like the fragile one here.

Fred: To put that a slightly different way—it's perfectly sensible to say that what needs to happen is for you to deepen your relationship as a precondition for her going into group. On the other hand, it also sounds like you're saying that you're not particularly deepening your relationship with her, perhaps for some sound reasons. But I think what you should do with that is say, "Well, maybe the group can do something with her that I can't do with her." The group might do a better job than you at discovering her fragility, or lack thereof. Because it sounds to me like you don't quite trust her, perhaps understandably. That's what I get. I think that also might be helped by the group. The group might be able to do a better job of exposing her emotionally than you seem able to do right now. We don't know if she wants to go into group, but it's worth a look at.

Groups are multipurpose. They can be used in different ways. When things are hard to do it might not be because we're bad therapists, but just that they're hard to do— given who she is, given who you are, given how the world is. It might be hard for you to convey a message something like, "I think you're fucking around a little bit." Maybe the group could do that more effectively. I've seen that happen with clients of mine all the time. I've had some people who I couldn't wait to bring into group because they had stymied me. And the group took them on in the first 20 minutes of the first group. I was indebted and amazed; I couldn't do it.

So maybe you can locate the discussion of her fragility in the context of a discussion about bringing her into group, finding out from her whether that would be something she might want to do.

I share your intuition that she needs to be pushed. And if you're tentative with her you're not going to help her. I think she needs to be pushed therapeutically, and what comes up when you talk about being "pushed therapeutically" is group.

from a supervisory session

Dialogue 52. *The Silent Client*

Therapist-in-training: How does a social therapist work with a silent client?

Fred: I have the privilege of doing only group therapy. I don't have to relate to individuals who are quiet, because I don't relate to individuals. I relate to the group. And the group is hardly ever quiet.

Every once in a while someone in group will ask, "How come these other people don't participate?" That usually lasts about 30 seconds in social therapy, and then everybody moves on because what we're working with is a collective creative activity in which people participate in all kinds of ways.

That doesn't mean that I don't periodically try to support someone who I think is having a difficult time. I can play a certain role in helping people to articulate something they have to articulate—not because it would be good for them in a narrow, individualistic sense to say something, but because it would be important in the creation of the group. Sometimes it's the body language or the look on their face, or because I'd like to hear a new voice, because a new voice would be another element for the group to make use of no matter what is said. Most people who are in group with me know that when those moments come up and I say to someone who hasn't said anything in a long time, "What do you think?," it's not as if they will suddenly spew out something brilliant. But it's useful and helpful to the process of the group. The help comes from the shared activity of what the group creates and everyone gets substantial, though varied, help from participating.

from a colloquium

Dialogue 53. The Dramatic Client

Summary of therapists' presentation. The supervision began with a therapist describing a session with a young woman who wanted to come back into therapy after a number of years. The therapy had been difficult: The client had gotten sick and was hospitalized; when she got out of the hospital she ran away from home and said her father had raped her. The parents felt that the therapist had taken the girl's side and took her out of therapy. The therapist found this extremely upsetting. There had been no contact between the client and therapist in the ensuing years. Now the woman has returned— still "out of her mind" but doing "better." She recently married a man she knew for only a short period of time, converting to his religion and way of life. She is taking medication, which she says helps her, and is in and out of the hospital. She said she wanted to get help with her relationships, that she's "really bad in them," gets in very bad moods, gets paranoid. She sees a psychiatrist who she thinks isn't helping her. The therapist described some of what she and the woman talked about in the session and her feelings about the conversation.

Therapist 1: The session seemed fine to me and yet I felt very upset and had very intense dreams about her the last few nights, so I wanted to talk about whether I have stuff left over from the last time she was in therapy with me.

Therapist 2: What are you upset about?

Therapist 1: I don't know. We have a very intense relationship and I felt upset about seeing her and I don't want to get caught up in the relationship the way I did before, which I think was problematic.

Therapist 2: What do you mean?

Therapist 1: I think I was into saving her. It's a different situation now. Her parents acted very, very crazy. They aren't in the picture now; she sees them very occasionally. I started thinking, can I handle seeing her, am I too upset, can I be of help to her? I feel vulnerable to getting invested in wanting her to get better.

Therapist 3: What would that look like?

Therapist 1: She's been in and out of the hospital so she'll probably go in again. That's very upsetting to me although this is the pattern, this is her life. I have to be prepared for that.

Therapist 4: On the one hand, she was saying that she wanted help with relationships. But it seemed like when you asked her questions, her answers seemed to have a quality of jerking you around, something like that, but what she wanted help with wasn't addressed at all.

Therapist 1: It's helpful what you are saying. In the first part of the session I think I was sitting there looking at her dressed in religious garb and thinking, what has happened to this gal, what has gone on? She seemed so much better; she was clear in the beginning, together. I did experience getting put off at the end of the session, feeling vulnerable to being seduced by her in some way, though I'm not sure what that means. She's very smart and very charming, so I don't know if this is what I get into with people who are very, very crazy, if there's some kind of attraction there.

Therapist 2: How is she crazy?

Therapist 1: She is self-destructive and unstable, she can't function in relationships, she's not in reality half the time, though for the first 45 minutes she was perfectly clear, insightful, said smart things about her parents. But her story is somewhat manipulative. I felt nervous about getting closer to her.

Fred: What's the big deal?

Therapist 1: I think I feel nervous about the impact she has on me, and I don't usually feel nervous about that with people.

Fred: It seems like you have some need to dramatize this situation.

Therapist 1: I feel like I don't know what it is other than from the history, it's a hard thing to go through.

Fred: Okay, so it's a hard thing to go through.

Therapist 3: It could be hard without dramatizing it.

Therapist 1: Do I feel like I've failed her—am I making that a big thing? I don't know. It's almost like there's a way that I feel spooked by her.

Fred: Why the drama? I don't understand it.

Therapist 5: I'm wondering about a "rescue dynamic." She's coming back saying you might be the only one who can help. Is she presenting herself as wanting to be rescued?

Fred: I'm not raising why she might be dramatic, I don't know her. What I'm reacting to is you [Therapist 1] being dramatic. Surely she isn't the first person you've seen who wants to be rescued.

Therapist 1: She is one of the more dramatic.

Fred: Just because *she's* dramatic, it doesn't follow that *you* have to be. How come you're getting dramatic? Do you think if you aren't dramatic, she won't be responsive to you? Are you excited about her coming back?

Therapist 1: Yes, I'm excited. I have a particular affection for her. I think about her.

Fred: Do you feel validated by her coming back?

Therapist 1: Do I feel validated?

Fred: "I guess this shows I was right . . ."

Therapist 1: Maybe momentarily, but I don't think I'm into that. I do question whether I can be of help to her . . . I feel validated by that . . .

Fred: I don't understand that.

Therapist 1: Oh, she's coming to me so I can help her.

Fred: I don't understand the relationship between those two. You are making it seem like there's a connection.

Therapist 1: I understand that what would be validating is that I'm the special person who can help this woman.

Fred: How are you saying that that's related to whether you can help her?

Therapist 1: I don't know how to pull it apart, it seems so logical. I wouldn't be so special if I can't help her.

Fred: So far, that hasn't happened yet. What's happened is that she's come back to you. The issue of whether you do or don't help her remains to be seen.

Therapist 1: I think the answer is, yes, I am validated by her.

Fred: I don't remember all the details of what happened years ago, but my memory is that you had a big investment in being right about how to play it with her. You had some definite opinions about what should be done and how it should happen. But other forces, namely, the family, were opposed to that. So this was kind of a set-up for feeling, "I guess I was right."

Therapist 1: That I'm right about her.

Fred: That you are right in what went down in her family. She didn't go back to the family; she came back to you.

Therapist 1: Yes, and things she said in the session were validating of that. She specifically said I was right about the family.

Fred: She was validating that.

Therapist 1: Are you saying that there is a relationship between this and my making it dramatic?

Fred: I think that is the drama. I think all that's bullshit and I think you have to get rid of it as quickly as possible and start working.

Therapist 1: I don't know what really went down with the family.

Fred: Why are you saying that? What does that have to do with what we're talking about?

Therapist 1: Because I thought what you were saying is that my thinking that I was right about the family is bullshit, is irrelevant.

Fred: What's irrelevant is the whole package, the feelings we just were talking about. If you can't get rid of them, you can't work with her.

Therapist 1: Getting rid of it is . . .

Fred: . . . forgetting about it. We don't know if you were right about the family then, we don't know if you're right now. It's dramatic bullshit.

Therapist 1: I'm getting glimmers here of being caught in that whole thing, I'm seeing it as you're saying this to me. I think I can let go of that.

Fred: What was her presenting problem, what does she want help with?

Therapist 1: Relationships.

Fred: That's not a presenting problem.

Therapist 1: She said she's getting better and she wants to keep getting better. She said she has difficulty getting a sense of herself, that she can take on the thoughts and values of other people, that she doesn't have any grounding. I didn't know whether it's her or her psychiatrist talking.

Fred: Is she in emotional pain?

Therapist 1: She doesn't seem to be. She has mood swings, and at the moment she is feeling euphoric.

Fred: Mood swings from what to what?

Therapist 1: To getting depressed and angry.

Fred: Does she get depressed and angry?

Therapist 1: Yes, she does. She hasn't for a while but it does happen.

Fred: And is taking the drugs helping her out?

Therapist 1: They somewhat even her out and she feels less paranoid. She also doesn't want to ruin her relationship with her husband and he wants her to stay on medication. She thinks he's right. She goes through these periods where she thinks no one knows what they are talking about, though she knows what she is talking about. For the last 6 months, she hasn't gone there. She thinks coming back to therapy will help her continue her steadiness.

I have a question. She is coming in and saying, "I can't get along with anyone, I can't maintain any friendships." Why are you saying that's not a presenting problem?

Fred: What if you can't get along with anyone and it doesn't bother you in the least? Maybe you don't know anyone you want to get along with. If you come in and say, "There's this person who I really care about and I can't get along with them," then that's a totally different story.

I really think you've got to take some deep breaths and relate to her as a run-of-the-mill patient and if you can't, you shouldn't see her. It sounds like she needs some run-of-the-mill good therapy.

from a supervisory session

Dialogue 54. Helping People in Crisis

Therapist-in-training: How do you help people in crisis?

Fred: What produces crisis is very complex, but very frequently what is central to it is a fear—almost a paralyzing fear—of chaos. Part of where crisis comes from is that people are constrained in their capacity to see potential ways of going in certain life situations. They become paralyzed with abject terror, and that creates a crisis—what some people in the field call crisis paralysis. People become so constrained because they don't see themselves as able to expand or grow or change, because that would involve a degree of chaos that they feel completely distant from.

When I work with people who feel destroyed by a situation, I often say to them, "Have you thought about doing such and such?" where the thing I am raising means a deconstructing and reconstructing of the situation that produced the crisis. When I say that, people look at me as though it's out of the question, as if to say, "I'd just as soon stay in the crisis as consider deconstructing the situation that produced it." Part of the way I try to help people in a crisis situation is to help them consider constructing something in a new way so as to engage the structural source of the crisis, while I support them through the chaos that they have to go through to do that. To me, that's a lot of how crisis resolution, in the best sense, works.

Therapist-in-training: So chaos is a way out of the paralysis?

Fred: Yes, where I take people when they're in crisis is to chaos. Chaos is my cure for crisis. I've been doing it for a long time and I think it's very effective and helpful, because the rigidity with which people are facing a given situation produces the crisis. Not that those situations can't be difficult, but in a crisis we become overwhelmed and unable to engage that the situation is difficult. Chaos, I think, is the cure. That's why I think history is the cure, because history is, in a way, pure chaos. If you really get into history, you go the route of chaos. So, to me chaos is a good thing. Chaos is a tool for me. I find it very useful.

Therapist-in-training: So, then, you don't deal directly with the crisis?

Fred: People often come into therapy and say, "I want to talk about crisis." I say, "I want to help you with chaos. You can talk about crisis. You're free to talk about whatever you want here. But where I'm coming from is not resolving the crisis, except by way of creating chaos. Let's create chaos."

Therapist-in-training 2: What does chaos mean to you? How do you deal with the kind of chaos that is closer to destruction than to creativity?

Fred: I don't see chaos as nearer to or further from destruction. I'm aware that that is a fairly traditional metaphor and that some call it a fact, but one person's fact can be another person's metaphor. To overstate it slightly, if something is, or is understood to be, truly chaotic I don't think you can simultaneously regard it as destructive because if it's chaotic you don't know where it's going. There is that kind of inconsistency in identifying chaos as destructive. Chaos is defined by its fundamental unpredictability; destruction or destructive is hardly defined by unpredictability.

This is not to say that people can't be destructive; they surely can. But I am not at all convinced that chaos leads to destruction. Other things can produce destructive behavior. You can see this in the All Stars program. It is a very successful antiviolence program in which chaos is very important in the creation of the program. If things get violent, that is, destructive, then the thing to do is stop the violence and stop people from getting hurt, but I don't think we have to impinge on the chaos to do that. Many people say to us, "If you allow this chaos to go on, it is going to get destructive." Our experience has been the other way around. More often then not, when things become violent or destructive, it has more to do with things impinging on the chaos of how the whole program is organized. I don't want to articulate that as an idealized theory; it is just our firsthand experience.

The same is true in social therapy. Frequently in my groups, when things are getting really provocative and open, I can usually tell something is happening because I look around the room and see many group members looking petrified that things are getting out of control. Out of control is what I am interested in. The chaos I am talking about is the chaos that results—to put it in vaguely functional terms—from reducing the inhibitory mechanisms that are characteristic of most people in most group situations. If you simply remove some of those inhibitions you start to see creativity, not just on a personal level but on a social level; people start to relate to each other in ways that are more creative. I don't mean creative as in writing a poem or play. I mean people are less constrained by their commitment to being who they are, which to me is the fundamental defense mechanism. Nothing leads to people being more defensive than having to perform as who one takes one to be. If people can break out of that, then they are able to perform other things they can't otherwise perform.

I'm not suggesting that the array of emotions changes—although I do believe there is the capacity to create new emotions—but that how one performs these emotions transforms radically. Sometimes it looks like people are doing something they've never done before. I think they are doing something without all of the inhibitors operative which characteristically have them do it in a certain kind of way. It's not that people are never passionate when inhibited; it's that the passion that they give expression to is different—inhibited, qualified. It's a different passion.

Do you know what I'm saying? If you've got your foot on the brake, acceleration is different than if it's off the brake. The car moves differently in each circumstance. Mechanical principles are also operative in human activity. If you are always repressing what is going on, then even when you do give expression to things, it is a totally different expression. Environments where those inhibitors are not so operative are experienced as chaotic because we all are very acclimated to these inhibitors. We come to rely on them and when they are not there it can become very frightening. In my groups, there is a kind of chaos that is collectively agreed to and created that makes room for people to feel free to do certain kinds of things emotionally that they would not ordinarily do. I don't mean something like, "Okay, this is the opportunity to be angry or to be whatever." That is not what it is about. It is not an individualistic activity.

It seems to me you cannot create chaos individualistically. Chaos is something that is created collectively. When people democratically agree to it, you can hit wonderful moments where the group is creating a new social performance. That has significance not only because people reach that place and make wonderful connections, but also because we come to discover that we are capable of doing that kind of thing. That is a central learning from social therapy—that you can create chaotic moments and create new things out of those chaotic moments. If people take that out of the work, then I feel like I have done pretty much as much as I can do.

from a colloquium

CHAPTER FIVE

Social Therapy
Integrated

A. SOCIAL THERAPY AND SPIRITUALITY

Dialogue 55. Humanizing Our Culture

Therapist-in-training: I am struck by the similarities I see between development in the social therapeutic community and what we in the faith community call formation. The old psychological methods of testing, categorizing, diagnosing, and treating people are reminiscent of the pre-1960s methods of teaching and doing religion. Also the question and answer rote method of learning, the idea of only good and bad behavior, the alienation of the members of the faith community from the knowers or leaders.

The social therapeutic approach—performance, being other than who one is as human activity (revolutionary activity)—seems akin to the new way of formation in the church—formation/development as human/spiritual activity, the performance that members of the community and leaders create together. I find that the development/performatory approach tremendously enriches the human and spiritual aspects of life. Would you comment?

Fred: I agree. I like to think that social therapy is but one element of a significant worldwide cultural transformation. It's kind of ironic. A humanizing process was supposed to be taking place coming out of the 19th century into the 20th. Well, clearly that was premature—bear witness to the 20th century. You can hardly look back on it and see it as a great humanizing century. If anything, you could make out a strong argument that it took the species down to the absolute bottom. And yet, there have been the beginnings of a sociocultural transformation in the last century. I think that the 60s were a big part of that. My experience of the 60s was cultural and spiritual more than it was political. At its best, and God knows it had its worst also, I think there was some kind of statement getting made in an

effort to speak to our spirituality and our humanity. But that's not the only
place it happened. It happened in lots of different areas. It happened in the
religious community. It happened in the cultural community. I think we're
barely beginning to see the impact of some of those transformations.

I think the dualistic, universalistic conception of science is beginning
to go through a cultural transformation of its own. Not to eliminate modern
science; that would be bizarre. Science has accomplished too much to eliminate. Its gains are profound and it will no doubt continue and I certainly
hope it continues. But human growth, which was a dominant social ideal in
the 19th century, was abandoned 20 or 30 years into the 20th century. The
intellectual writings of the last part of the 19th and early part of the 20th
century were filled with conceptions of the advancement of the human
being. But that was abandoned. Again, in some sense, with good reason.

One way of understanding science culturally is that it was an attack
on some of the worst features of the world. I for one feel grateful to science
for that and many other things. On the other hand there evolved over the
last 500 years of modern science a narrowness of its own that has left science wanting relative to certain human needs and certain forms of human
growth. But there is the beginning of a new form of critique—which I
think is cultural and spiritual—of what has been the dominant model of
understanding. There are many, many efforts under way to try to challenge
that. Social therapy is but one tiny little front in what I think is going to be
a long-term effort, but I remain vaguely optimistic that humanism might
have its best days in front of it. Of course, that might be utterly naïve on my
part.

I think that a lot of what's happening with modern technology is perfectly wonderful. I saw this show on PBS a few weeks ago on the so-called
"new news"—the news that's coming through the Internet. It's a whole
new phenomenon in which news is no longer determined simply by the
New York Times and the *Washington Post*. Some people are very up in arms
about this. But I think it's wonderful that there are new stories, some of
them bizarre, some of them ridiculous. That's fine. To me that's the price
that you pay for opening up democracy. I've long been devoted to the position that everybody has a right to be a fool. It's a fundamental human right
in this country. Everyone should have the right to be a fool as long as they
don't do any overt harm to other human beings. Technology is consistent
with this kind of broader sociocultural revolution that is gradually coming
into place. I for one feel happy to have lived long enough to fool myself
into thinking I'm seeing changes. Who knows? All of this will be determined long after I'm gone.

To return directly to your question, I'm hardly an expert on the faith
community. I think of myself as a spiritual person but I have very little to

do directly with the faith community. I have respect for it and love and caring for people involved in it. And there are some overlaps. It's just not been what I've been doing directly. I've not been part of the formal spiritual community. I'm part of the fringe. I'm just a fringy person altogether.

from a colloquium

Dialogue 56. *The Activity of Giving*

Therapist-in-training: I have been pursuing a spiritual path for many years and am currently a student of Siddha Yoga Meditation. As I learn about social therapy, I notice a similarity with some spiritual beliefs, specifically the theory of nondualism. Additionally, quantum physicists have discovered that the notion of separateness is an illusion. Can you please comment on this?

Fred: I agree with you. In the last few years, we've been discussing spirituality more and more self-consciously than we had before. I think there is a powerful and important connection between spirituality and human growth. For the bulk of this century, a lot of what orthodox psychology has done is try to understand change, development, growth, and so on in purely behavioral terms, in purely quantitative terms. I think it failed in large measure because human growth is in some fundamental sense spiritual. I don't mean by this to suggest any particular religious view. Rather, I mean that human beings grow in part by virtue of engaging in certain kinds of social life activities. Our nourishment as human beings is connected to our spiritual interconnectedness to other human beings and to the rest of the world. And if you stifle that, if you have what I would call an excess of individualism—which dominates our broader culture and dominates psychology even more so—then we have been deprived of this area of human life.

I don't mean to be anti-religious, but I think religion hasn't done terribly well either with advancing the notion of spirituality. So, religions don't do it; the schools don't do it; psychology doesn't do it. I'm a strong supporter of the separation of church and state, but what we're talking about here is not so much the separation of church and state, as it is the elimination of a whole component of human life which has to be dealt with somewhere or another.

For example, this might sound in some ways trivial and perhaps even unsophisticated scientifically speaking, but I think human beings have a psychological need to be giving. I don't think it's a moral issue. I think it's an emotive issue. To be deprived of the experience of giving is stultifying of human growth. And yet we live in a broader environment where in many ways what's reinforced constantly is to not be a giver but to be primarily a getter.

I think that no small part of what goes on in the therapy that I do is that people are learning something about how to give to each other and to give to the overall environment, and they come to see and experience what it means to grow in that kind of environment. That's a spiritual issue. I think psychology has performed a great disservice by shying away from it. Yes, I realize that there are dangers in certain attitudes toward spirituality, but there are dangers in certain attitudes about everything—I don't think we should shy away from the development of nuclear energy because there are dangers in it. I think we should find ways of doing things that are developmental and growthful.

Spirituality is one of those things. There has been a distinct misdirection in psychology in particular and science in general, away from spirituality. I think that is a cultural problem that ultimately needs to be corrected. Quite early in the 20th century there was a distinct turn in psychology in favor of the natural scientific model and away from things spiritual. And you could probably even make out a case that to some extent it was useful in certain kinds of ways. Some positive things came out of it, but much has been lost in my opinion. I think the spiritual is very much there in social therapy—with a small *s*.

from a colloquium

B. SOCIAL THERAPY AND BODY WORK

Dialogue 57. The Language of Massage

Therapist-in-training: How can I bring social therapy into the practice of therapeutic massage? What sorts of thoughts do you have about the language of touch? What kind of potential for a revolution of social relationships might an informed, developed, developing, developmental touch have?

Fred: Basically, I don't know. I'm sure you know much more about it than I do. I certainly wouldn't want to over-intellectualize that kind of work, because the beauty of it is that it is not intellectualized.

Maybe there is a way of doing more of the following: Maybe we could deepen the touch and the development that comes through touch if you and the person you are working with could find a way to creatively come to better understand the very process of that touching.

I've gotten a lot of massages. I've done a lot of that work with a lot of people and I think it's wonderful. One of the things I find lacking and try to bring to the work is to see if I and the person I'm working with could learn more about why and how this works, not from a distance, not just cognitively, but emotionally, humanly, in the very language of touch. I think that the language is, as you point out, a big part of the problem, as it tends to be distancing.

When I was writing this play, *The Store,* about a woman stripper, I worked with a group of people for 2 years in creating some of the background work for it. A lot of what we did—it was three good women friends and myself—was work hard on the language. We spent months talking dirty language to each other. We learned how we responded to hearing certain words, what emotions we had and so forth. That was a critical part of the process that I went through over the 2-year period in writing the play. I think the play was enormously helped by it.

That's something that has to be learned in the therapeutic process. People have to come to know each other better. And they have to learn it from each other, including learning language that both parties feel comfortable with. Sometimes we have to create language; we have to create meaning to learn how to talk to each other. And that can be a component of the process in learning more how something works and giving expression to how something works.

It might be helpful to deepen our understanding of our process within the very language of the activity of massage. I'm not talking about giving this muscle a pat. I'm talking about learning something about how touch works. We tend to be remarkably illiterate about touch in this culture. I worked back in the 60s and 70s with a very wonderful man who was one of my touch gurus for a period of 10 years. Alan was a lovely, lovely man, a wild, weird, crazy guy. Alan stood 5' 2." He was a former dancer who was then in his 60s and exceedingly powerful and incredibly eccentric. He was nothing less than a genius. When I first started seeing him, I could never allow people to touch my chest. I sort of had an analytical understanding of why it was, but I still could not do it.

The first time I went to see Alan, he spotted the thing with my chest instantaneously. There were four of us in the class at the time. The pattern was that we would do some motion work, then we'd fall down and he would do some individual massage work with each one of us. So I go through this and that motion, then I fall down. I just have on shorts, no shirt. And Alan comes at me like a madman. He goes right to my chest and starts tearing at it. It was extraordinary. I remember it as vividly as if it happened a minute ago. Then we worked for years on this. He subsequently cured me. Not by virtue of using distancing language but by virtue of what he was doing, and we worked through this together, what this was and how this worked. It was unbelievable. It made as big a difference as almost anything I have

experienced in my life. This might have no relevance to what you are doing, but it's what comes to mind.

There is this "letting go thing" that happens. My experience is that if
you don't do that, it is a waste of time. Again, it's like what I have said
about changing. If you are not into changing, don't bother asking to learn
something about change. It will not make a difference.

You have to be changing to change. That's the dialectical axiom of
development. You have to commit.

from a colloquium

Dialogue 58. *Minds, Bodies, and Subjectivity*

Therapist-in-training: The feet, the hands, the ears, the irises of the eye, the tongue,
the teeth—all these and more can provide pictures of the condition of the
human body that can help in assessment and treatment. In addition, blood,
urine, and stool are some of Western medicine's access points to reading
the state of the body.

Physicists say that the entire universe functions as a holographic image. Any part provides a picture of the whole. Given this, we can look at
human systems and see the condition of the earth itself. A few of the obvious correlations between the human body and the earth body are: the forests become the lungs; the rivers, streams, and inland running waters become
the circulatory system; the marshes, swamps, and wetlands become the
lymphatic system; the rocks become the bones and skeletal system; the soil
becomes the connective tissue.

All of this seems tied into the notions promoted here in this community—that the mind is not located within any individual, but is a shared
experience—and clearly the same reasoning holds true for the physical
world. For example, breathing is an experience the forests and the lungs
share and the conditions of the rivers are the conditions of our very own
blood.

Somewhere in here is a question. This is an idea I want to be developing, particularly as it relates to massage/bodywork/health/touch. I have been
approached to present a manuscript on "the how to" of giving massage,
directed at a general audience, and I would like to incorporate/integrate a
social therapeutic take on what or how I present this. What ideas do you
have about the holographic nature of social therapy and the nonseparateness
of the body and the mind and the planet and human relationships?

Fred: The very formulation "mind and body" is distorted, as is talking about
getting them back together again—my objection being that they are not
apart in the first place.

There is a tendency to think of nature as something other than human made. I don't agree that there is such a thing as an objectified nature. We cannot separate our comprehension of or our social connectedness to what is called nature from nature. I think that the tendency to reify nature, for nature to have a nonsubjective and a nonhistorical existence, is a serious problem. We see it manifested in many people's writings, including many Marxists. For example, Engels reifies nature in most of his writings, an unfortunate philosophical error. Marx, for the most part, didn't do that.

I don't think that there is any way out of the subjectivistic experience. Obviously, there is a very strong pull, not just in Western culture but also in other cultures, to create, by abstraction, a god figure, a nature figure, some kind of objectified figure. It's a strong human need to have that figure in order to make certain sets of appeals to it in certain kinds of situations. I just don't happen to think that is a healthy pull.

What we have is an ongoing and continuous historical process. This historical process has included, in certain periods, complex interpretations that have given objective qualities to certain beliefs. And I think it is dangerous when we come to believe the conclusions of that phenomenon. I think traffic lights are fine. They help us get across the street. It's good that we have them. But the moment we relate to a traffic light as something other than a merely utilitarian instrument *created by us* to help us negotiate a complex metropolis we get into trouble. I think we get into serious moral, social, and cultural trouble.

My difficulty with nature is similar. I am sympathetic to the unifying position you characterize but, for me, what is fundamental in terms of understanding the interconnectedness is the historical subjective. What we have are our historical, subjective life activities. Any effort to take out of that something that goes beyond that is, for me, problematic. Because I don't think there is anything "beyond that."

Regarding unification: unification doesn't require objectification of any kind. We can have unification in the historically subjective. We unify in our shared activities, in our subjectively historical activities. We unify in our life activity. We don't need, if you will, a third element to give unification to the other elements. We are unified by virtue of the fact that there is nothing else.

Now, people say, "How do you know?" I don't know. People say, "Might there be other things?" Of course there might be. I can only share what, to me, is the basis of a social unification that could be the root of further human development and growth.

To put it succinctly, I don't believe in mind and body at all, so I have no need to unify them.

Therapist-in-training: How can you say that there is no objective nature? Don't we see mountains because they're there?

Fred: Yes. I think we see mountains because they are there, but I don't think we know what "there" means. The pretentiousness of our species is to insist that we know what "there" means. I think there are mountains, I just don't know what that means. And I don't think I can know what it means. Mountains don't insist upon knowing that they are being seen. I don't know why we insist that we are seeing them. Mountains seem to get along quite well without knowing anything about us.

      I think we are very close to mountains, but we have this exceedingly clever, exceedingly brilliant, exceedingly interesting, and exceedingly pathological characteristic of being able to come up with complex interpretive descriptions. And even that seems perfectly fine to me. But then we tend to equate those descriptions with *what is*. That's the step I find very troublesome.

Therapist 1: "The mountain is there" seems kind of an innocuous statement.

Fred: I don't think it is innocuous. People have had their heads cut off for saying there were things there that others didn't see. Saying what is and what isn't has played an extraordinary role in people being either fortunate or destroyed: "If you say that the earth is not the center of the universe, you are a heretic and we will chop your head off!" What could be more obvious? We could be as absolutely certain that the mountain is there as the people in the 12th century were that the earth was the center of the universe. I'm not willing to fall prey to the simplicity of "The mountain is there." I don't think it is a simple statement at all. Existential statements are very complex statements, which have deep contextualized histories about which wars have been waged.

      One of my favorite quotes is from the great Native American hero, Crazy Horse. He said to the U. S. government, "One does not sell the land upon which the people walk." Now, he turned out to be wrong. But he was, of course, profoundly right. How do you sell land? It's what we walk on. That is what you do with land. You walk on it. You are stabilized by it. What does it mean to sell it? But one of the critical core elements of the current system that we have is that land can be sold. However, in order to sell it, one has to characterize it in a certain way; otherwise you can't sell it. So simple existential statements are very complex. And they cover up networks of deep conceptions that are hurtful and destructive.

      "There" is troublesome because it invokes complex, artificial, interpretive, and locative mechanisms. Wittgenstein had this wonderful section in his writings where he points out that even the simplest extensive definition involves conceptualizations of very sophisticated types. For example, pointing—I'm pointing at you only if you are interpreting my finger as going in the right direction. Locational terms require a whole mapping of the world in terms of its geography, which, in turn, is connected to all kinds of sociocultural interpretations and meanings. There are no simple things.

You can't isolate the simple statement from the entirety of cultural discourse—or the discourse of culture.

If you say to me, "Where is 57th Street?" I will tell you. I just don't know what I'm talking about. But it will suffice for what has to be accomplished to get somebody from 14th Street to 57th Street. That's fine. I have no objection to that. It is making the leap to considering what I said to be the objective truth that is troublesome. Objective truth gets us in trouble, in my opinion. Instructions to getting to 57th Street? No problem.

Therapist-in-training 1: In terms of applying what you are saying to the people I do bodywork with, then staying clear from objective truth might be an interesting way to go?

Fred: Yes. It might be an important way to go in terms of bodywork. I'm hardly a student of this as you are. I do think, though, that an important element in doing physical work with people is being more attentive to the history of that work, to the subjective history of that bodywork itself, if you will. Do not get caught up in reifying the body, but rather engage the subjective history.

For example, I'm currently on dialysis and go for treatment three times a week. I have many doctors, nurses, and technicians. They are wonderfully giving and decent people. I care about them. They care about me. They help me in many ways. But they have no historical sensibility; they have a "body" sensibility. I am the body in front of them on Tuesday. They know my name. They treat my body. And they are good at it. But they only treat the body. They don't care about their patient's subjective experiences; moreover, they don't care about history, which is inseparable from the patient's subjective experiences.

I am just a body up there. Again they are not bad people; they are nice and lovely people and care for my body. They know bodies; they don't know history. They don't know that there is a connection, a complex totality of subjective interconnectedness between what happened to you yesterday and the day before and what is happening all over the world and so on. That is not in their ontological scope. They feel an obligation to limit all of that. They do not want to hear the patient's subjective experiences because it gets in their way. That is their perspective. I have come to accept it.

But I think that these complex interrelated historical subjective features are a critical component, together with the other kinds of interpretive relationships. Yes, I think it's very important in helping people with their bodies to pay more attention to the relationships, not only between you and the person you are working with, but as part of a more human connected network.

I do a lot of yoga, which I love and which also is very helpful to me. I have a wonderful yoga teacher. One thing that I love in our work together is that we continuously try to discern in our relationship how we feel about bodies, our own and others, because that is a component of how you respond to, and in, your movement. How you respond to your body movement is a function of how you respond to all kinds of things, including what the relationship is historically to that movement, not just in that room, but in your life. If you want to put this in the simplest of terms, then how you are feeling, and how you are feeling about how you are feeling, is directly related to what you can do physically. I experience that all the time.

Our interrelationships—as part of a broader network of people, of what's happening in the room, in the building, in the world, and in our lives—are serious components of the work. It would be very interesting to see something written that takes this into account.

Therapist-in-training: That is helpful, because so often when you go to a yoga class, the instructor will say, "Now shut out everything else. This is your time to meditate, to just be here."

Fred: I have a different understanding of meditation. To me, meditation is not about shutting things out, but about letting things in. The "shut out theory" in meditation is not one I care for. I don't think it works on its own terms. What is extraordinary in meditation is the capacity to not censor and to not inhibit your mind but to be more at one with the world. I don't think you are at one with the world when you are shutting out the world.

When meditating, I think you should try not to think about *anything,* but rather to think about *everything.* Think about the totality. What is important in meditation is to find a way, if you can, to move beyond obsession. A lot of what we call thinking is obsessing. Obsession does not allow for keeping one's mind open to being a part of one's world. You have to get beyond obsession, because obsession is nothing but reifying the mind. When you obsess, you are taking the mind as fundamental and most important. People who are obsessive are sadly locked into their own minds.

Meditation is connecting to our world and allowing the mind to be free, to be a part of the free and dynamical process of being in the world. What I feel is most valuable to me when I'm meditating is that I am not controlling, by an obsessional process, what is going on in my mind. I feel a closeness to life.

How do you go beyond obsession? Socially. One has to come to terms with the fact that thinking, even if you do it by yourself, is social. Awareness is a subjective, social experience. Obsessing is a further effort in our culture to uniquely identify yourself; the underlying unit of obsessional processes is "This is mine, and mine alone." When I meditate it is an effort to get beyond that, with my mind being simply another element of the social world, a subjective, historical world in which things go on and are shared.

Just as when everyone is watching the same movie we each have a different experience but we would not then say we are all seeing different movies. I think that is true of life as well. But obsession is possessive. Meditation, as I understand it, is an effort to get beyond possessiveness, even the possessiveness of one's mind.

Therapist-in-training 2: Is what you're talking about "clearing the mind" versus "blocking the mind?"

Fred: Clearing the mind is an ambiguous term. We can clear the mind by trying to keep everything out, or clear the mind by letting things in.

Therapist 2: It seems that you could replace the word obsession with objectivity.

Fred: I think so. I think obsessing is the internal form of objectivity. It is how we objectify internally. Usually objectivity is taken to mean what we do externally. But there is an internal form to objectivity and I think you are right in identifying it with obsession. We have this strong pull—with some positive results, but also some very pathological results—to reify the particular. We create individuated particulars and then we go through the complicated process of trying to put them back together again, to see how things, which have never been disconnected, reconnect after we have taken them apart by individuation.

In some ways, that is my shortest formulation of the tragedy of humankind. We brilliantly separate everything and then try to be even more brilliant by discovering theories that reconnect everything. It is, no doubt, the source of our species hegemony, and also the source of our species pathology. It has put the species, in some respects, in a remarkably advantageous position—I don't want to use these terms morally, because I think that they are all relative to being human—but in some sense, in a position of power relative to other species. Unfortunately, what we have done with that power frequently is to destroy the environment, not to mention other species and other people. But it has had that positive impact, if you want to see that as positive. It is also profoundly pathological. Is there a way out of this fly bottle? It beats the hell out of me.

Therapist 1: Historically though, medical care wasn't always broken down to the particulars. Twenty-five hundred years ago, and even today still in some parts of the Eastern world, that model wasn't used. How did that come about?

Fred: Well, the particularistic model has done better. Science has done better in terms of some serious human needs. If you read *The Origins of Modern Science,* a wonderful book by the way, you see how this came to be. I'm

not questioning the success. I'm questioning *the price* of the success. I
don't think we have to throw away the success. I am not suggesting in
some idealistic fashion that we stop identifying the mountain as being there.
I am suggesting that we stop thinking that we know what we're talking
about when we do so. I have no problem with modern science. I think it is
an extraordinary accomplishment.

Maybe I'm the most naïve of idealists, but I think that the human
species can create things and not put them on pedestals or walls or turn
them, ultimately, into commodities. I think it's humanly possible to create
what we create without having to transform all that is created into a com-
modity. I believe it is a possibility. For tomorrow? No. Will it happen in my
lifetime? Certainly not. Could it occur? If it doesn't, if we don't move to
that place, then I think human development has reached its end.

from a colloquium

C. SOCIAL THERAPY AND MEDICINE

Dialogue 59. Creating Health

Therapist-in-training: I've been doing some work on including patients' narratives in the medical conversation—asking people about who they are, where
they're from, what they believe in, their family, their community, their culture, the roles they play at work and at home. Also, how their illness is
impacting upon their lives and their relationships. The research literature
on patient-physician interactions suggests that this type of intersubjective
interaction, in which the patient feels known as a person, improves health
outcomes. There is a field of narrative medicine that has developed around
this type of intervention—that is, looking at patients' stories with the hope
of clinicians seeing the patient as more of a person and less of an objectified clinical entity. What do you think about this work?

Fred: I couldn't agree more but let me take it a step further. Why couldn't that
interaction be about people creating health together? I wonder why that's
not on your list. It seems like you're still hearing through a quasi-
communicationalist position. My position is that doctors and nurses and
technicians and patients interrelating vis a vis activity can produce better
health for everybody and certainly for the person identifiable as the patient.
The deficiency in the medical model is that subjective factors that could be
provided uniquely by the patient are essentially left out of the model.

I think we have to move toward a more creative interaction that includes the subjective responses of the person with whom we're working. I

see this every day at the dialysis center. People are trained to not pay attention to the subjective factors that the patients could bring into the work. The patients know well how to describe it and the doctors know very much what they are talking about but it doesn't fit within the medical paradigm for that to be included. Therein lies the issue; it's an inferior medical situation.

So, agreeing with what you are saying, I would push you to take it all the way to producing health. I think that's what isn't sufficiently looked at in the existing model. Otherwise, we're vulnerable to just endorsing people talking better to each other in the abstract. I don't think we want to get people to talk better in the abstract; I think we want to get people to talk to each other for the concrete purposes that we engage in social activity together for, in this case, a social activity designed to help people with their physical condition.

Therapist-in-training: How do you see change coming about? What would change?

Fred: I'll give you a concrete example. I think that people shouldn't be trained to think that your blood pressure is what shows up every half-hour on the machine. I think that subjectively most people on dialysis have a pretty clear idea of what's happening with their blood pressure. A great deal of what's done in the treatment is literally done by accepting the record on that machine. These aren't bad technicians, they're good technicians, but they'll look at the machine and say, "Your blood pressure is fine, it's 153." And I want to say, because I'm a trained philosopher, "Now wait a second, you don't mean my blood pressure is 153, you mean the number on that machine is 153." In a way, this is a simple example and it sounds easy to correct, but it's not easy to correct because of how people are trained. The overidentification of what's recorded on the apparatus with what's going in the human body is so deeply entrenched that if I say to people, usually technicians, "Would you push the button and take it again because that's not where my pressure is now?" I can tell that they regard that remark as almost incomprehensible. There is a look on their face that says, "Wait a minute, that's what the numbers say."

We're challenging a paradigm. The way this appears is in endless trivial examples of this sort. I don't know if it's a memory issue, but doctors from week to week don't seem to remember . . . one week they are telling me they have to lower my dry weight and the following week, under pretty much the same conditions, they tell me they have to raise my dry weight. They have no memory of this. I know they see a lot of people, but why wouldn't they involve the experience of the patient? Some will occasionally ask, "How much fluid can you handle?" That's a moment of wonderful relief. Patients know exactly how much they can handle.

I'm not saying all these reports aren't important. What I'm saying is that we have to come up with a medical model that incorporates both of those things in some kind of interesting way and I think there is resistance to that because of the positivistic, empiricistic, reductionistic attitude which says essentially, "I don't really want to know what the patient thinks."

The difficult thing in creating this model is that you have to mix two different ontological kinds of things—namely, subjective reports and empiricistic, objective reports. We're going to have to find a way of coming up with determinations by mixing two distinctly different kinds of things and that's antithetical to the current methodology, not only in medicine, but in almost everything. The basic law of a positivistic approach is that you want to reduce everything to the same kind of thing and then you can mix them. So this is a violation of that because, to be sure, patients' subjective reports are different from readings on medical equipment. They aren't just different; they're different kinds of things. This is a creative task that progressive medicine has to come to terms with: how do we put those kinds of things together? At a theoretical level, that's a hard task.

from a colloquium

Dialogue 60. *Inside and Outside the Institution of Medicine*

Therapist-in-training 1: My current conversations with medical patients are more philosophical and less informational than they used to be, a change that's very important to me. There's a change in the nature of medicine going on—an increase in and recognition of medical uncertainty, a revisiting of the ethical and the human elements of doctoring. I read somewhere that the medical history hasn't changed since 1880! How do we teach physicians to have philosophical, methodological conversations with their patients?

Fred: I don't agree that there's been a change coming out of the institution of medicine. I think who is bringing about those changes you talk about are patients. I think society is moving through a postmodernization and that is impacting on everything. Relatively speaking, though, I don't think it's impacting that much on medicine. You point to the 1880 date for the model of the medical interview; medicine is very traditional and standardized. You see the same thing in the institutions of learning; endless studies have been done which show that the basic models of learning in our schools are the same as 150 years ago. I think that change of the kind we're talking about here has to come from a societal transformation, and then those institutions which are deadly self-perpetuative will have to have to, perhaps, give way to these kind of changes. I'm a great believer in paradigm shifts having to come from the masses; I don't think they come from self-perpetuating institutions because it's not in their interests to engage in paradigm shifts.

It's important to be clear on where the few changes you see are coming from. Otherwise, you create the illusion that you can go further than you can within the medical institution, and that leads to a big waste of important energy. This doesn't mean that we shouldn't write papers or give talks at conferences, but we shouldn't do them with illusions. In the simplest political terms, if we want to effect long-term changes, we have to look to people who are facilitating revolutionary organizing within the broad mass. It's got to come from there. There's got to be a process that is taking these postmodern transformations and trying to translate that into a popular revolutionary activity for further developed transformation. The notion that we are going directly to postmodern changes from existing modernist institutions is a great mistake. I don't think it will happen. I don't think it ever has and it never will. The existing institutions are a counterforce to social change. I know that's a sweeping generalization but my experience of this is that it doesn't happen that way.

Therapist-in-training 2: When I go to the doctor I want the doctor to talk to *me*. That hardly ever happens. People want something different from a doctor's visit, being listened to, being offered alternatives to the traditional model. . . .

Fred: Patients don't simply want something different; they are making a different set of demands off of a sweeping cultural postmodernization, but there isn't receptivity within the medical profession or any other profession. These institutions are not designed to be open to that; they are designed to be perpetuators of the existing cultural paradigms. I'm not critical of that but don't expect profound, qualitative and revolutionary change to come through that process. It doesn't. When people ask me what they should do in their hospital or school or mental health center, I say, "Do all you can to be humane and creative within your institution, but don't operate under the illusion that it's going to lead to change within your institution. If you want to do something about that, you have to do extracurricular work and support other efforts and join with each other." I don't think per se a revolution is going to do it either . . . it's mixing practical work within institutions with revolutionary work outside the institutions. I think Ken Gergen put that very well when he said we need a fringe to effect social change and we need people not on the fringe. One is not better or worse, but we need that dialectical combination. Where are we in that process in this country? I don't know.

from a colloquium

D. SOCIAL THERAPY AND SELF HELP

Dialogue 61. The Relational in Self Help

Therapist-in-training: On the back cover of your book *Let's Develop!* it says, "Beyond Self Help." Could you say something about what this means? How does or how can social therapy be integrated with a 12-step background and practice? How are they similar and how do they differ?

Fred: "Beyond self help"—I never want to be held responsible for what PR people put on books! I didn't write that but I won't cop a plea on that regard. I'll take responsibility for it. I think what was meant by "beyond self help" refers mainly to the word "self." What it is pointing to is a process of what we might call "social help," people helping each other, supporting each other, trying to find a social process of growth as opposed to simply an inner process of self expression. Social therapy is very much oriented toward social transformations—sociality as a self-conscious element in the process of growth as opposed to simply giving individualistic expression to who we are.

I guess that relates to the second part of your question as well. I think that, at its best, 12-step work does focus very much on interrelational matters. At its worst, I think it tends to be overly individualistic. But I think there's both sides. I don't think there is such a thing as the absolute 12-step model; it varies dramatically from situation to situation depending on who happens to be doing it. I think that, insofar as the relational approach that is fundamental to social therapy is made use of in 12-step work or any other approach, it's very positive and it is compatible. It is a focus on the relational, as opposed to simply the individual, that is so central to what social therapy is advocating. Social therapy is a challenge to what psychology itself is, not what this particular program or this particular approach or attitude or theory is. Social therapy is an attitude towards who we're helping and how we're helping them. It is exactly as the name suggests. It suggests that what you help people to do is to change their sociality and to help them to transform, even individually, by engaging their sociality rather than transforming the social by engaging their individuality.

So the approach of social therapy is distinctly group oriented. It's not as if we never do individual work but even the individual work is designed to help people go through a socialization process. It isn't designed to help someone to get more deeply into themselves and bring out their individual identity. It's rather to help people go through the intense process of recognizing our identity as profoundly social and of going through transformation and growth by virtue of transforming the sociality of who we are, rather than the pure individuality of who we are.

Yes, it's totally compatible and indeed there are people who have incorporated it into certain 12-step approaches in various areas of work and have learned from it. Social therapy is a funny kind of thing. A lot of people come to us and say, "Well, I've been doing something like that for a long time." To which we say, "That's great." We're not looking to have a competition. Insofar as people have been doing it, that's wonderful. We hope that we contribute something to understanding it a little better, because we've put so much energy into it, but I'm sure there are lots of people who are effectively focusing on the social as opposed to the individualistic in all areas of work. We feel very close to people who have been doing that.

from a colloquium

CHAPTER SIX

Social Therapy and
Philosophy (and Politics)

Dialogue 62. Paradigms and Paradigm Shifts

Therapist-in-training: What do we mean when we talk about paradigms? How do we challenge paradigms? How do we encourage paradigmatic changes? How do we as therapists continue this activity in our groups?

Fred: The functional definition of paradigms has a very long and varied history. Paradigm is a relatively "late modern" term. In this country it's associated with Thomas Kuhn, who wrote *The Structure of Scientific Revolutions*, a book that has had a huge intellectual impact. But the phenomenon had been talked about before, going way back to the Greeks, and certainly to Kant.

We don't see things in a pure visual sensory sense. The experience of seeing is some kind of combination of a conceptual and a visual experience. We have conceptions that we carry with us—models, if you will. And how do we carry them? This is a very complex question. According to people like Chomsky, we carry those models genetically. Other people think it's purely cultural. Others think it's a mixture of cultural and genetic. Some people think it's religious. There are endless stories of what these conceptions are. We bring to our perceptions models—physiological or psychological or cultural or whatever—of how things are supposed to look and be seen. We carry around views and attitudes about how things should look—not just how they should look in some evaluative sense, but what they should look like.

This goes all the way back to Plato's theory of ideas, where Plato insists that the perceptual experience was a rekindling of ideas that literally came into mind during a prelife period. Though I don't happen to agree with that way of formulating it, that's obviously part of the lineage of this mixture of perception and conception. In some sense, paradigms are nothing more than self-consciously developed conceptions.

What Kuhn writes about is how the scientific process goes back and forth between creating new conceptions during the paradigmatic period and then testing out those conceptions to see what their efficacy is during the observational period of science. At the simplest level, science is a two-cycled process (or maybe a three-cycled process), one being highly conceptual when we create paradigms, another being the testing of those paradigms, and the third being the interrelationship between the two. Simplistic.

So a paradigm is a self-consciously created new way of looking at things. You see it in science all over the place. One of the better examples is Harvey's discovery of circulation and the conceptual recognition—which was not purely conceptual, obviously, but for the moment bear with me—that the heart was functioning as a pump. This was obviously a significant breakthrough in that area of study, because a lot of people pondered endlessly over trying to understand where all that blood came from, or so the story goes. Out of this complicated social process there's a new conception for understanding—the heart as a pump—and now a lot of things are explained. But you still have to test them out. And you do test them out and they hold up empirically and on you go. So a new conception—not just for the heart but for a lot of things—enters in. I'm not a doctor. I don't know medicine. I don't know even now if the heart is used as a pump, but it seems useful to me. I remember it from junior high school At least it seemed like a big breakthrough in junior high school.

An area I do know something about is mathematics, where I've seen how new conceptions, new paradigms, play a part. For example, look at what proofs are. There are profound limitations in the foundations of mathematics and mathematical logic, which were broken through by discoveries of—not just new proofs—but new conceptions of what a proof was. Breakthroughs in the foundational areas of computer work and so-called recursive function theory came from new paradigms of proof. That's where I have the clearest understanding of it.

Roughly speaking, that's how paradigm has come down through the ages. It is taken as a modernist form. Postmodernism is often antiparadigmatic and offers very critical views of paradigm. Sometimes postmodernists hold onto critical views of certain paradigms, but are remarkably lenient relative to others. As always, I'm an extremist on these matters. I don't like paradigms altogether, because I think they distort. I think they are distortive of the actual process of human discovery and human growth. I certainly see how they are an interesting pedagogic device for explaining things. They make things comprehensible, but are distortive in being overdetermined in a mechanistic kind of way.

It's very hard to create the environments for paradigm shifts. Within therapeutic work, one creates it by a continuous effort to question the group's presuppositions about the conversations they are having. Constantly questioning to the point of saying, "Why are we having this conversation at all? Why is this what we're doing?" So much of getting caught up in paradigmism—at least emotionally—is the assumptions of meaning that people make about what people say. We say things and assume that we know what each other means. We assume we know what we mean. And if you try to explore that continuously—almost to the point of utter and complete frustration on the part of the group—I think people come to see that we often don't know what we mean. And we surely don't mean the same thing.

For example, some people think they mean the same thing if they use the same term. But they don't, because the process by which we learn meaning is not a repeatable process; people learn in different and nuanced ways. I don't think it's a defect of language. In fact, I think it's an interesting strength of language. I don't think it's a defect of poetry that you can't get absolutely clear objective meaning out of it. It is not designed to give you objective meaning. The same holds for emotionality. Emotionality and emotional language are best understood, in my opinion, artistically, not scientifically.

Art is no less clear than science; it's just different from science. You have to teach people something about the art of living, which, to me, means the art of functioning in a group. That's what I mean by the art of living. The art of living is not a series of techniques to make you a better individual, better at playing the game, better at winning. No, it's quite the contrary. The art of living seems to be the art of learning how to live as part of a social unit—to be a group member, to create a group, to create new group things.

No small part of what I do in therapy is engage this issue of paradigms at the level of emotional meanings. You can tell when someone is raising a problem from the point of view that they think everyone in the world understands what they are talking about. Red light for me. That's just the occasion on which I have to challenge. We have to take a look at those kinds of emotive assumptions and emotive paradigms, and question not only the correctness of the paradigm, whatever that means, but question even whether we want to understand this effort at communication in terms of paradigms.

Here's my biggest objection to *DSM–IV*. It's not just the particular things said. Those are sometimes helpful. It's that they would write that book at all, that they would convey that somehow this is a method for understanding human emotive communication. I don't believe it is. Human communication is far more poetic, far more artistic, and far less pseudo-scientific than the people who put together *DSM–IV* think. I think it's a dysfunctional methodology. That's my objection to it. Insofar as it's anecdotally interesting, it's not a bad compendium of different ways in which people use the word "blue." That's okay with me. I like intellectual efforts and if you want to have 73 different ways in which people use the word "blue" that's not bad. But what about the 74th? It's missing. And that's a problem. And what about the 75th? And what about the ways in which people are continuously creating? What's fundamental is the continuousness of that process. That's what is most significant to understand in understanding emotional discourse.

I sit around and do philosophy with the group. That's the method that I use. That's a whole lot of what social therapy is, that's the content of it. I'll do critical philosophy with you, and maybe we'll come to see together that emotional dialogue is not fully rule-governed. It's creative. It's artistic. And if we learn that and take control of that by learning how to function in a group, well, sometimes it happens that people get along better. On our worst days, not. But on our best days, that's what happens. And people learn something from that practical process.

from a colloquium

Dialogue 63. *Dualism and Connectionism*

Therapist-in-training: As a clinical psychologist with over 20 years of experience I've worked predominantly in an insight-oriented modality. My belief has been that internal cognitive/emotional changes and outer interpersonal life changes interact mutually to create development. The approach is, of course, the antithesis of social therapy. If my understanding is correct, social therapy theory states that only activity/performance can be developmental and that cognition, the self, the inner world, is superfluous. If so, then what is changing or developing in the individual if not oneself? How can development occur purely on a group activity level with no individual reference?

Fred: I don't think "the inner world is superfluous" is a social therapeutic position. What we are saying is that there is a dialectical unity—not a negation of the inner or of the outer. All is activity. The inside/outside distinction is troublesome because, for us, inside and outside are so interconnected that the effort to see them as two separate things is distortive. That, as I understand it, is the social therapeutic position. It may be very close to what you are saying, I don't know.

Therapist-in-training: If we start to believe that the self does not exist, then what exactly is development?

Fred: We agree with what we think is Vygotsky's position. Vygotsky writes very brilliantly of the social origins of individuation. For him and for us, it is not so much a denial of the individual as a denial of the fundamentality of the individual. We think of the individual or individuation as a by-product of the social rather than the other way around. So, it's not a denial of consciousness or the individual, but a denial of the individual as somehow primordial, as a basic unit, with everything else to be understood in terms of compounding individuals. It is this notion that we find problematic— not just abstractly, theoretically, and philosophically, but very practically.

Is a group to be simply understood in terms of its individuated membership? Or does a group have an existence independent of that, which gives meaning and definition to all kinds of things? What is the nature of a group? This is a big topic for us. Part of that comes from my own training and background in logic and mathematics; I find it an interesting philosophical and psychological question, which has been lost in contemporary psychology, if it was ever there. We're trying to offer a corrective.

It makes more sense to me to think in terms of the fundamentality of the social and to try to understand these other things in terms of how they evolved from sociality. What do you think of what I am saying? Does it make any sense at all?

Therapist-in-training: The whole issue of dualism has been difficult for me to understand. My position is that everything is interconnected, so my understanding goes in the direction of thinking you must mean the negation of the self, as opposed to thinking that self and the outer world are mutually connected to that original dualism.

Fred: This might sound a little paradoxical, but we think they're so connected that it does not even make sense to speak of them as connected. Because connectedness tends to imply a certain separation. Our commonsensical notion of connectedness is that there are two separate things and somehow they interconnect. This conception of connection has been a mistake within psychology and a lot of other fields. In physics there is a reexamination of connectedness going on that has led to breathtaking discoveries. I think that psychology needs to go through a similar thing.

from a colloquium

Dialogue 64. Dialectics and Contradiction

Therapist-in-training: As part of the therapist-training program, we have been reading and discussing different philosophers, including Wittgenstein,

Vygotsky, and Marx. These readings have generated considerable conversations. I have a question about dialectics.

In *Marx for Beginners*, the author defines dialectics as "the art of knowing truth by uncovering the contradictions in the reasoning of your adversary." He goes on to say: "Dialectics came to be transformed into a theory of development and universal relations. Dialectics consider all phenomena as being in movement, in the process of perpetual change. It views nature itself as a result of the struggle between contradictions within nature. Dialectics became a science when Marx and Engels liberated it from Hegelian idealism. It is a doctrine of development—a science of the universal laws governing the development of nature, human society, and thought."

In your article in *Postmodern Psychologies, Societal Practice and Political Life* [Holzman and Morss 2000], you write: "The well-suitedness of dialectics as a method of study is fully dependent on a new understanding of the proper object of study. It is not the object or the thing (large or small) which can be studied; it is activity, practice, subjectivity. Dialectical materialism does not, for Marx, mean the dialectical study of the material organized as things. This is the error of all prior forms of materialism. For not only is the physical object a cultural posit (in Quine's sense); so is object itself. Indeed, it is not the physicality of the object that is most insidiously mythical and, thereby, potentially metaphysical; it is its formal organization (its shape) as a discrete object of study or discernment. . . . And performance, in my opinion, will more and more become the practical-critical shape of activity even as dialectics replaces objectification as our mode of understanding."

These two excerpts seem to be contradictory. Could you say a little about this and possibly explain how they are related yet simultaneously different? And how does this relate to the social therapy practice of method?

Fred: How are they contradictory?

Therapist-in-training: They don't seem to mesh. I don't know, they seem to be opposed.

Fred: Well, I don't hear "opposed" from what you read, although there is a difference. The difference is that I think Marx, and more importantly Engels, was viewing dialectics as a characteristic of nature. He was very much determined by 19th-century science, where nature was understood in an objectified way. Nature was filled up with "things." Much has happened in science since the 19th century and now there is a deeper understanding, in pretty much all the sciences, that the stuff of nature is not "things" at all but some kind of process, not so much discrete objects as intertwined processes.

Note, however, that all of these conceptions have to do with some notion about how reality *is*. The notion of dialectics that we've developed relative to the shift in contemporary science has less to do with how reality is or with the object of study and more to do with the method of study. And so the dialectical conception that we put forth talks about the method for studying these processes that make up the world, and in particular these activities that make up human life. Ours is a definition of dialectics relative to method, not relative to object of study. So that's different.

That said, I think some of the basic things that Marx and Engels have to say are not incorrect, but 19th century-ish. That's because they are 19th century! They talk the language of 19th-century science, which isn't at all the language of 20th-century science. But given a liberal translation they come out to be very similar in their intent, having to do with contradictoriness. The contradictoriness of things has to do, as we now know, with the fact that the things that we study are processes, not discrete Aristotelian things.

I guess what I am saying is that I think there is a serious difference, but I wouldn't be inclined to call it a contradiction. Not that I have anything against contradictions. I just don't think it would be completely precise to relate to it as contradictory.

from a colloquium

Dialogue 65. *Particulars and Totalities*

Therapist-in-training: Lately I've noticed that a lot of conversations seem to follow an either/or duality model. For instance, is George Bush better than Al Gore? Is Sartre better than Heidegger? Or, is it this or that? I don't think these conversations are developmental because they seem to digress into some circular formulations. In observing these conversations I see my judgments and my frustrations; I react as if there's something wrong with them; why are they still bickering over the same thing and not progressing; how can I help them? I also realize that I fall into a dualistic mind frame as well, and think and say, "This is better than that . . ." I was wondering how you experience these kinds of conversations and how you participate and transform the conversation to "yes, and"?

Fred: There appear to be a number of questions here. One question, or one whole family of questions, relates to the issue of dualism. Another batch of questions relates to comparatives. And they are not always the same. Maybe I could say something about dualism and see where it gets us.

Dualistic formulations are fundamentally distorted. I don't believe in dualism. I don't adhere to and do not follow the law of the excluded middle. The law of the excluded middle has a long history and has been a foundational element of all kinds of scientific and logical advancements. Modern science was no less a distortion than other things; it just turned out to be an extraordinarily productive distortion and continues to be so. However, I don't think that science gives anything resembling a satisfactory picture of how things are—whatever that means.

Things seem to me to be so plainly interconnected. Wittgenstein is useful in this regard. The Wittgensteinian notion of "family resemblances" is a significant contribution to Western philosophical thought. The notion of things being discrete enough to be definable and to be individuated, Wittgenstein says, is a profound myth. At most, what we have is what he calls family resemblances—complex, interconnecting interrelationships that start out in perhaps a certain narrow way and then go beyond that to a more extended set of terms, concepts, and ideas, and then beyond that, ultimately, to a holism that includes everything.

The unit of discovery—to me—is not the discrete particular, nor what it excludes (the either/or of dualism's excluded middle). The unit of discovery, the unit of life, is the totality of life. Some people say, "Isn't that too big?" I don't think it's too big; it's only too big if you insist on knowing. As a matter of fact, my problem, generally speaking, has always been that discrete, individuated particulars are way too small, not that the totalities are too big. People who think that they can explain things or make things comprehensible in terms of an arbitrary interpretive relationship between discrete particulars are, in my opinion, fanciful or opportunists or looking for grants.

In theory, that is relatively easy. The really hard part is how to give expression to that in life, in practice. Because you can't do judgment making in quite the same way if you don't individuate. How do we avoid the pitfalls of judgment making based on an individuated sense of reality? A judgment is, after all, a description of something-or-other compared to a something. I guess you could say, "Can't you make judgments about the totality?" I suppose you could—and maybe you should—and maybe we do. But judgments about the totality of life don't have the same—what word to use?—nasty, blaming quality that judgments about discrete particulars do.

The practice of this is difficult. I work very hard at doing it. We had a very moving group last night. What ultimately came to be the subject matter of the group—and this is not infrequent in a social therapy group—was the struggle between insisting on comprehending what was happening in the group in terms of people's individuated selves, and comprehending and relating to the whole phenomenon that is the group.

That basic struggle is ongoing, not only in social therapy, but in life. In social therapy, it is self-conscious. In life, it's there all the time and creates very painful consequences, but I think it does not get to be identified as such. We tend to see the world in terms of every other particular's relationship to "me"—the "me" being whoever happens to be articulating "me." Every "me" differs somewhat, but nonetheless, it's all about me. The notion that there is a totality—whether it's a small totality, a medium-sized totality, a larger totality, or a universal totality—has been, philosophically speaking, discredited in favor of particularism.

In classical terms, realism has been thought of as having lost the battle against nominalism. I don't agree with that. I don't like this language, but, in the classical philosophical sense, I am and remain a realist—meaning that I believe in the existence of totalities. I haven't the need to think that the totality is comprehensible only if you can reduce it to particulars. Particulars have been an unfortunate and destructive feature of Western thought for the last several hundred and, perhaps, for the last several thousand years. Particulars are now so pervasive in our culture and so much in our language that people can't talk without them.

In a sense, the answer is all in the practice. If social therapy is any kind of significant breakthrough, it has to do with its capacity, almost in an engineering sense, to put into practice this kind of holistic perspective or totalistic understanding. A lot of people think that the "social" of social therapy is simply that we do social things. That is not it at all. The "social" of social therapy is the acceptance of the fact that the fundamental unit of human intercourse is social. That is why, to me, social therapy and group therapy are synonymous. Yes, we have therapists who do individual therapy. I think they're very skillful, although—maybe this is my own mythology— I persist in thinking that they do the individual work to help people do better in group.

from a colloquium

Dialogue 66. Undecidability and Emotions

Therapist-in-training: In "Undecidable Emotions" [Newman, 2003], you write: "Social therapy is, among other things, an effort to create a therapy which is not overdetermined by a metaphor or a model of decidability." You go on to say, "We are a decision-making species. And we decide much more than important matters. We continuously decide what to do with the endless impingements on consciousness that make up daily life including, most importantly, what we call our emotions. But that we make endless decisions should no longer be understood to mean that the totality of our decision making is itself decidable." Can you say this in another way that I might better understand? How does this philosophical understanding find expression in the life of the social therapy group?

Fred: A basic methodological assumption that comes down to us in Western cul-
        ture is that if you had enough words and enough time and enough energy,
        you could ultimately come up with the final answer. In some ways that's a
        credo of the Enlightenment—that human beings can know all of the de-
        tailed information about the universe. But what if some of the answers are
        beyond us? What if we're not smart enough? What if it's not a question of
        having enough time or energy?

           Now, within the Enlightenment framework that's impossible, because
        the center of the universe is the human being; the human being mediates all
        of this, and she or he can ultimately understand everything. But what if we
        deny that assumption? What if we deny the assumption of an infinitude of
        knowledge, which is central and core to the Enlightenment model? What if
        it's all too damn complex for us? Isn't it possible that we can create some-
        thing that is too complex for us to understand? The Enlightenment assump-
        tion—if we created it, it must be that we can understand it—permeates our
        culture. People create families, nations, factories, all kinds of things, and
        then by virtue of our creating them we believe that we know or can know
        how they all work. But what if we have this remarkable skill—and in fact
        we do—to create things that we cannot comprehend?

           Children have this delightful way of playing games that don't require
        rules for every situation. Adults don't do it so well. Adults want decidable
        systems; they need to have a rule to cover every situation. When we get
        older we conform to rule-governed behavior. But life is not governed by
        rule-governed behavior. This is not an argument against rule-governed be-
        havior where it is appropriate. But I think there's something profoundly
        liberating in recognizing, as in the case of emotional activity, that there are
        significant areas of our lives that are not rule governed. I think people have
        so much trouble with emotions because they have trouble with non-rule-
        governed aspects of life

           It is distortive of life to insist that rules govern what is not rule gov-
        erned. It leads to all kinds of personal problems—in families, with chil-
        dren. The child will say, quite justifiably, "Who made up these rules? Where
        did they come from?" Well, that's the moment of dread for many parents.
        But it can be a moment of wonder, where we can say, "Let's reconstruct the
        whole thing. This is a beautiful time to construct something new." People
        can learn how to do that, how to deal with non-rule-governed situations
        more creatively.

           That's what I mean in talking about undecidability. The illusion that
        we will find the absolute answer is just that—an illusion. People say, "I
        have to know the answer!" From my point of view you might as well say I
        have to fly to the moon. You can feel frustrated by that, but the fact is there
        are lots of areas of human life that are not decidable, and you have to learn

how to develop and grow given that. I have found that once we accept that, it opens up lots of doors. After all, just look at children. There's a profound element of creativity that's lost once they adapt to rules. Is it adaptive? Absolutely. Is it good? To some extent yes and to some extent no. But something is lost. We are eager to have adults not be children again, but to participate in activity which is very, very different from the overly rule-governed activity in the rest of their lives. What social therapy does is to help people to deal with situations that are non-rule-governed. Social therapy urges people to be unnatural. It's an undecidable world—there are many answers we will never know.

from a colloquium

Dialogue 67. Alienation and Humiliation

Fred: We live in a culture, sadly enough, where people try to stop other people from doing things by, among other things, embarrassing them. Even more than guilt, ours is a culture of embarrassment. I think the culture of guilt was a 19th- and early 20th-century European phenomenon. America is now a culture of embarrassment. That's very sad and painful. My own personal reaction to this is the more people try to embarrass me, the louder I talk. In part, it's a pure arrogance in response to it, because the thing that gripes me most in the world is people trying to get other people to do what they want them to do by virtue of embarrassing them. I find it particularly inhuman.

I know the feeling when people effectively say to you, "Aren't you ashamed of yourself for doing this? Why did you waste your life this way? Don't you know you could have done this and that . . . ?" And it's vaguely effective. I have to take a moment before I say, "Because I don't want to be doing that. I don't want to be in that kind of environment—it inhibits development. I want to be right here. This is what I love to do." But you can really feel the weight of people's efforts to embarrass you.

Student: How is this culture of embarrassment that you're talking about connected to alienation? I was in a conversation with a woman who I would say is one of the most alienated people that I know. All she did was talk about how alienated she was and all the things that she didn't have. But she was perfectly comfortable saying to me after she asked me questions about my work as a human rights lawyer, "When you start practicing law again, this time you're going to make some money, right?" And it was humiliating, a moment of embarrassment, an arrow thrown across the table. So what is this connection between that power of somebody to use humiliation like that and alienation?

Fred: I think humiliation is the subjective emotional experience that comes of living in a culture that is super-alienated. It's the emotional counterpart to it. Alienation, as I understand it, and as Marx understood it—and I think that Marx was right about this, not about everything, but about this—is an objective characteristic of the world. Alienation means the separation of the process of production from the product of production. That means living in a world that is commodified; living in a world in which we take the things which are produced and somehow tear them away from the human process which led to their being created, and then relate to them as having an independent existence.

Living in a world of that kind, which is a fictionalized, artificial, alienated world, what happens is that over time people become increasing vulnerable to being humiliated. Because we lose our connectedness to the life processes. And once we lose our connectedness to the processes by which we create things, we're very vulnerable to being embarrassed by them. People can hold them up to you. You can't embarrass people who know what they've created, who are connected to what they've created, who understand their relationship to the process of creating something. But if something is created and it's torn away from people so they no longer realize that they're connected to it and then you push it back into their face, you can humiliate the hell out of them.

We have forgotten as a species that it's we who have created all that is wonderful. To be sure, all that is awful as well. But we have forgotten that, and it leaves us incredibly vulnerable. In order to do something about that vulnerability, we have to come to better understand and appreciate our relationship to the culture, to all that we've created.

from a seminar

Dialogue 68. On Not Making Distinctions

Therapist-in-training: In social therapy is there is a distinction between change, growth, and development? If so, what is it?

Fred: Well, those terms are used in various ways and, of course, context determines what words mean. In general, though, I would warn against making the assumption that all change or development or growth is, in some kind of moral sense, necessarily positive—whatever that might mean. Transformation goes in many different directions.

I find your question hard to answer because in our approach, we don't introduce the distinction of the distinction. That is not just being glib. Making distinctions is a major part of conditional theorizing, but it's not part of our approach. Social therapy is radically monistic; it's an effort to engage issues without resting on the whole edifice of distinction, as well as on the kind of conditional theorizing that is constructed around distinctions. That isn't to say that we don't ever do that because we are a part of the culture, but this is what we continually strive for. And I think this is a lot of what makes our work incomprehensible to lots of people. Many tell us that they have no idea what we are talking about. That makes perfectly good sense because as long as you stay in the confines of traditional theorizing—not even traditional theories, but traditional theorizing—it is very difficult to grasp what we are talking about.

I think it is difficult to grasp in the way that grasping impressionistic art was very difficult for some people. It was not lined design, and if your notion of figure was determined by line and all you had were dabs of paint, then you might have wondered, "Where are the figures? All I see is dabs of paint." In a sense, I think of social therapy as a new art form, and some people are not going to see it. They might decide they are not going to see it; they are not going to look at this new kind of thing; it does not fit into their ontological view of their world. They say, "We don't know what things are. You don't make distinctions; you don't introduce theoretical constructs; you don't distinguish between cause and effect, between which comes first and which comes second, et cetera. But those are the very things that you have to do in order for what you do to be comprehensible." And we say, "If that is your definition of comprehensible, then you are right, then social therapy will turn out to be incomprehensible."

from a colloquium

Dialogue 69. Beyond Postmodernism?

Therapist-in-training: I've heard it said that social therapy goes "beyond" postmodernism. Can you talk a little bit about that?

Fred: In some ways I am not sympathetic to that formulation. It has a labeling quality to it, a taxonomical quality. I don't even know if it makes any sense. The "beyond" question is very much associated with the modernist narrative. After all, modernism, like all full-blown ideologies or meta-narratives, doesn't simply define itself; it defines everything else relative to itself. Maybe there's a way to stop talking about these things as if there were some fixed points relative to which there are points before, and points beyond. Maybe that's not a useful way of looking at things.

I don't know if I'd want to say that social therapy is beyond—or before—anything. It is what it is. We're all pulled to try to locate it because location is a central component of the modernist and postmodernist narrative—things come from somewhere, they fit in there, they are composed of a little of this, a little of that, and so on. It is a constructive narrative—constructive in the sense of "here are the elements that make it up." That way of talking is often used in the heat of debates—you establish location. But I don't know if that really gets to what something *is*. It seems too "labelist," if that's a word.

Now, if we mean to say that insofar as postmodernism has itself transformed into a new narrative, and that social therapy is an effort to break from that narrative, well in some ways yes, I think it is "beyond postmodernism." But the caution here is that social therapy is an effort to break from that narrative as part of breaking, in some respects, from all narratives. Now, some people say you can't do that since we're a narrative-inclined species. And I don't know, maybe they're right.

This is not a particularly new way of thinking about things for me. My inclinations and training have leaned heavily in this direction. The first course I ever taught after I got my PhD was a course in Greek philosophy, about which I knew relatively little at the time. I made it plain that I didn't pretend to be teaching about Greek philosophy; I was trying to teach philosophy by taking a look at some of the people who were Greek philosophers. That seemed to me to be an important distinction even then. I don't know what "Greek philosophy" is, what it means to ascribe Greekness to a philosophy, or any other nationality or time or whatever.

So this position didn't come when I officially got designated as a postmodernist. I was kind of unhappy with a lot of that stuff a long time ago. Not because I think it is wrong, but because I just don't think it's very useful. It feels like the academic equivalent of diagnosis. Some people disagree with that; some people find diagnosis to be the cat's meow. I do not. I don't find it at all useful in helping people. The academic analog is the classification of periods and times—hours of talk about the Greek and Romans and so on: "Here's what the American pragmatists believe, and some of the pragmatists follow this school, and they're different from the Continental rationalists," et cetera. I just don't tend to see things that way.

Therapist-in-training: Does what you said about challenging "going beyondism" apply to development in social therapy? Does "beyondism" regarding development also entail motion relative to some fixed point?

Fred: If you're saying that in our culture it invariably does, I agree completely. But I don't think it has to entail that. I think it's possible to have a notion of development without a fixed point. Many postmodernists say to us, "We don't understand how you can support development because it involves fixed points and a value notion of gradation from that fixed point." What we've tried to say is that we don't think that has to be the case. I don't know that creation has to involve gradation, which implies the ability to measure and describe. We can have a notion of development as the creation of otherness.

We can create theater and beautiful music without critics. After all, creativity came into existence long before there were critics. We have to find a modality of development, of growth, a language for all of this that makes it possible for us to be liberated from the constraint of gradation, of value-laden notions of development. I think that's certainly true of the education system in this country, which is fundamentally a graded phenomenon. It isn't simply that learning goes on and then it is graded. It is that learning is overdetermined by the grading of it. To me, that's the single most inhibitory element of the educational process in this country and in the world.

from a colloquium

Dialogue 70. It's All Activity

Therapist-in-training: I believe every therapist has seen himself or herself as making mistakes in the therapy room, for example, stunting the growth of the session or of relational activity. Can you share some of those moments in your therapeutic developmental lifeline?

Fred: My first intuitive answer is—all of what we do is a mistake. Therapy is a process of regularly making mistakes from which we try to figure out what to do next, and what we wind up doing next is simply a next order of mistake. The backdrop of your question suggests that there is some notion of correctness and then there are some times when mistakes occur. It's *all* a mistake—or it's all *not* a mistake. It's all an activity. And activities don't come with little labels saying "right" or "wrong," "correct" or "incorrect."

There is a sufficient internal dynamic in physical chemistry, for example, so that you can speak of what is correct or incorrect; that's no small part of how come it is a science. You can introduce language from which you can make deductions that give certain kinds of objective explanations and accounts. But there is no descriptive system, it seems to me, for human activity. The attempts to do so, like *DSM–IV*, are obviously foolish. It's a pretense, which is why they seem so distortive and silly. Human activity is not classifiable in this way. Yet this is difficult to come to terms with because we have been so taught, so conditioned into thinking that this is the only way of understanding anything. It's perfectly fine to raise these kinds of questions, except that there are absolutely no answers. And the search for answers takes you away from what can be developmentally accomplished in the carrying out of therapeutic activity.

The real issue here is coming to terms with and understanding what activity is. Not surprisingly, there is a profound pull in our culture to objectifying everything as a precondition for understanding it. If you seek to understand activity by going through that kind of process of objectification you lose activity. It is not the kind of thing that can be understood objectively. Now, the positivist response would suggest that, therefore, activity cannot be understood and studied and advanced. I would not agree with that. We have done 30 years of successful therapy without saying a single objective word about it. And yet there is reason to believe that it is developmental.

from a colloquium

EPILOGUE

Therapists' Comments

What do social therapists and social therapists-in-training do with the all this talk of methodology? Do they find it useful? How do they put it into practice? How do they work to relate to their therapy sessions as the improvisational creating of a collective play? What does it look like when they try to "speak to the group?" How do they "practice method?"

Social therapy doesn't have techniques to speak of, so a therapist can't identify a particular "move," practice it and, at some point, say, "Aha, I've got it!" And yet, social therapists do continuously transform the way they practice and they do get better at doing social therapy. Next we offer some of their own accounts of the impact of their training and supervision.

I.

I had wanted some help with a woman who came back to therapy after a period of several years. The help I got was to look at my own vulnerability to being dramatic with dramatic clients. First, let me say that the woman in question just began group after a few months of seeing me individually. A lot has happened with her and with me.

After the supervisory dialogue, I worked self-consciously to not get hooked into a particular thing that she might say or do, or a way she might look. I was focusing on and working to deal with the totality of our relationship, the history of our relationship. So she would say provocative things and I would feel all the pulls in the world to get into some dramatic thing with her. Instead, I would use those moments to say something very banal.

I worked to engage her philosophically, and if you're having a philosophical conversation it's hard to get into dramatics. Some of those conversations had to do with her dealing with the contradiction of being a woman whose religion forbids her talking to men unless her husband is present and her being in a day treatment program where she encounters and talks to men regularly. What did she mean that she couldn't talk with men; what was she really saying about that—since it was the case that she did talk to them? We talked of her spirituality, the guidelines of her religion, how she decides how to live using those guidelines, what that has to do with her actual life, what her husband thinks about all of this.

I worked with her to create something new out of what she was giving. Creating something small, not creating a drama. We were able to talk about our history from 5 years ago, all its craziness and drama. And we were able to talk about that in ordinary ways. She was able to say how bad she felt about that, how crazy she was then—"ordinary" crazy. So I invited her to come to the group, and it was so lovely. She just became very happy and she said, "I just have to say I feel very cared for by you. And I feel I really want to do that." And we talked about her being an ordinary person there. She would be an ordinary group member. She said she knew she was special to me, and we were able to deconstruct that in some sense. We meant a lot to each other, but the specialness was problematic. We did a lot of work on that before I invited her into group.

II.

I was feeling stuck in one of my groups. There was one man in particular I needed help with relating to, someone I was identifying with and always trying to be there for. We discussed me needing to get a little distance in order to help him and the group. Fred had suggested that if I was "a little more smug" I might achieve that distance. I literally used that as theatrical direction. What did that look like? I told the group I wasn't there to attend to things individuals wanted help with. I was smug about it—not a bitch or anything, but I just proceeded to attend to what I wanted to attend to, namely, the group.

III.

B, a longtime member of my group, is talking about her ex-lover M, who recently had a heart attack. B is very upset and concerned that M recently left therapy because of the heart attack. She's angry at M because she wants her to be somebody else, to do this heart attack in a different way. The group gets into pursuing with B how come she wants that, how does she feel about M, what does the heart attack raise for her? It's a long, drawn-out conversation that is becoming more and more psychological.

I begin to participate in it myself. And then I start thinking about a supervision when Fred talked about people needing to take responsibility for making decisions. So in the middle of the group I said, "Let me tell you something. We are doing the very activity that we are complaining B is doing with M. B is into being the person who's going to help M out of her situation, and I think the group is invested in doing that with B, and I've participated in it. But the fact is we can't help B, it's not what we do here. But you know, even if we wanted to help her we can't, because the question is whether B wants to do anything about it or not. She's been doing this with M for 20 years, and how she presented it and talked about it tonight is the way she's done it over and over. So, what are we all doing here?"

B and some others said, "What should we do?" I said, "What do you want to do? What, if anything, does the group want to do with this?" This turned out to be very engaging of the group. Group members began to talk about how uncomfortable they were with what I was saying, about all kinds of things that they are going through, and about their conflicts about taking responsibility for creating their life. B said that she was really mad at me for stopping the scripted play we were in and urging the group to do something new—and even though she was mad, she thought it was good.

People talked about their conflicts about getting closer to each other. They would have to go through something emotionally; they would have to feel things that they are trying not to feel; they would have to say more about what's going in their lives without cleaning it up in order to get closer to the group, and people don't want to expose what a mess their life is, they want to look much more together than that.

B said that she would be very upset and incredibly sad about what she and M had not been able to do in their lives. She added that she thought that she was in a lot of danger in her life emotionally—going along and living her life as she has been, she is risking losing things that are very important to her. She said she was feeling frightened and needed and wanted to do something. At that point in the conversation she was much more concrete and much more with us than earlier. B had been trying to get help from the group from a great distance. Part of the distance were these scripted ways of talking, ways of talking that were very self-protective. The message was "Stay away from me" but at the same time "I'm in a lot of pain about this; I really need help." There was a long history of her talking about M in the group, including times when she has been much closer to the group and talked about her and M in a different way. But that night she was on another planet. And the group was saying, after we reorganized things, "You're still on that planet. So if you want to come in here and be with us maybe we can do something together."

IV.

This was a woman who had suffered very severe sexual abuse. The supervision was about being ordinary with her and not getting caught up in making her special because of her painful past. She came in to the next individual session and said,

"I'm just distraught, I'll never have a relationship. I can never be with a man." So I listened to her, and had a very different response this time. I said, "What are you talking about? You could be with a man if you wanted to. I guess you're choosing not to—and that's fine." The dialogue continued along these lines—"I'll never have any friends, I'll never get help." It was something of a litany. And I continued to respond in a way that challenged this way of talking—"I don't know where you're coming from in saying that." And then she said, "What happened to you yesterday? Did you talk with Fred Newman?" And I said, "As a matter of fact, I did." And she said, "I could tell. What's going to happen now? You're going to start treating me like everybody else in the group? Is that how it works around here?" I said, "That's exactly how it works." She said, "Who else did you get help from?" I told her, "Bette." So she came into group that week and said, "Just watch out everybody, 'cause she's getting help from Fred Newman and Bette Braun." It was great! It was a complete turning point in the therapy.

V.

In one supervision meeting about women being reactive to men, we talked about how I was dealing with S, a man in one of my groups who was nasty and antagonistic, and we identified that I was substituting myself for the women in the group. So at the beginning of the next group I told the group that I realized I had made a mistake in my relationship with S. I said that I had brought him into the group too soon, that my relationship with him hadn't been built enough. And I had done a disservice to him and the group. I felt bad and wanted to do something about it. We had to go through some kind of process that would help S decide whether or not he wanted to be in therapy with me.

In this group session, some individual work we did together, and a few subsequent groups, S was very impacted on by what I said. He was very emotional about my taking responsibility for there being something amiss in our relationship, and it opened up for him whether or not he wanted to be in therapy with me—he said he hadn't ever thought about it. We talked about what he wanted to do.

Over the next month and a half the work with him got much better; he stopped playing the role of the antagonist. A lot of stuff was raised with him about whether or not he wanted to learn how to be a man in a different way. And what came out of that was that he said no, he didn't. And he left therapy. It was great. I was so happy that he decided what he wanted to do. I think he left well.

VI.

Two issues we talk a lot about in our training—taking care of people and buying into their pathology—have helped me with a particular client. I had been waiting for E to raise his issue—going to prostitutes and his feelings about that—in group. He's young, very working class, very Catholic, very guilty. Every week in our individual sessions I "pitched" him on raising it in group. But he wouldn't. In a training session, we explored why I was waiting for his permission. We identified that I was buying into his pathology and that it was a mistake to wait for E to bring it up—Why wasn't *I* doing it?

At the next individual session with him I told him I was going to raise this in the group rather than working with him on it alone week after week. So I did that. I told the group, "E and I have been working on some stuff, and it's very hard to talk about. E has been afraid to talk about his visits to prostitutes." He was blown away, he just turned white—and was completely helped by it! The group was very interested, asking questions of him and he was responding—he was having a *conversation.* I think that blew him away too, that he was able to do that, that people were not rejecting of him as this pervert who went to prostitutes, that people were interested in him and his sex life. And people pushed him as they would with any other issue: "How come you didn't raise this with the group? Tell us why you were having a hard time doing that. How do you feel with _____ [therapist] raising this—she just said that this was something you didn't want to raise." None of this was said antagonistically.

VII.

There was a client who I was very paranoid about. He was taking notes in sessions and in a lot of ways his story didn't add up. I thought he might be a reporter or something. One of the things that came out of supervision was that I needed to find a way of letting him know that I was suspicious, that I didn't trust him. This was difficult at first to hear—I didn't want to expose to him that I felt paranoid, that I couldn't be of help to him.

But it wound up freeing me up to build my relationship with him. In our next session, he came in and was raising how he didn't trust people, how he has a hard time remembering things. And I was saying that I felt uncomfortable with him, that a lot of things he said didn't add up. For example, that he'd been in 8 years of traditional therapy but never got help with any of the things he was raising—his isolation and what he called his "social phobia."

We started to take a look at what he did in his previous therapies, and basically what he said was what he did in those sessions was to outsmart his therapists, and that he'd never talked about this before. What we got to was how he was in a competitive battle with everybody, that you were either a winner or a loser. And he liked therapy because that's a place where he can win, where he can control the dialogue. This was so different from the way he'd talked about himself before, as being the victim of his "social phobia," how that paralyzed him, and so on. So we talked a lot about his competitiveness in social situations—how you're either one up or one down—and how paralyzing that whole activity was, and how it was all about him. In a later session he said that no therapist had called him on that before. He said that if anybody could help him it would be me—he went to many kinds of therapists and no one had ever helped him look at things in ways that I did, and the way we talked about things helped him to see them in a way he'd never seen before.

VIII.

I've gotten a lot of help from work we've done on "liberal authoritarianism." One time was when a therapist was talking about being frustrated with what one of his groups was doing. He spoke in critical terms about the group. We explored how come the therapist was critical of the group and how he understood that. What came from this was that he was trying to get the group to act in a certain way, to get people to do what he wants—which is authoritarian. Fred told us it was important in doing therapy to make a distinction between what clients do and what therapists do. Clients will do whatever they do and it's the therapists' job to build with that, not to critique it. Our job is to build with what the group is doing, whatever that is. When social therapy groups work well, the group members do whatever they do, but the therapist doesn't swerve from building the group. Social therapists need to make demands on *themselves* to help the group. They need to consistently convey that they won't help people individually.

What we call the "community group" has been a marvelous training ground for me. This is a large weekly group (at any one time, it has 50 to 70 people) that serves as Fred's collective therapist. I supervise the group every other week when Fred isn't there. I help the group work collectively as a unit to be Fred's therapist, and in this particular environment I'm never pulled to help individual people with their problem; it's not relevant to what they're doing there. I've learned to work very, very hard to make demands on myself to create with what the group is giving me. These supervisions show me the way.

I do sometimes feel the pull to help individuals to relate to the group if they're having a hard time doing that. You might ask, "Isn't that what you're supposed to do—help them break out of their individualistic ways of relating, particularly if they ask for help to do that?" Well, my job is to help them with that *only in a way that helps the group*. And the more I do that, the more the group has said to me, "You're really growing—this is much more challenging, much more helpful."

IX.

I've brought several new people into one of my groups. This is a group with very strong leaders in it. The new people who have come in have never been in group therapy, and they learned rather quickly that they're not there to get help with their individual problems but to build the group. And I'm convinced that how quickly this gets conveyed and taught is off of my getting better at doing group therapy, getting more creative at helping the group to build, in other words, seeing that the group is my patient.

In a recent group two new people (who've been in the group for about 3 months) said they noticed that the group only made use of me or asked for my help when the group was stuck. It seemed to them that the group was stuck at growing because they didn't ask for things from me when the group was doing well. So they wanted to "up the ante" in the group. That kind of blew everybody away, because most of the time new people come in and say, "I don't know what's going on here!" But these were people who were relatively new, and they were pushing the group to use me more, to get closer to me. It was really a testament to the environment that the group had created.

X.

E was a long-time member of a group who had gotten a lot of help with his depression and feelings of failure. At a certain point he said he wanted to go further, to explore new ways to grow. I suggested that he work on how he relates to women and how he feels about himself as a man. That's when he balked. Increasingly, he became defensive and combative when the women in the group pushed him. He said he was being criticized and attacked, that he couldn't hear what was being said. He said he wanted to leave the group and do individual therapy with me. I agreed to this.

Our dialogue in a supervisory session helped me see that our individual work was going nowhere and I needed to have been more intimate by helping him deal with his difficulties in the group. When I saw E again, I told him that we had gone as far in our work as I thought we could, and that my recommendation was to stop therapy with me and to work with a male therapist who could push him and engage him harder. He became very upset and angry, said he didn't trust where I was coming from, that I was just trying to get rid of him. I suggested we work on this in the group to get help to have this conversation.

The group raised whether E wanted their help so that he and I could have this dialogue, because ours had been such an important relationship. E said he wanted to do that because he loved me and cared for me. And so the group, in a very moving and intimate way, helped me to create the environment where I could say to him that I didn't feel right about his continuing individual therapy with me when for months and months he kept telling me in group that he wasn't getting help. That I had to come to terms with the fact that I wasn't helping him, even though he kept relating to me as the only one who could "save him." I said I had to have a hard look at my ego needs to save him. I said that as a woman and a therapist you can get seduced by that—when someone tells you you're their only shot left in life, you want to help them and you can also get ego-involved.

What was so helpful was that the group said that I was being distant from him and he from me. And I knew that I was—in the face of his being so angry at me and hurt, I was trying to "stick to my guns" and kept repeating what he had been saying for months about his not getting help, what I thought would be best for him, et cetera—and that was distancing. The group told me that I needed to be more open about what was happening with me. Doing that—being more open about my limitations as a therapist, in part because of my vulnerabilities as a woman and my ego need to rescue him—helped him to be open about his vulnerabilities.

E said that he was upset that I called him over the phone to "fire him" from therapy. I said that I understood, and then I reiterated my reasons for doing so. One group member said, "The two of you aren't having the same conversation and maybe we can help." Another told me I wasn't hearing that E was upset that I called him on the phone, that I was acknowledging it but only giving lip service to his reaction. Similarly, E was told that he needed to work to hear me, that *I* was having a hard time with something—namely, my need to want to save someone, particularly when it's a man, and that that was a vulnerability of mine. It wasn't about something that was wrong about him. And the group talked about how hard it was for him to hear that. I was able in this context to describe my experience of wanting to save someone I'm working with, again, especially in the case of a man. One woman said that what was so growthful about my being able to share this was that they were willing to give me what I needed to help E in the group, instead of trying to get something from me. They created the environment for me to go further and were able to see that when they go further it enables me to go further and give more to them—as opposed to them needing or expecting me to give more so they can go further.

APPENDIX

Readings in Social Therapy and the Social Therapeutic Method

BOOKS

Holzman, L. (1997). *Schools for growth: Radical alternatives to current educational models.* Mahwah, NJ: Lawrence Erlbaum Associates.

Holzman, L., ed. (1999). *Performing psychology: A postmodern culture of the mind.* New York: Routledge. [A collection of writings by and about Fred Newman, including three of his stage plays]

Holzman, L., & Morss, J., eds. (2000). *Postmodern psychologies, societal practice and political life.* New York: Routledge. [Contains Holzman, "Performance, Criticism and Postmodern Psychology"; and Newman, "The Performance of Revolution (More Thoughts on the Postmodernization of Marxism)"]

Holzman, L., & Polk, J., eds. (1987). *History is the cure: A social therapy reader.* New York: Practice Press. [Contains new and previously published essays, including "History as an Anti-Paradigm"]

Newman, F. (1991). *The myth of psychology.* New York: Castillo. [Contains unpublished essays: "Patient as Revolutionary"; "Talkin' Transference"; "Crisis Normalization and Depression"; "Panic in America"; "The Myth of Addiction"; "Community as a Heart in a Havenless World"; and "Vygotsky's Method"]

Newman, F. (1994). *Let's develop! A guide to continuous personal growth.* New York: Castillo International.

Newman, F. (1996). *Performance of a lifetime: A practical-philosophical guide to the joyous life.* New York: Castillo International.

Newman, F., & Holzman, L. (1993). *Lev Vygotsky: Revolutionary scientist.* London: Routledge. [Portuguese translation, *Lev Vygotsky: Cientista revolucionário*, 2002, Edições Loyola, São Paolo, Brasil]

Newman, F., & Holzman, L. (1996). *Unscientific psychology: A cultural-performatory approach to understanding human life.* Westport, CT: Praeger.

Newman, F., & Holzman, L. (1997). *The end of knowing: A new developmental way of learning.* London: Routledge.

BOOK CHAPTERS AND JOURNAL ARTICLES

Holzman, L. (1985). Pragmatism and dialectical materialism in language development. In *Children's language*, K. E. Nelson (ed.), 345–367. Hillsdale, NJ: Lawrence Erlbaum Associates. Reprinted in H. Daniels (ed.), 1996. *Introduction to Vygotsky*, 75–98. London: Routledge.

Holzman, L. (1986). Ecological validity revisited. *Practice, The Journal of Politics, Economics, Psychology, Sociology and Culture 4:*95–135.

Holzman, L. (1987). People need power: An introduction to the Institute for Social Therapy and Research. *The Humanistic Psychologist 15:*105–113.

Holzman, L. (1990). Lev and let Lev: An interview on the life and works of Lev Vygotsky. *Practice, The Magazine of Psychology and Political Economy 7*(3):11–23.

Holzman, L. (1992). When learning leads development: Work-in-progress toward a humane educational environment. *Community Psychologist 25*(3):9–11.

Holzman, L. (1993). Notes from the laboratory: A work-in-progress report from the Barbara Taylor School. *Practice, The Magazine of Psychology and Political Economy 9*(1):25–37.

Holzman, L. (1993). The Rainbow Curriculum in democracy-centered schools: A new approach to helping children learn. *Inquiry: Critical Thinking Across the Disciplines 11*(3):3–5.

Holzman, L. (1994). Stop working and get to play. *Lib Ed 11:*8–12.

Holzman, L. (1995). Creating developmental learning environments: A Vygotskian practice. *School Psychology International 16:*199–212.

Holzman, L. (1995). Creating the zone: Reflections on the International Conference on L.S. Vygotsky and the Contemporary Human Sciences. *School Psychology International 16:*213–216.

Holzman, L. (1995). "Wrong," said Fred. A response to Parker. *Changes, An International Journal of Psychology and Psychotherapy 13*(1):23–26.

Holzman, L. (1996). Newman's practice of method completes Vygotsky. In *Psychology and society: Radical theory and practice*, I. Parker and R. Spears (eds.), 128–138. London: Pluto Press.

Holzman, L. (1997). The developmental stage. *Special Children* June/July:32–35.

Holzman, L. (1999). Psychology's untold stories: Practicing revolutionary activity. In *La psicologia al fin del siglo*, 141–156. Caracas: Sociedad Interamericana de Psicologia.

Holzman, L. (2000). Performing our way out of postmodern paralysis. *Psychologie in Österreich* 1/2000:11–17.

Holzman, L. (2000). Performative psychology: An untapped resource for educators. *Educational and Child Psychology 17*(3):86–103.

Holzman, L., & Braun, B. (1983). Reorganizing psychology. *Issues in Radical Therapy 7:*4–11.

Holzman, L., & Newman, F. (1987). Language and thought about history. In *Social and functional approaches to language and thought*, M. Hickmann (ed.), 109–121. London: Academic Press.

Hood [Holzman], L., Fiess, K., & Aron, J. (1982). Growing up explained: Vygotskians look at the language of causality. In *Verbal processes in children*, C. Brainerd and M. Pressley (eds.), 265–286. New York: Springer-Verlag.

LaCerva, C., Holzman, L., Braun, B., Pearl, D., & Steinberg, K. (2002). The performance of therapy after September 11. *Journal of Systemic Therapies 21*(3):30–38.

Newman, F. (2003). Undecidable emotions (What is social therapy? And how is it revolutionary?). *Journal of Constructivist Psychology*, in press.

Newman, F. (2000). Does a story need a theory? (Understanding the methodology of narrative therapy). In *Pathology and the postmodern: Mental illness as discourse and experience,* D. Fee (ed.), pp. 248–261 London: Sage.

Newman, F. (1999). One dogma of dialectical materialism. *Annual Review of Critical Psychology 1:*83–99.

Newman, F., &. Holzman, L. (2003). Power, authority and pointless activity (The developmental discourse of social therapy). In *Furthering talk: Advances in the discursive therapies,* eds. T. Strong and D. Paré. New York: Kluwer/Academic Press.

Newman, F., & Holzman, L. (2000). Against against-ism: *Theory & Psychology 10*(2):265–270.

Newman, F., & Holzman, L. (2000). The relevance of Marx to therapeutics in the 21st century. *New Therapist 5:*24–27.

Newman, F., & Holzman, L. (2000). Engaging the alienation. *New Therapist 8:*16–17.

Newman, F., & Holzman, L. (1999). Beyond narrative to performed conversation ('In the beginning' comes much later). *Journal of Constructivist Psychology 12*(1):23–40.

Strickland, G., & Holzman, L. (1989). Developing poor and minority children as leaders with the Barbara Taylor School Educational Model. *Journal of Negro Education 58*(3):383–398.

MONOGRAPHS

Newman, F. (1974). *Power and authority: The inside view of class struggle.* New York: Centers for Change.

Newman, F. (1977). *Practical-critical activities.* New York: Institute for Social Therapy.

Hood [Holzman], L., & Newman, F. (1979). *The practice of method: An introduction to the foundations of social therapy.* New York: Institute for Social Therapy and Research.